CLONE
BREWS

Homebrew Recipes for
150 Commercial Beers

Tess and Mark Szamatulski

Storey Publishing

*The mission of Storey Publishing is to serve our customers
by publishing practical information that encourages personal independence
in harmony with the environment.*

Dedication

We dedicate this book to the memory of Tess's father, Arthur Paul Demcsak.
We have felt his love and support shining down on us through the many months
we have spent researching and writing *CloneBrews*. We wish he could be with us
to share a beer in celebration of our first book. Cheers, Dad!

Edited by Brad Ring and Julia Rubel
Cover design by Rob Johnson, Johnson Design
Cover photographs: (top) © Foodpix, (bottom) © SuperStock
Text design by Mark Tomasi
Text production by Eileen M. Clawson
Drawing on page 7 by Kay Holmes Stafford and drawing on page 9 by Christine Erikson
The Beer Style Guidelines chart on page 162 is used by permission of
Charlie Papazian and the Association of Brewers.

Printed in the United States by Banta
20 19 18 17 16 15 14 13 12 11 10 9

Library of Congress Cataloging-in-Publication Data

Szamatulski, Tess, 1954–
    CloneBrews : homebrew recipes for 150 commercial beers / Tess and Mark Szamatulski.
        p.   cm.
    Includes index.
    ISBN 1-58017-077-3 (pbk. : alk. paper)
    1. Beer. 2. Brewing—Amateur's manuals. I. Szamatulski, Mark, 1957–   . II. Title.
TP577.S985 1998
    641.8'73—dc21   98-23752
                                                                              CIP

Contents

Preface

I n the beginning . . . there were two beers for us, a light and a dark. Slowly we evolved. We discovered that there is more to beer than light and dark. A new world awaited us, a world full of Belgian abbey ales, Tripels, smoked beer from Germany, heather ales from Scotland, IPAs from England, tropical stouts, beers brewed with maple sap, honey, candi sugar, spices. Long gone are the days of light and dark. We are in beer heaven. Now, as never before, we have access to so many unique, well-brewed, delicious beers from all over the world! Brewing is steeped in tradition, and we, as homebrewers, must continue the tradition.

We would like to acknowledge the following people and companies for helping us with this book. We are eternally grateful to all of them. Many thanks to our family for all of their support and encouragement: our children, Noella, Paulette, and Rob, our mom, Bess Demcsak, who at the age of 79 realizes she loves beer, Sharon and Michael Demcsak for all their love and support, and the Szamatulski family for all of their enthusiasm. To all of our loyal customers and friends who have sampled beers with us, brewed our recipes, shared them with us, and brought us back beers from all over the United States and the world. Mike Sebas, Gary Chase, Tom Conti, Naheel and Jim Norton, Blake Brown, Mark Labell, Eric Condo, Jim Mitchell, Dominik Wellman, John and Mimi Mudrick, Mike Novak, Lauren Mazurok, Tom Remilard, Mark Tomasco, Gino Gaucher, Diana Durden, Bill Breen, Paul Duh, Joe Burton, "Dude" Nelson, Keats Gill, Doug Wilborne, Drew Rosenberg, W. Neville, Kate Chase, Charlie Versaci, and all the other homebrewers and friends from Maltose Express. Special thanks to Terry Boyd of Mountview Wines in Naugatuck, CT, for all the help in finding every beer we needed to sample, Doug Hamm, former brewer at Elm City, Johnny Fincioen of Global Beer Network for sending samples of all of his wonderful Belgian beers, Jeff Browning of Spring Street Brewing, Yuengling Brewing Co., Bill Fadeley of Bulunda Import Co., Antonio Abraham of Balearic Beverage Dist., Yasuyuki "Yas" Shimauchi of Sapporo, Drew Behr of Magic Hat Brewing Co., Anne Latchis of Amazon Inc., Wasfi Skaff of American Fidelity Trading, Guinness Importing Co., the helpful people at Pilsner Urquell, the Athenée Importing Co., Dave Logsdon of Wyeast Laboratories, Charlie Papazian of the Association of Brewers, the very helpful people at Merchant du Vin for sending us samples and information, and the very knowledgeable people at Vanberg and DeWulf. Also thanks to Fireworks Brewery, White Plains, NY, and Ed Cody and Ken Espenak of Photographic Images. Thank you to all of the unknown people who have dropped off beer for us to sample, the beer from Portugal, Spain, Poland, England, and Czechoslovakia. We were not there to thank you in person, so we hope you read this. There are many more customers and friends who have helped and supported us. We are sorry if we have left anyone out, but please accept our heartfelt thanks. We would also like to thank Michael Jackson for all of his great books. They were a wealth of information for us. Last of all we would like to thank our first editor, Pamela Lappies, for providing us the opportunity to write this book.

We hope you enjoy our book as much as we have enjoyed writing it and may Gambrinus, the legendary patron of beer, watch over you and your brews always.

The Art of Cloning a Beer

CLONING BEER IS MUCH MORE FUN than cloning sheep, and a lot easier! You will have to forgo that warm wool sweater and some nice juicy lamb chops, but you get something even better — five gallons of fresh, delicious clonebrew! The best part of this whole process is that you can make your clonebrew just like the commercial brew or you can adjust it to your own taste. For example, suppose you want to clone your favorite pale ale but lately have come to enjoy hoppier beers. The solution to your dilemma is to make a hoppier clone of your favorite commercial beer. Tweak the recipe to just the way you like it. That's the beauty of homebrewing — you are in charge.

We will provide information in this section to help you clone your favorite beers. It does take practice. Some of the world's great breweries have been brewing for hundreds of years. The more beers that you sample, evaluate, and research, the more experienced you become. Tough work, cloning. Soon you will be able to identify hops, specialty malts, yeasts, and even spices. The more information that you can acquire before you begin to clone, the more accurate you will be. It's best to concentrate on one style at a time. The art of cloning simply boils down to researching the beer and knowing your beer styles, hop varieties, grains, specialty ingredients, and yeasts. Remember that practice makes perfect. Drink up, and let the cloning begin . . .

Know Your Clone Subject

Books and Magazines

Now more than ever there is a wealth of information about beer. Many magazines are devoted to homebrewing and beer appreciation, and hundreds of books have been written about the subject. One of the best sources for accurate information is Michael Jackson, British author of many beer books. In many instances he provides original gravity, color ratings, alcohol content, and types of grains and hops used in brewing a specific commercial beer. He even has a book devoted just to Belgian beers. His *Pocket Guide to Beer* is invaluable, especially if you travel and are sampling beers in another state or country.

Read Your Beer Bottle

You will find, especially with American microbrews, there is valuable information printed on the labels. Look for alcohol content and mention of the types of malts and hops used. Determine if it is a lager or an ale. If the beer is imported, in what part of the country is the brewery located? This can help you to determine ingredients. For example, if you are sampling a lager from Bavaria, Germany, you will be considering a Bavarian lager yeast, regional Spalt or Tettnanger hops and some German light crystal and Pilsner malt. You have applied your knowledge of hops, malt, yeast, and style of beer before even opening the bottle.

Ask Questions

Many brewers or beer importers are more than willing to share information about their brews. We have found that they are flattered that you enjoy their beer enough to want to copy it. Nine times out of ten they will offer you some helpful tips in recreating their recipes. Remember that many of these talented people started out as homebrewers!

Another resource is the knowledgeable person at your local homebrew supply store. There is a chance that he or she has been asked about the beer before, and if not, they should have many books right at their fingertips to find information. They can also help you out with bittering amounts, hops, and grains. Homebrewing clubs are another good source of information to tap into for your cloning projects. Don't be afraid to ask questions.

Know Your Beer Styles

It is helpful if you can determine the style of the beer you are trying to clone. Style clues are often provided on bottle labels or in published reviews of the beer you are copying. You can also work on identifying different styles by studying and learning what characteristics define particular styles. Once you know what the style of your particular beer is, you can look it up in the style guideline charts (see pages 162–164 in appendix 1) developed by Charlie Papazian and the Association of Brewers, headquartered in Boulder, Colorado. The charts will provide you with not only the characteristics of the beer, but also a range of specific gravity, color, and bitterness. You can then use this information as a starting point to build your clone recipe.

Know Your Hops

It is important to know your hop varieties and characteristics when cloning a commercial beer. Hops are the female cones of the hop vine and have lupulin glands that contain alpha and beta resins and essential oils. Alpha and beta resins are measured as their weight percentage of the hop cone and expressed as alpha acids and beta acids. The higher the alpha acid percentage, the more bitter that hop will be in your brew kettle. These acid percentages change from year to year and even crop to crop within the same hop varieties. It is important to keep accurate records of your calculations so that you can duplicate your bittering units the next time you brew the same recipe.

Alpha resins are not very soluble in water and must be boiled at least 60 minutes to contribute bitterness. Hop oils are soluble in water but will quickly boil off with the steam of the boil. They contribute flavor if they are in the boil for 5 to 15 minutes and aroma if they are in the boil for 1 to 3 minutes.

Using the hop chart on page 165 in appendix 2 and your taste buds, you can determine what hops you will need for bittering, flavor, aroma, and dry hopping your clonebrew. For example, if you are cloning a German Pilsner, depending on your research, you might pick out Spalt for bittering, Tettnang for flavor, and Saaz for aroma. These choices would be reasonable because Spalt is a German bittering hop, Tettnang is a hop used in many German lagers, and Saaz is a very popular German aroma hop. With a little research, a hop chart, and your taste buds, you shouldn't be too much off the mark!

Calculating Bittering Units

Home Bittering Units (HBUs) — For a 5 gallon (18.9 L) batch, simply multiply the ounces of hops used for bittering by their alpha acid number. For example: 2 ounces of Kent Goldings hops at 5% alpha acid per ounce equals 10 HBU. 2 oz. x 5% AAU = 10 HBU. All the recipes in this book use HBUs.

International Bittering Units — International Bittering Units (IBUs) are a more accurate measurement of bitterness than HBUs. IBUs are measured in parts per million (ppm) or milligrams per liter (mg/L). All the recipes in this book list a target IBU. You can estimate IBUs by using this formula:

IBU = (ounces of hops x % alpha acid of hop x % utilization) / (gallons of wort x 1.34)

Percent utilization varies with wort gravity, boiling time, wort volume, and other factors. Home-brewers obtain approximately 25% utilization for a 1-hour boil, 15% for a 30-minute boil and 5% for a 15-minute boil. Here's an example: 1 ounce of Challenger hops at 6% alpha acid in 5 gallons of wort boiled for 1 hour would end up with a beer with 22 IBUs.

22 IBU = (1 oz. x 6% AA x 25% utilization)/(5 gallons of wort x 1.34)

Know Your Grains and Specialty Ingredients

The grains and specialty ingredients you choose for your cloning project will determine the flavor, aroma, body, strength, and color of your brew. If you are a specialty grain and extract brewer, use an extra-light dried malt extract (DME) as a base for lagers, and a light malt extract as a base for ales. (We suggest English malt, unless you are brewing Belgian or wheat beers.) You should color and flavor this base with specialty malts. It is much easier to tweak a recipe and see what effect different grains and adjuncts have on a beer if you have a consistent base. Refer to our grains and adjuncts chart on page 167 in appendix 3 for complete descriptions of color, gravities, and common uses. This chart will help with your clone recipe building.

Determining the Amount of Grains and Malt to Use

After looking through our ingredient chart, you need to know how much of each to use to clone your beers accurately. All you need is a little bit of information about the beer you want to clone, such as original gravity or alcohol by volume, to get your shopping list together. The original gravity of many commercial brands can be found in Michael Jackson's *New World Guide to Beer and Beer Companion* and his *Pocket Guide to Beer*, as well as Fred Eckhard's *The Essentials of Beer Styles*, and most beer imported into the United States has its alcohol content printed on the label.

USING EXTRACTS

If you know the original gravity of the beer you wish to clone, subtract 1 from it, multiply it by 5, for 5 gallons, and then divide it by the gravity of the malt you are going to use. One pound of dry malt extract (DME) has a gravity of 1.044 if dissolved in 1 gallon of water. One pound of malt extract syrup has a gravity of 1.037 if dissolved in 1 gallon of water. To the right are some helpful formulas you can use to determine how much extract to use for a 5-gallon batch.

If the only information available about the beer you want to clone is the alcohol by volume percentage off the bottle's label, you can still

Using Extracts

$[(\text{Original Gravity} - 1) \times 5]/.044 =$ Approximate number of pounds of DME required to achieve correct original gravity

$[(\text{Original Gravity} - 1) \times 5]/.037 =$ Approximate number of pounds of malt extract syrup required to achieve correct original gravity

$[(\text{Original Gravity} - 1) \times 5]/.097 =$ Approximate number of kilograms of DME required to achieve correct original gravity

$[(\text{Original Gravity} - 1) \times 5]/.082 =$ Approximate number of kilograms of malt extract syrup required to achieve correct original gravity

come up with your total extract needed. Divide the alcohol by volume by the figures given to the right to determine how much malt extract to use in a recipe.

Here is a quick example: In New England Brewing's Atlantic Amber, the original gravity is 1.050, therefore using the formula:

[(Original Gravity-1) X 5]/.044 = pounds of DME required.

[(1.050-1)5]/.044 = 5.7 pounds of DME required.

However, if the only information you have about Atlantic Amber is a 4.8 percent alcohol by volume:

Alcohol by Volume/.84 = Pounds of DME required.

4.8/.84 = 5.7 pounds of DME required.

Either of these methods will closely approximate the amount of extract required.

Using Grains

If you are creating your recipe using grains rather than malt extract, the procedure is similar to determine the amount of grain you'll need. Each grain has a specific gravity that it will yield when mashed in 1 gallon of water. This varies from grain to grain. You'll find that gravity reading listed in the grains and adjuncts chart in appendix 3 (see pages 167–169). For example, British 2-row pale malt has a reading of 1.038 sg (specific gravity) when mashed in 1 gallon of water. An extra factor in grain brewing is the efficiency of your mash. Most homebrewers mash at 65 percent to 75 percent efficiency. In this book we assume a 70 percent efficiency for our all grain and partial grain recipes. The only exception are fermentables in the brew pot that are not going to be mashed, such as cane sugar or honey. In this case, the mash efficiency for these particular ingredients needs to be calculated at 100 percent.

For example, Harp Lager has an original gravity of 1.051 and you want to use British 2-row pale malt for the recipe, therefore:

[(1.051-1)5]/(1.038-1)(.7) = 9.6 lb. of British 2-row pale malt

Alcohol by Volume

Alcohol by Volume/.84 = Approximate number of pounds of DME to use in a recipe
Alcohol by Volume/.71 = Approximate pounds of malt extract syrup to use in a recipe
Alcohol by Volume/1.85 = Approximate number of kilograms of DME to use in a recipe
Alcohol by Volume/1.57 = Approximate number of kilograms of malt extract syrup to use in a recipe

Using Grains

If you know the original gravity of the beer you are trying to make:
[(Original Gravity-1) x 5]/(Grain gravity-1)*(efficiency) = Approximate number of pounds of grain required to achieve correct original gravity

If you want to mix and match various grains and extracts for your clone recipe, simply divide up the total original gravity for your clone beer by the percentage you want to allocate to your list of ingredients. The key is for all fermentable ingredients in the brew kettle to always add up to the target original gravity.

How to Determine the Color of Your Recipe

The type and quantity of the grains and malts you choose will also determine how close you come to copying the color of your commercial beer. In the beer style guidelines and in each recipe we list the target color of the beer using the Standard Research Method (SRM) scale of color. To estimate color using the European system to evaluate color, European Brewing Convention scale (EBCs), multiply the SRMs by 2.65 and then subtract 1.2 from the total. If you want to convert EBCs to SRMs, multiply the EBC number by 0.375 and add 0.46. Use our recipe ratings along with the chart to the right to know what color you are after with your clonebrew.

SRM Ratings	
Color	SRM number
Clear	0
Light straw	1–2.5
Pale straw	2.5–3.5
Dark straw	3.5–5.5
Light amber	5.5–10
Pale amber	10–18
Dark amber or copper	18–26
Very dark amber	26–40
Black	40+

We also earlier listed the Lovibond or SRM number for each individual brewing ingredient. Lovibond and SRM are measured on the same scale. Brewers use Lovibond to describe malts, while SRM is more often used to describe the color of the finished beer. You can use this Lovibond number to help predict the final color of your recipe. Multiply the amount of pounds being used of each grain or malt by the Lovibond of that grain or malt, then divide it by the total gallons of wort. Here is an example for our Bass Ale recipe:

(14 oz. crystal malt @ 55 Lovibond plus 6 lbs. M&F Light DME @ 3.5 Lovibond) divided by 5 gallons. [(14/16)(55)+(6)(3.5)]/5=13.8 SRM or Lovibond

Know Your Yeast

Commercial Liquid Yeasts

The advent of liquid yeast strains is what separates homebrewing today from homebrewing fifteen years ago. We can now choose from the dozens of yeast strains of liquid yeast available in homebrewing shops. There is a type of liquid yeast for almost every style of beer and more and more hit the market each year. If you know what style of beer you are trying to clone, match it up with the same style of yeast. Each of these strains has different properties reaching far past the basics of being an ale or lager yeast. If you can match styles, you are well on your way to success. Your homebrew supplier should have updated lists of what is currently available from the professional yeast manufacturers. With all these specific strains available, we strongly recommend avoiding dry yeast whenever possible. You'll notice the quality of your clonebrews increase dramatically.

Reculturing Yeast from Bottles

In addition to using the commercially available liquid yeasts, we also reculture the yeast from a bottle of beer that we are cloning if we are sure that the brewery used the same strain of yeast in priming as in fermenting the beer. Often a different yeast is used in bottle conditioning so that the brewery protects the exclusivity of their primary yeast. Yeasts provide the valuable signature taste for many beers and sometimes breweries do not want someone else using their primary yeast strain, whether it be a homebrewer or another commercial brewery.

The commercial bottle of beer needs to have been bottle-conditioned just like any bottle of your homebrew. This means there is live yeast in the bottle creating carbonation and that telltale yeast sediment at the bottom of the bottle. To culture yeast from a bottle of commercial beer, pour out eighty percent of the beer leaving the yeast in the bottle. Mix together a yeast starter by bringing to a boil ½ cup of dry wheat malt extract, 8 ounces of water, and 2 hop pellets of any variety (for a 12-ounce bottle). Boil for 10 minutes, cover the pot, and cool it in the sink in a bath of ice and water. While the starter is cooling, impeccably sanitize the mouth of the beer bottle, a #2 drilled rubber stopper, and an airlock. Pour the cooled starter (cooled to below 80°F) through a sanitized funnel into the bottle. Keep the bottle at room temperature, 68°F to 75°F. Allow 3 to 4 days for the recultured yeast to start. After the yeast begins to come back to life, you can either use it or put it in the refrigerator to render the yeast dormant for use at a later date. Among the commercial beer yeasts we recommend reculturing for use in clonebrews are Chimay, Westmalle, Orval, and Sierra Nevada Pale Ale.

Yeast Starter

When you are using yeast of any kind it is very important to always use a starter culture before pitching (or adding) it into the cooled wort. The procedure is almost the same as reculturing yeast. Begin with an expanded packet of liquid yeast that you have activated 1 to 2 days before. Boil the same reculturing starter mixture of dry wheat malt extract, water, and hops for 10 minutes before cooling to 80°F. Sanitize a beer bottle or half-gallon jug, a rubber stopper, and an airlock. Pour in the starter followed by the liquid yeast and put in the stopper and airlock. Gently shake to mix. Leave it at room temperature (around 70°F) regardless of whether the yeast is an ale or lager strain. Activity should begin within 12 hours. Yeast starters will ensure that you have viable yeast and will increase the pitching rate of your yeast. The larger and more active your yeast starter is, the less chance there is of an undesirable yeast fermenting your beer. Starters also allow you to brew on the spur of the moment. Yeasts can also be split into two starter bottles, enabling you to brew two beers for the price of one yeast!

Know Your Water

Water, since it is the primary ingredient in your beer, is very important. Certain beer styles are associated with certain types of water found near the style's birthplace. For example, the hard water found near Burton-on-Trent, England, is now a key factor in many commercial British-style Pale Ales. Ingredients can be added to your brew water to help replicate the water qualities of these famous brewing centers. We include such advice where needed in our clone recipes. If you know the beer you are copying was made with water having certain characteristics, you can alter your water accordingly.

However, for most homebrewed cloning, it is not mandatory to try to duplicate the brewery's original water source. Your tap water is usually fine unless you can smell or taste chlorine in it. If you like the way your water tastes and you drink it every day, then you should brew with it. If not, the best way around this is to install a charcoal filtration system or use bottled spring water for your brewing. If you have city water, call your water company and ask for an analysis of your water. In most cases the analysis is free. If you have well water it should be tested during the summer when the water levels drop and possible infection takes place. If your water is questionable, boil all your water for at least 15 minutes before using it for brewing to help eliminate the risk of bacteria or chlorine ruining your batch.

Ready, Set, Clone!

Now that we have covered beer styles, hops, grains, and yeast, we are finally ready to clone. Begin with a fresh sample of the beer you want to clone. It should be cellar temperature (55–60°F) so that all the flavors and aromas are evident. The best glasses to evaluate beer are either goblet or champagne tulip glasses. These glasses give you an opportunity to really capture the aroma because of their shape. They should be "beer clean," meaning never washed with soap. Soap will impact the taste and head of a beer. The glass should be rinsed with cold water and the beer poured into a wet glass.

The Head

When pouring the beer, turn the bottle upside down (unless it is bottle-conditioned) and pour directly into the middle of the glass. This allows the head to form completely so that an accurate evaluation can be made. What color is the head? Is it creamy or frothy? Does it have big bubbles or small, tightly beaded ones? Does the head dissipate quickly or is it long lasting? Look for "Belgian lace" by tipping the glass and seeing if the head leaves a lacelike pattern on the side of the glass.

The Color

Now determine the color. Color can range from the palest straw to the deepest black, with many shades in between — remember the SRM chart (see page 6). Don't just look for the obvious, yellow, gold, amber, brown, or black. Are shades of ruby present in that dark amber beer? Is there an almost greenish tint to that straw-colored lager? Is there a hint of garnet in that dark brown brew? Evaluate not just for color, but for depth of color. Clarity is also an observation you should make. Is the beer brilliant? Does it have a haze or particles floating in it? Beer should be brilliant, unless it is a wheat, white, or Belgian beer.

The Aroma

Sniff the beer, swirl the glass, and sniff again. Your nose should be attuned to three different smells. Aroma is a non-hop odor of grains, roasted malts, biscuit or freshly baked bread, alcohol, or spices. Bouquet is the smell of bubble gum, yeast, and fruit you inhale from the yeast strains. Bouquet is from esters that are products of the yeast metabolism. They are most evident in Belgian beers with their intense and complex bouquets. The nose of the beer is the aroma you receive from the hops. If it is an English ale, you might find Fuggles or Kent Goldings hops. German beers might be hopped with Spalt, German Hallertauer, or Tettnang. The first hop that comes to mind in many American brews is Cascade, with its fruity, citrus aroma. Train your sense of smell. Never drink a beer without deeply sniffing it first!

The Taste

Finally, it's time to taste. For a better understanding of taste, you must get to know your tongue better. The very back of your tongue is where you taste bitterness, on each side you taste sourness, on the very tip, sweetness and on each side of the tip of your tongue you will taste salt. Now, take a big sip of beer and swirl and slosh it so that the whole mouth is washed with beer. Take another sip, this time inhaling air along with the beer. This excites the olfactory region at the base of your nose, which heightens your sense of flavor. Record what you taste from each area of your tongue. Do you get a

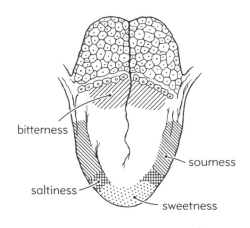

bitter taste from the hops or roasted malts? Is there a sweet malt taste? Swish some beer between your bottom teeth and lip. Do you taste or feel any astringency from the hops? Take another sip and swallow the beer slowly. Is there any aftertaste or tail? Is the finish dry, or sweet, or do hops linger on the palate? As a rule of thumb, the hoppier the beer, the longer and spicier the finish. The sweeter and maltier beers tend to finish quickly.

The Body

Now determine the body of the beer. Is it light in body like an American Pilsner, medium as in India Pale Ale, or heavy as in a barley wine? How does the beer feel in your mouth? The carbon dioxide has a lot to with this. Is it highly carbonated and fizzy? Is it creamy, grainy, dry, vinous, smooth, or neutral? These are all characteristics that you can actually feel.

Putting It All Together

What's your final impression? Tie all you have experienced together. Look at your notes, sip the beer again to verify your findings, alter your observations if necessary, and finish your beer. Put together a recipe based on your tasting notes, research, and our list of beer styles, hops, and ingredients.

After you have formulated your recipe with an eye on matching all the beer's attributes, it is time to actually brew the beer. Be consistent with temperatures when brewing and fermenting, following the information you have gleaned from your research. When your creation is ready to be tasted, have the commercial beer that you have cloned ready to be tasted in side-by-side comparison. They should both be at the same temperature and poured into the same style glass. Compare the head, color, aroma, bouquet, nose, flavor, mouthfeel, and aftertaste. Take notes and tweak your recipe. Brew the beer again to perfect your recipe. Cloning takes practice. Awaken all your senses and let them be your guide.

Disclaimer

Although we have obtained some information through brewers, breweries, and importers, these recipes were created by us and in no way do we claim that these are the exact ingredients, techniques, and formulas that are used by the breweries. These are homebrew recipes created by homebrewers for homebrewers.

CloneBrew
Recipes

About Our Recipes

All of our recipes assume the following:

- All extract and partial mash recipes require a 2.5- to 4-gallon boil, depending on the specific gravity of the wort. Each recipe specifies the amount of total volume of the boil. An easy way to measure volume is to mark the measurement on the outside of your pot with permanent marker.
- The full mash recipes are calculated with a 70 percent mash efficiency.
- Ingredients are given in US gallons and Liters, teaspoons and grams.
- The total boil time (from the time the wort actually comes to a boil) is 60 minutes for all recipes except full mash versions where indicated.
- All statistics (such as alcohol by volume, color, IBUs, and gravities) are for the home-brewed recipe and are not necessarily the brewery's statistics.
- Bittering is given in International Bittering Units (IBUs) and Home Bittering Units (HBUs) with alpha acids provided.
- Color is measured in SRMs, the U.S. measurement for color. To estimate EBCs, multiply the SRMs by 2.65, then subtract 1.2 from the total. To convert EBCs to SRMs, multiply the EBC number by 0.375 and add 0.46.
- Our recipes use pellet hops. If you are using leaf hops, add 10 percent more for bittering.

Have Fun

Homebrewing is a hobby, not a job. Enjoy our recipes and let your family and friends reap the benefits of the beer you have so lovingly brewed.

Mamba Malt Liquor

Solibra Brewery, Abidjan, Ivory Coast

Bright gold Mamba has a creamy white, tightly beaded head enticing you with a rich malt nose. This clean-tasting lager features a balancing act of malt and light hop flavor. Smooth, full-bodied with fine carbonation, it finishes long with hints of malt. Mamba stands up well to the spicy food of the Ivory Coast.

Yield: 5 gallons (18.9 L)	Final gravity: 1.011–1.012	SRM 4.5
Original gravity: 1.055–1.056	IBU 19	5.5% alcohol by volume

Crush and steep in ½ gallon (1.9 L) 150°F (65.5°C) water for 20 minutes:

> **½ lb. (.23 kg) 10°L crystal malt**
> **3 oz. (85 g) Belgian aromatic malt**

Strain the grain water into your brew pot. Sparge the grains with ½ gallon (1.9 L) water at 150°F (65.5°C). Add water to the brew pot for 1½ gallons (5.7 L) total volume. Bring the water to a boil, remove the pot from the stove, and add:

> **5.5 lb. (2.5 kg) M&F extra-light DME**
> **1 lb. (.45 kg) corn sugar**
> **2 oz. (57 g) Czech Saaz @ 2.5% AA (5 HBU) (bittering hop)**

Add water until total volume in the brew pot is 2.5 gallons (9 L). Boil for 45 minutes then add:

> **½ oz. (14 g) Czech Saaz (flavor hop)**
> **1 tsp. (5 ml) Irish moss**

Boil for 15 minutes, remove pot from the stove, and cool for 15 minutes. Strain the cooled wort into the primary fermenter and add cold water to obtain 5 gallons (18.9 L). When the wort temperature is under 80°F (26.6°C), pitch your yeast.

> **1st choice: Wyeast's 2007 Pilsen lager yeast**
> **(Ferment at 42–52°F [6–11°C])**
> **2nd choice: Wyeast's 2278 Czech Pilsner yeast**
> **(Ferment at 42–52°F [6–11°C])**

Ferment in the primary fermenter for 5–7 days or until fermentation slows, then siphon into the secondary fermenter. Bottle when fermentation is complete with:

> **¾ cup (180 ml) corn sugar**

 Serve in a Pilsner glass at 45°F (7°C).

 **Alternate Methods**

Mini-mash Method: Mash 2.5 lb. (1.1 kg) 2-row lager malt with the specialty grains at 150°F (65.5°C) for 90 minutes. Then follow the extract recipe omitting 2 lb. (.9 kg) DME at the beginning of the boil.

All-grain Method: Mash 8.25 lb. (3.7 kg) 2-row lager malt, 1.5 lb. (.68 kg) flaked maize, and 1 lb. (.45 kg) rice hulls with the specialty grains at 122°F (50°C) for 30 minutes and 150°F (65.5°C) for 60 minutes. Add 4 HBU (20% less than the extract recipe) for the last 90 minutes of the boil. Add the flavor hops and Irish moss for the last 10 minutes of the boil.

Tafel Pilsner Lager

Hansa Breweries, Swakopmund, Namibia

Tafel is a golden Pilsner displaying a tight, white head of small bubbles. Soft and round on the palate, it is light in body and hops. Smooth and refreshing, it quenches your thirst with a light malt flavor and imparts a pleasant malt aroma. Namibia, having been a German colony in the 1800s, still shows a German influence in its beer styles.

Yield: 5 gallons (18.9 L) Final gravity: 1.010–1.012 SRM 3.5
Original gravity: 1.045–1.048 IBU 16 4.5% alcohol by volume

Crush and steep in ½ gallon (1.9 L) 150°F (65.5°C) water for 20 minutes:

> **6 oz. (170 g) 2.5°L German light crystal malt**
> **2 oz. (57 g) Belgian aromatic malt**

Strain the grain water into your brew pot. Sparge the grains with ½ gallon (1.9 L) water at 150°F (65.5°C). Add water to the brew pot for 1.5 gallons (5.7 L) total volume. Bring the water to a boil, remove the pot from the stove, and add:

> **5.5 lb. (2.5 kg) M&F extra-light DME**
> **1 oz. Tettnanger @ 4% AA (4 HBU) (bittering hop)**

Add water until total volume in the brew pot is 2.5 gallons (9 L). Boil for 45 minutes then add:

> **¼ oz. (7 g) Czech Saaz, and ¼ oz. (7 g) Tettnanger (flavor hop)**
> **1 tsp. (5 ml) Irish moss**

Boil for 15 minutes, remove pot from the stove, and cool for 15 minutes. Strain the cooled wort into the primary fermenter and add cold water to obtain 5 gallons (18.9 L). When the wort temperature is under 80°F (26.6°C), pitch your yeast.

> **1st choice: Wyeast's 2278 Czech Pilsner lager yeast (Ferment at 42–52°F [6–11°C])**
> **2nd choice: Wyeast's 2007 Pilsen lager yeast (Ferment at 42–52°F [6–11°C])**

Ferment in the primary fermenter 5–7 days or until fermentation slows, then siphon into the secondary fermenter. Bottle when fermentation is complete with:

> **¾ cup (180 ml) corn sugar**

 Serve in a Pilsner glass at 45°F (7°C).

 **Alternate Methods**

Mini-mash Method: Mash 2.5 lb. (1.1 kg) German 2-row Pilsner malt with the specialty grains at 150°F (65.5°C) for 90 minutes. Then follow the extract recipe omitting 2 lb. (.9 kg) dry malt extract at the beginning of the boil.

All-grain Method: Mash 8.25 lb. (3.7 kg) German 2-row Pilsner malt with the specialty grains at 122°F (50°C) for 30 minutes and 150°F (65.5°C) for 60 minutes. Add 3 HBU (25% less than the extract recipe) for 90 minutes of the boil. Add the flavor hops and Irish moss for the last 15 minutes of the boil.

Windhoek Special

Namibia Breweries Ltd., Windhoek, Namibia

Namibia Breweries have been in operation since 1920 and the German colonial influence is still apparent. Windhoek Special is a pale gold color with a tight-knit, white head. It gives off a mild, slightly sweet fruit aroma. This light-bodied lager begins with a light initial bitterness followed by a slightly fruity, light malt flavor. It finishes with a short, dry malt aftertaste.

Yield: 5 gallons (18.9 L)	Final gravity: 1.011–1.014	SRM 3.5	
Original gravity: 1.054–1.055	IBU 20	5.3% alcohol by volume	

Crush and steep in ½ gallon (1.9 L) 150°F (65.5°C) water for 20 minutes:

6 oz. (170 g) 2.5°L German light crystal malt

Strain the grain water into your brew pot. Sparge the grains with ½ gallon (1.9 L) water at 150°F (65.5°C). Add water to the brew pot for 1.5 gallons (5.7 L) total volume. Bring the water to a boil, remove the pot from the stove, and add:

6.25 lb. (2.8 kg) M&F extra-light DME
2 oz. (57 g) German Hallertau Hersbrucker @ 2.5% AA (5 HBU) (bittering hop)

Add water until total volume in the brew pot is 2.5 gallons (9 L). Boil for 45 minutes then add:

¼ oz. (7 g) Czech Saaz (flavor hop)
¼ oz. (7 g) German Hallertau Hersbrucker (flavor hop)
1 tsp. (5 ml) Irish moss

Boil for 13 minutes then add:

¼ oz. (7 g) Czech Saaz (aroma hop)
¼ oz. (7 g) German Hallertau Hersbrucker (aroma hop)

Boil for 2 minutes, remove pot from the stove, and cool for 15 minutes. Strain the cooled wort into the primary fermenter and add cold water to obtain 5 gallons (18.9 L). When the wort temperature is under 80°F (26.6°C), pitch your yeast.

1st choice: Wyeast's 2007 Pilsen lager yeast
(Ferment at 42–52°F [6–11°C])
2nd choice: Wyeast's 2035 American lager yeast
(Ferment at 42–52°F [6–11°C])

Ferment in the primary fermenter 5–7 days or until fermentation slows, then siphon into the secondary fermenter. Bottle when fermentation is complete with:

1¼ cup (300 ml) M&F extra-light DME

 Serve this refreshing beer in a Pilsner glass at 45°F (7°C).

Alternate Methods

Mini-mash Method: Mash 3 lb. (1.36 kg) German 2-row Pilsner malt with the specialty grain at 150°F (65.5°C) for 90 minutes. Then follow the extract recipe omitting 2 lb. (.9 kg) DME at the beginning of the boil.

All-grain Method: Mash 10 lb. (4.5 kg) German 2-row Pilsner malt with the specialty grain at 122°F (50°C) for 30 minutes and 150°F (65.5°C) for 60 minutes. Add 4 HBU (20% less than the extract recipe) for 90 minutes of the boil. Add the flavor hops and Irish moss for the last 15 minutes of the boil and the aroma hops for the last 2 minutes.

Gulder Export Premium

Nigerian Breweries, PLC, Nigeria

Gulder Export Premium is one of the two largest selling beers in Western Africa. Displaying a snow-white head and a pale straw color, light-bodied Gulder has a light, fruity hop nose with traces of malt in it. The flavor profile integrates a distinctive, light grape taste with other tropical fruits and finishes with a trace of malt and hops.

Yield: 5 gallons (18.9 L)　　Final gravity: 1.010–1.011　　SRM 3
Original gravity: 1.049–1.051　　IBU 19　　5% alcohol by volume

Crush and steep in ½ gallon (1.9 L) 150°F (65.5°C) water for 20 minutes:
> **4 oz. (113 g) 2.5°L German light crystal malt**
> **3 oz. (85 g) Vienna malt**

Strain the grain water into your brew pot. Sparge the grains with ½ gallon (1.9 L) water at 150°F (65.5°C). Add water to the brew pot for 1.5 gallons (5.7 L) total volume. Bring the water to a boil, remove the pot from the stove, and add:
> **5 lb. (2.3 kg) M&F extra-light DME**
> **1 lb. (.45 kg) corn sugar**
> **2 oz. (57 g) Czech Saaz @ 2.5% AA (5 HBU)**
> **(bittering hop)**

Add water until total volume in brew pot is 2.5 gallons (9 L). Boil for 45 minutes then add:
> **½ oz. (14 g) Czech Saaz (flavor hop)**
> **1 tsp. (5 ml) Irish moss**

Boil for 15 minutes, remove pot from the stove, and cool for 15 minutes. Strain the cooled wort into the primary fermenter and add cold water to obtain 5 gallons (18.9 L). When the wort temperature is under 80°F (26.6°C), pitch your yeast.
> **1st choice: Wyeast's 2124 Bohemian lager yeast**
> **(Ferment at 42–52°F [6–11°C])**
> **2nd choice: Wyeast's 2206 Bavarian lager yeast**
> **(Ferment at 42–52°F [6–11°C])**

Ferment in the primary fermenter 5–7 days or until fermentation slows, then siphon into the secondary fermenter. Bottle when fermentation is complete with:
> **¾ cup (180 ml) corn sugar**

 Serve at 45°F (7°C) in a Pilsner glass.

Alternate Methods

Mini-mash Method: Mash 2.5 lb. (1.1 kg) German 2-row Pilsner malt with the specialty grains at 122°F (50°C) for 30 minutes and 150°F (65.5°C) for 60 minutes. Then follow the extract recipe omitting 2 lb. (.9 kg) DME at the beginning of the boil.

All-grain Method: Mash 7.25 lb. (3.3 kg) British 2-row lager malt, 1.5 lb. (.68 kg) flaked maize, and 1 lb. (.45 kg) rice hulls with the specialty grains at 122°F (50°C) for 30 minutes and 150°F (65.5°C) for 60 minutes. Add 4 HBU (20% less than the extract recipe) of bittering hops for 90 minutes of the boil. Add the flavor hop and the Irish moss for the last 15 minutes of the boil.

Castle Lager

South African Breweries Ltd., Johannesburg, South Africa

This pale yellow, light-bodied lager has a frothy white head and is finely carbonated. It makes a lively entrance with bright hop aroma. The initial flavor is slightly sweet followed by a slightly bitter hop prickle on the tongue before finishing with a hop aftertaste. This beer has been brewed since 1895 and is one of the best known beers in South Africa.

Yield: 5 gallons (18.9 L)	Final gravity: 1.010–1.011	SRM 3	
Original gravity: 1.050–1.051	IBU 20	5% alcohol by volume	

Crush and steep in ½ gallon (1.9 L) 150°F (65.5°C) water for 20 minutes:

4 oz. (113 g) 2.5°L German light crystal malt
4 oz. (113 g) German Vienna malt

Strain the grain water into your brew pot. Sparge the grains with ½ gallon (1.9 L) water at 150°F (65.5°C). Add water to the brew pot for 1.5 gallons (5.7 L) total volume. Bring the water to a boil, remove the pot from the stove, and add:

5 lb. (2.3 kg) M&F extra-light DME
1 lb. (454 g) corn sugar
1 oz. (28 g) Spalt @ 5% AA (5 HBU) (bittering hop)

Add water until total volume in brew pot is 2.5 gallons (9 L). Boil for 45 minutes then add:

¼ oz. (7 g) Tettnanger (flavor hop)
¼ oz. (7 g) German Hallertau Hersbrucker (flavor hop)
1 tsp. (5 ml) Irish moss

Boil for 13 minutes then add:

¼ oz. (7 g) Tettnanger (aroma hop)

Boil for 2 minutes, remove pot from the stove, and cool for 15 minutes. Strain the cooled wort into the primary fermenter and add cold water to obtain 5 gallons (18.9 L). When the wort temperature is under 80°F (26.6°C), pitch your yeast.

1st choice: Wyeast's 2007 Pilsen lager yeast
(Ferment at 42–52°F [6–11°C])
2nd choice: Wyeast's 2278 Czech Pilsner lager yeast
(Ferment at 42–52°F [6–11°C])

Ferment in the primary fermenter 5–7 days or until fermentation slows, then siphon into the secondary fermenter. Bottle when fermentation is complete with:

¾ cup (180 ml) corn sugar

 Serve at 45°F (7°C) in a Pilsner glass.

Alternate Methods

Mini-mash Method: Mash 2.5 lb. (1.1 kg) German 2-row Pilsner malt with the specialty grains at 150°F (65.5°C) for 30 minutes and 150°F (65.5°C) for 60 minutes. Then follow the extract recipe omitting 2 lb. (.9 kg) DME at the beginning of the boil.

All-grain Method: Mash 7.5 lb. (3.4 kg) German 2-row Pilsner malt, 1.5 lb. (.68 kg) flaked maize, and 1 lb. (.45 kg) rice hulls with the specialty grains at 122°F (50°C) for 30 minutes and 150°F (65.5°C) for 60 minutes. Add 4 HBU (20% less than the extract recipe) of bittering hop for 90 minutes of the last 15 minutes of the boil and the aroma hops for the last 2 minutes.

Lion Lager

South African Breweries Ltd., Johannesburg, South Africa

Lion Lager is one of the best known beers between the Cape and the Zambezi. This crisp, light golden lager has a creamy white head composed of small bubbles and has a faint hop and malt aroma. The flavor is fruity and dry.

Yield: 5 gallons (18.9 L) Final gravity: 1.010–1.011 SRM 3
Original gravity: 1.049–1.051 IBU 15 5% alcohol by volume

Crush and steep in ½ gallon (1.9 L) 150°F (65.5°C) water for 20 minutes:

4 oz. (113 g) 2.5°L German light crystal malt

Strain the grain water into your brew pot. Sparge the grains with ½ gallon (1.9 L) water at 150°F (65.5°C). Add water to the brew pot for 1.5 gallons (5.7 L) total volume. Bring the water to a boil, remove the pot from the stove, and add:

5 lb. (2.3 kg) M&F extra-light DME
1 lb. (.45 kg) corn sugar
1 oz. (28 g) Czech Saaz @ 2% AA (2 HBU)
(bittering hop)
½ oz. (14 g) Tettnanger @ 4% AA (2 HBU)
(bittering hop)

Add water until total volume in brew pot is 2.5 gallons (.9 L). Boil for 45 minutes then add:

¼ oz. (7 g) Tettnanger (flavor hop)
1 tsp. (5 ml) Irish moss

Boil for 15 minutes, remove pot from the stove, and cool for 15 minutes. Strain the cooled wort into the primary fermenter and add cold water to obtain 5 gallons (18.9 L). When the wort temperature is under 80°F (26.6°C), pitch your yeast.

1st choice: Wyeast's 2007 Pilsen lager yeast
(Ferment at 42–52°F [6–11°C])
2nd choice: Wyeast's 2035 American lager yeast
(Ferment at 42–52°F [6–11°C])

Ferment in the primary fermenter 5–7 days or until fermentation slows, then siphon into the secondary fermenter. Bottle when fermentation is complete with:

¾ cup (180 ml) corn sugar

 Serve in a Pilsner glass at 45°F (7°C).

 **Alternate Methods**

Mini-mash Method: Mash 2.75 lb. (1.25 kg) German 2-row Pilsner malt with the specialty grain at 122°F (50°C) for 30 minutes and 150°F (65.5°C) for 60 minutes. Then follow the extract recipe omitting 2 lb. (.9 kg) DME at the beginning of the boil.

All-grain Method: Mash 7.5 lb. (3.4 kg) German 2-row lager malt, 1.5 lb. (.68 kg) flaked maize, and 1 lb. (.45 kg) rice hulls with the specialty grain at 122°F (50°C) for 30 minutes and 150°F (65.5°C) for 60 minutes. Add 3 HBU (25% less than the extract recipe) of bittering hops for 90 minutes of the boil. Add the flavor hop and Irish moss for the last 15 minutes of the boil.

Ngoma Malt Liquor Awooyo Special

BB Brewery, Lomé, Kara, Togo. Ngoma is also brewed in South Africa, Kenya, Mozambique, and Nigeria.

This traditionally brewed, amber Oktoberfest has a light tan head and a balance in the aroma of hops and malt. The taste has hop bitterness blended with toasted malt followed by a dry aftertaste. This lager is very smooth and rich on the palate. Awooyo is brewed with very soft water. It was initially brewed for the President of Togo. "Ngoma" means "the drum" in the Tsheluba language.

Yield: 5 gallons (18.9 L)	Final gravity: 1.013–1.016	SRM 11
Original gravity: 1.061–1.063	IBU 24	6% alcohol by volume

Crush and steep in ½ gallon (1.9 L) 150°F (65.5°C) water for 20 minutes:

6 oz. (170 g) Belgian Cara-Munich malt

Strain the grain water into your brew pot. Sparge the grains with ½ gallon (1.9 L) water at 150°F (65.5°C). Add water to the brew pot for 1.5 gallons (5.7 L) total volume. Bring the water to a boil, remove the pot from the stove, and add:

6.6 lb. (3 kg) Ireks light malt extract syrup
1.5 lb. (.68 kg) M&F light DME
1 oz. (28 g) Northern Brewer @ 7% AA (7 HBU) (bittering hop)

Add water until total volume in the brew pot is 2.5 gallons (9 L). Boil for 45 minutes then add:

½ oz. (14 g) German Hallertau Hersbrucker (flavor hop)
1 tsp. (5 ml) Irish moss

Boil for 15 minutes, remove pot from the stove, and cool for 15 minutes. Strain the cooled wort into the primary fermenter and add cold water to obtain 5 gallons (18.9 L). When the wort temperature is under 80°F (26.6°C), pitch your yeast.

1st choice: Wyeast's 2206 Bavarian lager yeast (Ferment at 42–52°F [6–11°C])
2nd choice: Wyeast's 2124 Bohemian lager yeast (Ferment at 42–52°F [6–11°C])

Ferment in the primary fermenter 5–7 days or until fermentation slows, then siphon into the secondary fermenter. Bottle when fermentation is complete with:

1¼ cup (300 ml) M&F extra-light DME

 Serve in a pub mug at 55°F (13°C).

 **Alternate Methods**

Mini-mash Method: Mash 2.5 lb. (1.1 kg) German 2-row Pilsner malt at 150°F (65.5°C) for 90 minutes. Then follow the extract recipe omitting 6.6 lb. (3 kg) Ireks light malt syrup and add 3.3 lb. (1.5 kg) Bierkeller light malt syrup and an additional 1 lb. (.45 kg) M&F extra-light DME at the beginning of the boil.

All-grain Method: Mash 11.25 lb. (5.1 kg) German 2-row Pilsner malt and the specialty grain at 122°F (50°C) for 30 minutes and 150°F (65.5°C) for 60 minutes. Add 5 HBU (28% less than the extract recipe) of bittering hops for 90 minutes of the boil. Add the flavor hop and Irish moss for the last 15 minutes of the boil.

Ngoma Togo Pils

BB Brewery, Lomé, Kara, Togo. Also brewed in South Africa, Kenya, Mozambique, and Nigeria.

This pale gold German-style Pilsner is brewed in the Nuremberg style with soft water. It displays a compact white head of small bubbles and is lightly carbonated. Ngoma Togo Pils imparts a fruity aroma with a pleasant hop and toasted malt nose. It pleases the palate with a balanced hop flavor.

Yield: 5 gallons (18.9 L)   Final gravity: 1.012–1.015   SRM 4–6
Original gravity: 1.057–1.060   IBU 29   5.7% alcohol by volume

Crush and steep in ½ gallon (1.9 L) 150°F (65.5°C) water for 20 minutes:

> **4 oz. (113 g) 2.5°L German light crystal malt**
> **4 oz. (113 g) German Vienna malt**

Strain the grain water into your brew pot. Sparge the grains with ½ gallon (1.9 L) water at 150°F (65.5°C). Add water to the brew pot for 1.5 gallons (5.7 L) total volume. Bring the water to a boil, remove the pot from the stove, and add:

> **3.3 lb. (1.5 kg) Bierkeller light malt extract syrup**
> **4 lb. (1.8 kg) M&F extra-light DME**
> **2 oz. (55 g) Spalt @ 4.25% AA (8.5 HBU) (bittering hop)**

Add water until total volume in the brew pot is 2.5 gallons (9 L). Boil for 45 minutes then add:

> **¼ oz. (7 g) German Hallertau Hersbrucker (flavor hop)**
> **¼ oz. (7 g) Tettnanger (flavor hop)**
> **1 tsp. (5 ml) Irish moss**

Boil for 15 minutes, remove pot from the stove, and cool for 15 minutes. Strain the cooled wort into the primary fermenter and add cold water to obtain 5 gallons (18.9 L). When the wort temperature is under 80°F (26.6°C), pitch your yeast.

> **1st choice: Wyeast's 2124 Bohemian lager yeast**
> **(Ferment at 42–52°F [6–11°C])**
> **2nd choice: Wyeast's 2278 Czech Pilsner lager yeast**
> **(Ferment at 42–52°F [6–11°C])**

Ferment in the primary fermenter 5–7 days or until fermentation slows, then siphon into the secondary fermenter. Bottle when fermentation is complete with:

> **1¼ cup (300 ml) M&F extra-light DME**

 Serve in a Pilsner glass at 45°F (7°C).

 **Alternate Methods**

Mini-mash Method: Mash 2.5 lb. (1.1 kg) German 2-row Pilsner malt with the specialty grains at 150°F (65.5°C) for 90 minutes. Then follow the extract recipe omitting 2 lb. (.9 kg) DME at the beginning of the boil.

All-grain Method: Mash 10.5 lb. (4.8 kg) German 2-row Pilsner malt with the specialty grains at 122°F (50°C) for 30 minutes and 150°F (65.5°C) for 60 minutes. Add 6 HBU (27% less than the extract recipe) of bittering hops for 90 minutes of the boil. Add the flavor hops and the Irish moss for the last 15 minutes of the boil.

Zambezi Premium Export Lager

Natbrew, Zimbabwe

Zambezi is named after Africa's fourth largest river, which runs over the spectacular Victoria Falls. Golden Zambezi displays a frothy, off-white head with low carbonation. A pronounced, sharp hop aroma is followed by an earthy, slightly bitter flavor and a dry aftertaste. This is a lively, interesting, medium-bodied brew.

Yield: 5 gallons (19 L) Final gravity: 1.009–1.010 SRM 2.5
Original gravity: 1.045 IBU 22 4.5% alcohol by volume

Crush and steep in ½ gallon (1.9 L) 150°F (65.5°C) water for 20 minutes:

4 oz. (113 g) 2.5°L German light crystal malt

Strain the grain water into your brew pot. Sparge the grains with ½ gallon (1.9 L) water at 150°F (65.5°C). Add water to the brew pot for 1.5 gallons (5.7 L) total volume. Bring the water to a boil, remove the pot from the stove, and add:

4.5 lb. (2 kg) M&F extra-light DME
¾ lb. (.34 kg) corn sugar
2 oz. (55 g) Spalt @ 2.75% AA (5.5 HBU) (bittering hop)

Add water until total volume is 2.5 gallons (9 L). Boil for 45 minutes then add:

¼ oz. (55 g) German Hallertau Hersbrucker (flavor hop)
¼ oz. (55 g) Czech Saaz (flavor hop)
1 tsp. (5 ml) Irish moss

Boil for 15 minutes, remove pot from the stove, and cool for 15 minutes. Strain the cooled wort into the primary fermenter and add cold water to obtain 5 gallons (18.9 L). When the wort temperature is under 80°F (26.6°C), pitch your yeast.

1st choice: Wyeast's 2007 Pilsen lager yeast
(Ferment at 42–52°F [6–11°C])
2nd choice: Wyeast's 2278 Czech Pilsner lager yeast
(Ferment at 42–52°F [6–11°C])

Ferment in the primary fermenter 5–7 days or until fermentation slows, then siphon into the secondary fermenter. Bottle when fermentation is complete with:

¾ cup (180 ml) corn sugar

 Serve in a Pilsner glass at 45°F (7°C).

 **Alternate Methods**

Mini-mash Method: Mash 3 lb. (1.36 kg) British 2-row Pilsner malt with the specialty grain at 150°F (65.5°C) for 90 minutes. Then follow the extract recipe omitting 2 lb. (.9 kg) of DME at the beginning of the boil.

All-grain Method: Mash 7.25 lb. (3.3 kg) British 2-row lager malt, 1 lb. (.45 kg) flaked maize, and ½ lb. (.23 kg) rice hulls with the specialty grain at 122°F (50°C) for 30 minutes and 150°F (65.5°C) for 60 minutes. Add 4.5 HBU (18% less than the extract recipe) of bittering hops for 90 minutes of the boil. Add the flavor hops and the Irish moss for the last 15 minutes of the boil.

Tsing-Tao

Tsing-Tao Brewery Co. Ltd., Quingdao, China

Tsing-Tao, China's super premium beer, is brewed in Quingdao Shandong. This medium-bodied lager has a finely beaded white head, and is tawny gold in color. It has a satisfying light malt and good hop flavor, finishing with a mild malt nose.

Yield: 5 gallons (18.9 L)   Final gravity: 1.010–1.011   SRM 3–4
Original gravity: 1.047–1.048   IBU 18   4.7% alcohol by volume

Crush and steep in ½ gallon (1.9 L) 150°F (65.5°C) water for 20 minutes:

> **½ lb. (.23 kg) 10°L crystal malt**

Strain the grain water into your brew pot. Sparge the grains with ½ gallon (1.9 L) water at 150°F (65.5°C). Add water to the brew pot for 1.5 gallons (5.7 L) total volume. Bring the water to a boil, remove the pot from the stove, and add:

> **4.5 lb. (2 kg) M&F extra-light DME**
> **1 lb. (.45 kg) rice syrup solids**
> **½ oz. (14 g) Tettnanger @ 5.0% AA (2.5 HBU) (bittering hop)**
> **1 oz. (28 g) Czech Saaz @ 2.5% AA (2.5 HBU) (bittering hop)**

Add water until total volume in the brew pot is 2.5 gallons (9 L). Boil for 50 minutes then add:

> **¼ oz. (7 g) Czech Saaz (flavor hop)**
> **1 tsp. (5 ml) Irish moss**

Boil for 10 minutes, remove pot from the stove, and cool for 15 minutes. Strain the cooled wort into the primary fermenter and add cold water to obtain 5 gallons (18.9 L). When the wort temperature is under 80°F (26.6°C), pitch your yeast.

> **1st choice: Wyeast's 2007 Pilsen lager yeast (Ferment at 42–52°F [6–11°C])**
> **2nd choice: Wyeast's 2035 American lager yeast (Ferment at 42–52°F [6–11°C])**

Ferment in the primary fermenter 5–7 days or until fermentation slows, then siphon into the secondary fermenter. Bottle when fermentation is complete with:

> **¾ cup (180 ml) corn sugar**

 Pour into a Pilsner glass and serve at 45°F (7°C).

Alternate Methods

Mini-mash Method: Mash 2.75 lb. (1.25 kg) British 2-row lager malt with the specialty grain at 122°F (50°C) for 30 minutes and 150°F (65.5°C) for 60 minutes. Then follow the extract recipe omitting 2 lb. (.9 kg) DME at the beginning of the boil.

All-grain Method: Grind 1.5 lb. (.68 kg) rice, then cook for 20 minutes until soft. Mash 6.75 lb. (3.1 kg) American 6-row pale malt with the rice and 1 lb. (.45 kg) of rice hulls with the specialty grain at 122°F (50°C) for 30 minutes and 150°F (65.5°C) for 60 minutes. Use 4 HBU (20% less than the extract recipe) bittering hops for 60 minutes of the boil. Add the flavor hops and Irish moss for the last 10 minutes of the boil.

Bin Tang Pilsner Lager

Pt. Multi Bintang, Tangerang, China

This pale golden lager has a creamy white head, medium body, crackling carbonation, and a sweet, fruity flavor. Bin Tang leaves you with a light hop aroma reminiscent of sweet herbs and fruit. It finishes with a dry, light aftertaste.

Yield: 5 gallons (18.9 L)   Final gravity: 1.009–1.011   SRM 2.5
Original gravity: 1.042–1.043   IBU 21   4.1% alcohol by volume

Crush and steep in ½ gallon (1.9 L) 150°F (65.5°C) water for 20 minutes:

½ lb. (.23 kg) 2.5°L German light crystal malt

Strain the grain water into your brew pot. Sparge the grains with ½ gallon (1.9 L) water at 150°F (65.5°C). Add water to the brew pot for 1.5 gallons (5.7 L) total volume. Bring the water to a boil, remove the pot from the stove, and add:

4 lb. (1.8 kg) Alexander's pale malt syrup
2 lb. (.9 kg) M&F extra-light DME
2 oz. (57 g) Czech Saaz @ 2.5% AA (5 HBU)
(bittering hop)
1 tsp. (5 ml) kosher salt

Add water until total volume in the brew pot is 2.5 gallons (9 L). Boil for 45 minutes then add:

½ oz. (14 g) Czech Saaz (flavor hop)
1 tsp. (5 ml) Irish moss

Boil for 12 minutes then add:

½ oz. (14 g) Czech Saaz (aroma hop)

Boil for 3 minutes, remove pot from the stove, and cool for 15 minutes. Strain the cooled wort into the primary fermenter and add cold water to obtain 5 gallons (18.9 L). When the wort temperature is under 80°F (26.6°C), pitch your yeast.

1st choice: Wyeast's 2565 Kölsch yeast
(Ferment at 50–62°F [10–17°C])
2nd choice: Wyeast's 2007 Pilsen lager yeast
(Ferment at 42–52°F [6–11°C])

Ferment in the primary fermenter 5–7 days or until fermentation slows, then siphon into the secondary fermenter. Bottle when fermentation is complete with:

⅞ cup (202 ml) corn sugar

 Serve in a Pilsner glass at 45°F (7°C).

 **Alternate Methods**

Mini-mash Method: Mash 2.25 lb. (1 kg) British 2-row lager malt and the specialty grains at 150°F (65.5°C) for 90 minutes. Then follow the extract recipe omitting 2 lb. (.9 kg) DME at the beginning of the boil.

All-grain Method: Mash 7.5 lb. (3.4 kg) 2-row British lager malt with the specialty grain at 150°F (65.5°C) for 90 minutes. Use 4 HBU (20% less than the extract recipe) of bittering hops for 60 minutes of the boil. Add the flavor hops and Irish moss for the last 15 minutes of the boil and the aroma hops for the last 3 minutes.

Golden Eagle Lager Beer

Mohan Meakin Limited, Ghaziabad, India

A deep golden lager with a snow-white head, Golden Eagle leads into its light taste with hints of fruit, malt, smoke, and a vague, light, salty sensation. It is extremely light in the hop department and finishes short and dry.

Yield: 5 gallons (18.9 L)	Final gravity: 1.010–1.012	SRM 5–6
Original gravity: 1.050–1.052	IBU 22	5% alcohol by volume

Crush and steep in ½ gallon (1.9 L) 150°F (65.5°C) water for 20 minutes:

½ lb. (.23 kg) 20°L crystal malt
1 oz. (28 g) peat-smoked malt
2 oz. (57 g) German Munich malt

Strain the grain water into your brew pot. Sparge the grains with ½ gallon (1.9 L) water at 150°F (65.5°C). Add water to the brew pot for 1.5 gallons (5.7 L) total volume. Bring the water to a boil, remove the pot from the stove, and add:

5.5 lb. (2.5 kg) M&F light DME
½ lb. (.23 kg) rice syrup solids
1 tsp. (5 ml) kosher salt
1 oz. (28 g) Tettnanger @ 6% AA (6 HBU)
 (bittering hop)

Add water until total volume in the brew pot is 2.5 gallons (9 L). Boil for 45 minutes then add:

¼ oz. (7 g) German Hallertau Hersbrucker (flavor hop)
1 tsp. (5 ml) Irish moss

Boil for 15 minutes, remove pot from the stove, and cool for 15 minutes. Strain the cooled wort into the primary fermenter and add cold water to obtain 5 gallons (18.9 L). When the wort temperature is under 80°F (26.6°C), pitch your yeast.

1st choice: Wyeast's 2206 Bavarian lager yeast
 (Ferment at 42–52°F [6–11°C])
2nd choice: Wyeast's 2124 Bohemian lager yeast
 (Ferment at 42–52°F [6–11°C])

Ferment in the primary fermenter 5–7 days or until fermentation slows, then siphon into the secondary fermenter. Bottle when fermentation is complete with:

¾ cup (180 ml) corn sugar

 Serve in a Pilsner glass at 45°F (7°C).

Alternate Methods

Mini-mash Method: Mash 3.25 lb. (1.5 kg) 2-row British lager malt and the specialty grains at 150°F (65.5°C) for 90 minutes. Then follow the extract recipe omitting 2.5 lb. (1.1 kg) DME at the beginning of the boil.

All-grain Method: Grind 1 lb. (.45 kg) rice, then cook it for 20 minutes until soft. Mash 7.5 lb. (3.4 kg) 2-row British lager malt, the rice, ½ lb. (.23 kg) of rice hulls, and the specialty grains at 122°F (50°C) for 30 minutes and 149°F (65°C) for 60 minutes. Use 4.5 HBU (25% less than the extract recipe) of bittering hops and 1 tsp. (5 ml) kosher salt for 90 minutes of the boil. Add the flavor hops and Irish moss for the last 15 minutes of the boil.

Asahi Dry Draft Beer

Asahi Breweries, Tokyo, Japan

*Asahi is a light, straw-colored lager with a small-beaded, white head, light body, and a
delicate bitterness. It has a light, clean-tasting malt flavor and nose. The Asahi Brewery is
one of the world's most technologically advanced breweries. In the brewery, as in all Japanese
breweries, there is a shrine. Once a month a new beer is left for the god of the brewery.*

Yield: 5 gallons (18.9 L)	Final gravity: 1.007–1.009	SRM 2
Original gravity: 1.040–1.041	IBU 14	4.1% alcohol by volume

Crush and steep in ½ gallon (1.9 L) 150°F (65.5°C) water for 20 minutes:

½ lb. (.23 kg) 2.5°L German light crystal malt

Strain the grain water into your brew pot. Sparge the grains with ½ gallon
(1.9 L) water at 150°F (65.5°C). Add water to the brew pot for 1.5 gallons
(5.7 L) total volume. Bring the water to a boil, remove the pot from the
stove, and add:

3.5 lb. (1.6 kg) M&F extra-light DME
1.25 lb. (.57 kg) rice syrup solids
  1 oz. (28 g) Czech Saaz @ 3.5% AA (3.5 HBU)
    (bittering hop)

Add water until total volume in the brew pot is 2.5 gallons (9 L). Boil for
45 minutes then add:

¼ oz. (7 g) Czech Saaz (flavor hop)
1 tsp. (5 ml) Irish moss

Boil for 15 minutes, remove pot from the stove, and cool for 15 minutes.
Strain the cooled wort into the primary fermenter and add cold water to
obtain 5 gallons (18.9 L). When the wort temperature is under 80°F
(26.6°C), pitch your yeast.

    1st choice: Wyeast's 2007 Pilsen lager yeast
      (Ferment at 42–52°F [6–11°C])
    2nd choice: Wyeast's 2035 American lager yeast
      (Ferment at 42–52°F [6–11°C])

Ferment in the primary fermenter 5–7 days or until fermentation slows,
then siphon into the secondary fermenter. Bottle when fermentation is
complete with:

¾ cup (180 ml) corn sugar

Serve in a Pilsner glass chilled to 45°F (7°C).

Alternate Methods

Mini-mash Method: Mash
2.25 lb. (1 kg) 2-row
German Pilsner malt and
the specialty grain at 150°F
(65.5°C) for 90 minutes.
Then follow the extract
recipe omitting 1.75 lb.
(.8 kg) DME at the begin-
ning of the boil.

All-grain Method: Grind
1.75 lb. (.8 kg) rice, then
cook it for 20 minutes until
soft. Mash 5 lb. (2.3 kg)
6-row pale malt, the rice,
1 lb. (.45 kg) rice hulls, and
the specialty grain at 122°F
(50°C) for 30 minutes and
150°F (65.5°C) for 60 minutes. Use 3 HBU (15% less
than the extract recipe) of
bittering hops for 60 minutes of the boil. Add the
flavor hops and Irish moss
for the last 15 minutes of
the boil.

Kirin Lager

Kirin Brewing Co. Ltd., Tokyo, Japan

This popular lager is named after a creature of Chinese mythology, half horse, half dragon. It is a very clean, medium-bodied, bright yellow lager with a grain and light hop flavor. Kirin Lager has a sprightly carbonation and finishes with a rice, malt, and hop aroma.

Yield: 5 gallons (18.9 L)	Final gravity: 1.010	SRM 3
Original gravity: 1.045–1.046	IBU 17	4.5% alcohol by volume

Crush and steep in ½ gallon (1.9 L) 150°F (65.5°C) water for 20 minutes:

⅓ lb. (.15 kg) 2.5°L German light crystal malt

Strain the grain water into your brew pot. Sparge the grains with ½ gallon (1.9 L) water at 150°F (65.5°C). Add water to the brew pot for 1.5 gallons (5.7 L) total volume. Bring the water to a boil, remove the pot from the stove, and add:

4.25 lb. (1.9 kg) M&F extra-light DME
1 lb. (.45 kg) rice syrup solids
1 oz. (28 g) Czech Saaz @ 2% AA (2 HBU)
(bittering hop)
1 oz. (28 g) German Hallertau Hersbrucker @ 2% AA
(2 HBU) (bittering hop)

Add water until volume in the brew pot is 2.5 gallons (9 L). Boil for 45 minutes then add:

¼ oz. (7 g) Czech Saaz (flavor hop)
¼ oz. (7 g) German Hallertau Hersbrucker (flavor hop)
1 tsp. (5 ml) Irish moss

Boil for 13 minutes then add:

¼ oz. (7 g) Czech Saaz (aroma hop)
¼ oz. (7 g) German Hallertau Hersbrucker (aroma hop)

Boil for 2 minutes, remove pot from the stove, and cool for 15 minutes. Strain the cooled wort into the primary fermenter and add cold water to obtain 5 gallons (18.9 L). When the wort temperature is under 80°F (26.6°C), pitch your yeast.

Wyeast's 2007 Pilsen lager yeast
(Ferment at 42–52°F [6–11°C])

Ferment in the primary fermenter 5–7 days or until fermentation slows, then siphon into the secondary fermenter. Bottle when fermentation is complete with:

¾ cup (180 ml) corn sugar

 Serve in a Pilsner glass at 45°F (7°C).

 **Alternate Methods**

Mini-mash Method: Mash 2.25 lb. (1 kg) 2-row German Pilsner malt and the specialty grain at 150°F (65.5°C) for 90 minutes. Then follow the extract recipe omitting 1.5 lb. (.68 kg) DME at the beginning of the boil.

All-grain Method: Grind 1.5 lb. (.68 kg) rice, then cook it for 20 minutes until soft. Mash 7.5 lb. (3.4 kg) 6-row pale malt, the rice, 1 lb. (.45 kg) rice hulls, and the specialty grain at 122°F (50°C) for 30 minutes and 150°F (65.5°C) for 60 minutes. Use 3 HBU (25% less than the extract recipe) of bittering hops for 90 minutes of the boil. Add the flavor hops and Irish moss for the last 15 minutes of the boil and the aroma hops for the last 2 minutes.

Sapporo Black Stout Draft

Sapporo Breweries Ltd., Tokyo, Japan

Sapporo uses ceramic cold filtration to filter their beers instead of pasteurization. The beer is slowly passed through ceramic filtration rods to remove the yeast. Sapporo's Black Stout Draft has a creamy, light tan head, a smooth roasted malt flavor with hop overtones, and roasted malt bitterness. Light in body, it finishes with a dry aftertaste and a big, toasted, roasted malt aroma.

Yield: 5 gallons (18.9 L)	Final gravity: 1.012–1.014	SRM 80
Original gravity: 1.055–1.057	IBU 40	5.5% alcohol by volume

Crush and steep in 1 gallon (3.8 L) 150°F (65.5°C) water for 20 minutes:

⅔ lb. (.3 kg) 65°L German dark crystal malt
½ lb. (.23 kg) German Munich malt
⅔ lb. (.3 kg) black malt

Strain the grain water into your brew pot. Sparge the grains with ½ gallon (1.9 L) water at 150°F (65.5°C). Add water to the brew pot for 1.5 gallons (5.7 L) total volume. Bring the water to a boil, remove the pot from the stove, and add:

6.5 lb. (3 kg) M&F light DME
1.25 oz. (35 g) Northern Brewer @ 9% AA (12 HBU)
(bittering hop)

Add water until total volume in the brew pot is 2.5 gallons (9 L). Boil for 55 minutes then add:

½ oz. (14 g) Czech Saaz (aroma hop)
1 tsp. (5 ml) Irish moss

Boil for 5 minutes, remove pot from the stove, and cool for 15 minutes. Strain the cooled wort into the primary fermenter and add cold water to obtain 5 gallons (18.9 L). When the wort temperature is under 80°F (26.6°C), pitch your yeast.

1st choice: Wyeast's 2308 Munich lager yeast
(Ferment at 47–52° [8–11°C])
2nd choice: Wyeast's 2124 Bohemian lager yeast
(Ferment at 42–52°F [6–11°C])

Ferment in the primary fermenter 5–7 days or until fermentation slows, then siphon into the secondary fermenter. Bottle when fermentation is complete with:

1¼ cup (300 ml) M&F extra-light DME

 Serve at 55°F (13°C) in a pint glass or goblet.

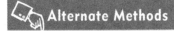 **Alternate Methods**

Mini-mash Method: Mash 1.75 lb. (.8 kg) British 2-row pale malt and the specialty grains at 150°F (65.5°C) for 90 minutes. Then follow the extract recipe omitting 2 lb. (.9 kg) DME at the beginning of the boil.

All-grain Method: Mash 8.75 lb. (4 kg) British 2-row pale malt with the specialty grains at 150°F (65.5°C) for 90 minutes. Use 9 HBU (25% less than the extract recipe) of bittering hops for 90 minutes of the boil. Add the aroma hops and Irish moss for the last 5 minutes of the boil.

ABC Extra Stout

Archipelago Brewery Co., Malayan Breweries Pte. Ltd., Singapore, Malaya

Opaque, brown ABC Extra Stout is topped with a dark tan head. It imparts to the palate a complex mix of light herbs with roasted barley overtones. This heavy-bodied brew finishes long with a dry, slightly burnt aroma and a rich, toasted, roasted malt and coffee nose. This is a very different stout, well worth brewing!

Yield: 5 gallons (18.9 L)	Final gravity: 1.018–1.019	SRM 64
Original gravity: 1.081–1.082	IBU 52	8.1% alcohol by volume

Crush and steep in 1 gallon (3.8 L) 150°F (65.5°C) water for 20 minutes:

> **²⁄₃ lb. (.3 kg) roasted barley**
> **³⁄₄ lb. (.34 kg) 120°L crystal malt**

Strain the grain water into your brew pot. Sparge the grains with ½ gallon (1.9 L) water at 150°F (65.5°C). Add water to the brew pot for 1.5 gallons (5.7 L) total volume. Bring the water to a boil, remove the pot from the stove, and add:

> **8.5 lb. (3.9 kg) M&F light DME**
> **1 lb. (.45 kg) corn sugar**
> **2.5 oz. (71 g) Northern Brewer @ 8% AA (20 HBU)**
> **(bittering hop)**

Add water until total volume in the brew pot is 2.5 gallons (9 L). Boil for 45 minutes then add:

> **½ oz. (14 g) German Hallertau Hersbrucker (flavor hop)**
> **1 tsp. (5 ml) Irish moss**

Boil for 15 minutes, remove pot from the stove, and cool for 15 minutes. Strain the cooled wort into the primary fermenter and add cold water to obtain 5 gallons (18.9 L). When the wort temperature is under 80°F (26.6°C), pitch your yeast.

> **1st choice: Wyeast's 2308 Munich lager yeast**
> **(Ferment at 47–52° [8–11°C])**
> **2nd choice: Wyeast's 2206 Bavarian lager yeast**
> **(Ferment at 42–52°F [6–11°C])**

Ferment in the primary fermenter 5–7 days or until fermentation slows, then siphon into the secondary fermenter. Bottle when fermentation is complete with:

> **1¼ cups (300 ml) M&F extra-light DME**

 Serve in a pint glass at 60°F (16°C).

 **Alternate Methods**

Mini-mash Method: Mash 2.5 lb. (1.1 kg) British 2-row pale malt and the specialty grains at 150°F (65.5°C) for 90 minutes. Then follow the extract recipe omitting 2.25 lb. (1 kg) DME at the beginning of the boil.

All-grain Method: Mash 12.75 lb. (5.8 kg) British pale malt, 1.5 lb. (.68 kg) flaked maize, and 1 lb. (.45 kg) rice hulls with specialty grains at 122°F (50°C) for 30 minutes and 150°F (65.5°C) for 90 minutes. Use 13 HBU (35% less than the extract recipe) of bittering hops for 60 minutes of the boil. Add the flavor hops and Irish moss for the last 15 minutes of the boil.

O. B. Lager Beer

Oriental Brewing Co., Ltd., Seoul, South Korea

Pale gold in color with a finely beaded white head and lively carbonation, this crisp, light-bodied lager imparts a light malt and apple aroma. It entices your palate with a fruity, light malt flavor and a dry malt aftertaste.

Yield: 5 gallons (18.9 L) Final gravity: 1.008–1.009 SRM 2–3

Original gravity: 1.044–1.045 IBU 14 4.6% alcohol by volume

Crush and steep in ½ gallon (1.9 L) 150°F (65.5°C) water for 20 minutes:

½ lb. (.23 kg) 2.5°L German light crystal malt

Strain the grain water into your brew pot. Sparge the grains with ½ gallon (1.9 L) water at 150°F (65.5°C). Add water to the brew pot for 1.5 gallons (5.7 L) total volume. Bring the water to a boil, remove the pot from the stove, and add:

4 lb. (1.8 kg) M&F extra-light DME
1.33 lb. (.6 kg) corn sugar
¾ oz. (21 g) Tettnanger @ 4.5% AA (3.5 HBU)
(bittering hop)

Add water until total volume in the brew pot is 2.5 gallons (9 L). Boil for 45 minutes then add:

½ oz. (14 g) German Hallertau Hersbrucker (flavor hop)
1 tsp. (5 ml) Irish moss

Boil for 15 minutes, remove pot from the stove, and cool for 15 minutes. Strain the cooled wort into the primary fermenter and add cold water to obtain 5 gallons (18.9 L). When the wort temperature is under 80°F (26.6°C), pitch your yeast.

1st choice: Wyeast's 2565 Kölsch yeast
(Ferment at 50–62°F [10–17°C])
2nd choice: Wyeast's 2112 California lager yeast
(Ferment at 57–62° [14–17°C])

Ferment in the primary fermenter for 5-7 days or until fermentation slows, then siphon into the secondary fermenter. Bottle when fermentation is complete with:

⅞ cup (200 ml) corn sugar

 Serve at 45°F (7°C) in a Pilsner glass.

Alternate Methods

Mini-mash Method: Mash 2.75 lb. (1.25 kg) British 2-row lager malt and the specialty grain at 150°F (65.5°C) for 90 minutes. Then follow the extract recipe omitting 2 lb. (.8 kg) DME at the beginning of the boil.

All-grain Method: Mash 5.5 lb. (2.5 kg) American 6-row pale malt, 2 lb. (.9 kg) flaked maize, and 1 lb. (.45 kg) rice hulls with the specialty grain at 122°F (50°C) for 30 minutes and 150°F (65.5°C) for 90 minutes. Use 3 HBU (15% less than the extract recipe) of bittering hops for 90 minutes of the boil. Add the flavor hops and Irish moss for the last 15 minutes of the boil.

Singha Malt Liquor

Boon Rawd Brewing Co. Ltd., Bangkok, Thailand

Singha beer is named after a lionlike character in Thailand's mythology. Singha Malt Liquor is brilliant gold in color and displays a tightly beaded, off-white head. Well carbonated with a medium body, this brew performs a balancing act with its bitter and strong hop character and flavors. The aroma is an assertive bouquet of both hops and malt and ends with a dry malt finish.

Yield: 5 gallons (18.9 L)	**Final gravity:** 1.016	**SRM** 4–5
Original gravity: 1.063	**IBU** 43	6% alcohol by volume

Crush and steep in ½ gallon (1.9 L) 150°F (65.5°C) water for 20 minutes:

> **¾ lb. (.34 kg) 2.5°L German light crystal malt**
> **¼ lb. (113 g) German Munich malt**

Strain the grain water into your brew pot. Sparge the grains with ½ gallon (1.9 L) water at 150°F (65.5°C). Add water to the brew pot for 1.5 gallons (5.7 L) total volume. Bring the water to a boil, remove the pot from the stove, and add:

> **6 lb. (2.7 kg) M&F extra-light DME**
> **1 lb. (.45 kg) corn sugar**
> **6 oz. (.17 kg) Malto-dextrin**
> **1.5 oz. (42 g) Northern Brewer @ 9% AA (13 HBU)**
> **(bittering hop)**

Add water until total volume in the brew pot is 2.5 gallons (9 L). Boil for 50 minutes then add:

> **½ oz. (14 g) German Hallertau Hersbrucker (flavor hop)**
> **½ oz. (14 g) Czech Saaz (flavor hop)**
> **1 tsp. (5 ml) Irish moss**

Boil for 10 minutes, remove pot from the stove, and cool for 15 minutes. Strain the cooled wort into the primary fermenter and add cold water to obtain 5 gallons (18.9 L). When the wort temperature is under 80°F (26.6°C), pitch your yeast.

> **1st choice: Wyeast's 2206 Bavarian lager yeast**
> **(Ferment at 42–52°F [6–11°C])**
> **2nd choice: Wyeast's 2007 Pilsen lager yeast**
> **(Ferment at 42–52°F [6–11°C])**

Ferment in the primary fermenter 5–7 days or until fermentation slows, then siphon into the secondary fermenter. Bottle when fermentation is complete with:

> **⅞ cup (200 g) corn sugar**

 Serve at 50°F (10°C) in a Pilsner glass.

 **Alternate Methods**

Mini-mash Method: Mash 2.25 lb. (1 kg) British 2-row pale malt, ½ lb. (.23 kg) dextrin malt and the specialty grains at 150°F (65.5°C) for 90 minutes. Then follow the extract recipe omitting 2 lb. (.9 kg) DME and the Malto-dextrin at the beginning of the boil.

All-grain Method: Mash 9.25 lb. (4.2 kg) British 2-row pale malt, 1.5 lb. (.68 kg) flaked maize, 1 lb. (.45 kg) rice hulls, and ½ lb. (.23 kg) dextrin malt with the specialty grains at 122°F (50°C) for 30 minutes and 150°F (65.5°C) for 60 minutes. Use 9 HBU (30% less than the extract recipe) of bittering hops for 90 minutes of the boil. Add the flavor hops and Irish moss for the last 10 minutes of the boil.

33 Export

B. G. I. Tien Giang, Vietnam

Golden-colored 33 Export has a creamy, white head, good carbonation, and light body. It has a floral hop aroma which is initially slightly bitter. This is followed by a floral taste and a dry aftertaste.

Yield: 5 gallons (18.9 L)
Original gravity: 1.052

Final gravity: 1.011–1.012
IBU 20

SRM 2–3
5.2% alcohol by volume

Crush and steep in ½ gallon (1.9 L) 150°F (65.5°C) water for 20 minutes:

½ lb. (.23 kg) 2.5°L German light crystal malt

Strain the grain water into your brew pot. Sparge the grains with ½ gallon (1.9 L) water at 150°F (65.5°C). Add water to the brew pot for 1.5 gallons (5.7 L) total volume. Bring the water to a boil, remove the pot from the stove, and add:

5 lb. (2.3 kg) M&F extra-light DME
1 lb. (.45 kg) rice syrup solids
1 oz. (28 g) Tettnanger @ 5% AA (5 HBU)
   (bittering hop)

Add water until total volume in the brew pot is 2.5 gallons (9 L). Boil for 45 minutes then add:

¼ oz. (7 g) Czech Saaz (flavor hop)
¼ oz. (7 g) Tettnanger (flavor hop)
1 tsp. (5 ml) Irish moss

Boil for 13 minutes then add:

¼ oz. (7 g) Czech Saaz (aroma hop)

Boil for 2 minutes, remove pot from the stove, and cool for 15 minutes. Strain the cooled wort into the primary fermenter and add cold water to obtain 5 gallons (18.9 L). When the wort temperature is under 80°F (26.6°C), pitch your yeast.

1st choice: Wyeast's 2007 Pilsen lager yeast
   (Ferment at 42–52°F [6–11°C])
2nd choice: Wyeast's 2124 Bohemian lager yeast
   (Ferment at 42–52°F [6–11°C])

Ferment in the primary fermenter 5–7 days or until fermentation slows, then siphon into the secondary fermenter. Bottle when fermentation is complete with:

¾ cup (180 ml) corn sugar

 Serve at 45°F (7°C) in a Pilsner glass or frosty mug.

 **Alternate Methods**

Mini-mash Method: Mash 2.75 lb. (1.25) British 2-row lager malt and the specialty grains at 150°F (65.5°C) for 90 minutes. Then follow the extract recipe omitting 2 lb. (.9 kg) DME at the beginning of the boil.

All-grain Method: Grind 1.5 lb. (.68.) rice, then cook it for 20 minutes until soft. Mash 7.75 lb. (3.5 kg) British 2-row lager malt, the rice, and 1 lb. (.45 kg) rice hulls with the specialty grains at 122°F (50°C) for 30 minutes and 150°F (65.5°C) for 60 minutes. Use 3.5 HBU (30% less than the extract recipe) of bittering hops for 90 minutes of the boil. Add the flavor hops and Irish moss for the last 15 minutes of the boil and aroma hops for the last 2 minutes.

Cooper's Best Extra Stout

Coopers Brewery Ltd., Leabrook, South Australia, Australia

Coopers Brewery, founded in 1862, is the oldest independent brewery in Australia. This dark brown stout sports a creamy, compact, light tan head. This hefty, chewy beer imparts a dry coffee and malt flavor with a slightly sweet malt aftertaste. It has a fruit and roasted barley aroma.

Yield: 5 gallons (18.9 L)   Final gravity: 1.011–1.014   SRM 87
Original gravity: 1.064–1.067   IBU 41   6.8% alcohol by volume

Crush and steep in 1 gallon (3.8 L) 150°F (65.5°C) water for 20 minutes:

> ¾ lb. (.34 kg) 120°L crystal malt
> 10 oz. (.28 kg) roasted barley
> 6 oz. (.17 kg) chocolate malt

Strain the grain water into your brew pot. Sparge the grains with ½ gallon of 150°F (65.5°C) water. Add water to the brew pot for 1.5 gallons (5.7 L) total volume. Bring the water to a boil, remove the pot from the stove, and add:

> 6.6 lb. (3 kg) Coopers light malt syrup
> .75 lb. (.34 kg) M&F light DME
> 1.25 lb. (.57 kg) cane sugar
> 1.3 oz. (37 g) @ 10% AA (13 HBU) Pride of Ringwood
>   (bittering hop)

Add water until total volume in the brew pot is 2.5 gallons (9 L). Boil for 45 minutes then add:

> ½ oz. (14 g) Styrian Goldings (flavor hop)
> 1 tsp. (5 ml) Irish moss

Boil for 15 minutes, remove pot from the stove, and cool for 15 minutes. Strain the cooled wort into the primary fermenter and add cold water to obtain 5 gallons (18.9 L). When the wort temperature is under 80°F (26.6°C), pitch your yeast.

> 1st choice: Wyeast's 1084 Irish ale yeast
>   (Ferment at 68–72°F [20–22°C])
> 2nd choice: Wyeast's 1098 British ale yeast
>   (Ferment at 68–72°F [20–22°C])

After fermentation is complete, bottle with:

> ¾ cup (180 ml) corn sugar

 Serve in a pint glass at 55°F (13°C).

 **Alternate Methods**

Mini-mash Method: Mash the specialty grains and 1.75 lb. (.8 kg) British 2-row pale malt at 150°F (65.5°C) for 90 minutes. Then follow the extract recipe omitting 3.3 lb. (1.5 kg) Coopers light malt syrup and add and additional 1 lb. (.45 kg) M&F light DME at the beginning of the boil.

All-grain Method: Mash 8.75 lb. (4 kg) British 2-row pale malt and the specialty grains at 150°F (65.5°C) for 90 minutes. Add 9.5 HBU (27% less than the extract recipe) of bittering hops and 1.25 lb. (.57 kg) cane sugar for 60 minutes of the boil. Add the flavor hops and Irish moss for the last 15 minutes of the boil.

Cooper's Sparkling Ale

Coopers Brewery Ltd., Leabrook, South Australia, Australia

It is with much Australian irony that Cooper's Sparkling Ale is labeled "sparkling," because in truth it is heavily sedimented and very cloudy. Fermented in open wooden vessels, this brew displays a white head with small beads and is hazy gold in color. The flavor is a complex blend of yeast, spice, and fruit. It finishes on the nose with spicy hops, bananas, and apples.

Yield: 5 gallons (18.9 L)   Final gravity: 1.010–1.011   SRM 18
Original gravity: 1.055–1.056   IBU 47   5.8% alcohol by volume

Crush and steep in ½ gallon (1.9 L) 150°F (65.5°C) water for 20 minutes:

½ lb. (.23 kg) 120°L crystal malt
½ lb. (.23 kg) Belgian aromatic malt

Strain the grain water into your brew pot. Sparge the grains with ½ gallon (1.9 L) water at 150°F (65.5°C). Add water to the brew pot for 1.5 gallons (5.7 L) total volume. Bring the water to a boil, remove the pot from the stove, and add:

3.3 lb. (1.5 kg) Coopers light malt syrup
2.25 lb. (1 kg) M&F light DME
1.33 lb. (.6 kg) cane sugar
1 oz. (28 g) @ 10% AA (10 HBU) Pride of Ringwood (bittering hop)

Add water until total volume in brew pot is 2.5 gallons (9 L). Boil for 45 minutes then add:

1 oz. (28 g) Pride of Ringwood (flavor hop)

Boil for 12 minutes then add:

½ oz. (14 g) Pride of Ringwood (aroma hop)

Boil for 3 minutes, remove pot from the stove, and cool for 15 minutes. Strain the cooled wort into the primary fermenter and add cold water to obtain 5 gallons (18.9 L). When the wort temperature is under 80°F (26.6°C), pitch your yeast.

1st choice: Wyeast's 1098 British ale yeast
(Ferment at 67–75°F [19–24°C])
2nd choice: Wyeast's 1028 London ale yeast
(Ferment at 67–75°F [19–24°C])

Ferment in primary fermenter 5–7 days or until fermentation slows, then siphon into secondary fermenter. After fermentation is complete, bottle with:

¾ cup (180 ml) corn sugar

 Serve in a Pilsner glass at 45°F (7°C).

 **Alternate Methods**

Mini-mash Method: Mash the specialty grains and 2 lb. (.9 kg) 2-row British pale malt at 152°F (66.6°C) for 90 minutes. Then follow the extract recipe omitting 1.75 lb. (.8 kg) DME at the beginning of the boil.

All-grain Method: Mash 7.25 lb. (3.3 kg) 2-row British pale malt with the specialty grains at 150°F (65.5°C) for 90 minutes. Add 8 HBU (20% less than the extract recipe) of bittering hops and 1.33 lb. (.6 kg) cane sugar for 60 minutes of the boil. Add the flavor hops for the last 15 minutes of the boil and the aroma hops for the last 3 minutes.

Foster's Lager

Carlton & United Breweries, Melbourne, Australia

Foster's lager was first brewed by the Foster brothers 100 years ago in Melbourne. Sold in a hefty 25.4-ounce can, it is affectionately referred to by Aussies as a "stubby," or a "tall frosty." The straw-yellow lager has a bright white head, zesty carbonation, and a light body. Pure and well balanced with an enticing malt and hop taste and light hop aftertaste, it finishes with a mild, clean aroma.

Yield: 5 gallons (18.9 L)   Final gravity: 1.008–1.009   SRM 4–5
Original gravity: 1.047–1.048   IBU 22   4.9% alcohol by volume

Crush and steep in ½ gallon (1.9 L) 150°F (65.5°C) water for 20 minutes:

> **½ lb. (.23 kg) 20°L crystal malt**

Strain the grain water into your brew pot. Sparge the grains with ½ gallon of 150°F (65.5°C) water. Add water to the brew pot for 1.5 gallons (5.7 L) total volume. Bring the water to a boil, remove the pot from the stove, and add:

> **3.3 lb. (1.5 kg) Coopers light malt syrup**
> **1.25 lb. (.57 kg) M&F extra-light DME**
> **1.25 lb. (.57 kg) cane sugar**
> **2 oz. (57 g) @ 2.5% AA (5 HBU) German Hallertau Hersbrucker (bittering hop)**

Add water until total volume is 2.5 gallons (9 L). Boil for 45 minutes then add:

> **¼ oz. (7 g) German Hallertau Hersbrucker (flavor hop)**
> **1 tsp. (5 ml) Irish moss**

Boil for 13 minutes then add:

> **1 oz. (28 g) Styrian Goldings (aroma hop)**

Boil for 2 minutes, remove pot from the stove, and cool for 15 minutes. Strain the cooled wort into the primary fermenter and add cold water to obtain 5 gallons (18.9 L). When the wort temperature is under 80°F (26.6°C), pitch your yeast.

> **1st choice: Wyeast's 2007 Pilsen lager yeast (Ferment at 42–52°F [6–11°C])**
> **2nd choice: Wyeast's 2035 American lager yeast (Ferment at 42–52°F [6–11°C])**

Ferment in the primary fermenter 5–7 days or until fermentation slows, then siphon into secondary fermenter. After fermentation is complete, bottle with:

> **¾ cup (180 ml) corn sugar**

 Serve at 45°F (7°C) in a frosty mug.

 **Alternate Methods**

Mini-mash Method: Mash 1.25 lb. (.57 kg) 2-row Pilsner malt and the specialty grain at 150°F (65.5°C) for 90 minutes. Then follow the extract recipe omitting 1.25 lb. (.57 kg) DME at the beginning of the boil.

All-grain Method: Mash 6.5 lb. (2.9 kg) German 2-row Pilsner malt and the specialty grain at 122°F (50°C) for 30 minutes and 150°F (65.5°C) for 60 minutes. Add 4 HBU (20% less than the extract recipe) of bittering hops and 1.25 lb. (.57 kg) cane sugar for 60 minutes of the boil. Add the flavor hops and the Irish moss for the last 15 minutes of the boil and the aroma hops for the last 2 minutes.

Razor Edge Lager

Esk Brewing, Launceston, Tasmania, Australia

This Tasmanian lager introduces itself with a tight, white head, and a straw-gold color. Smooth and clean on the palate, it sneaks in some subtle malt overtones before finishing with a mild malt nose. Light in body, this is an easy sipper from the land of the Tasmanian devil!

Yield: 5 gallons (18.9 L)	Final gravity: 1.009–1.011	SRM 4–5
Original gravity: 1.050–1.051	IBU 24	5.2% alcohol by volume

Crush and steep in ½ gallon (1.9 L) 150°F (65.5°C) water for 20 minutes:

> **½ lb. (.23 kg) 20°L crystal malt**

Strain the grain water into your brew pot. Sparge the grains with ½ gallon (1.9 L) water at 150°F (65.5°C). Add water to the brew pot for 1.5 gallons (5.7 L) total volume. Bring the water to a boil, remove the pot from the stove, and add:

> **3.3 lb. (1.5 kg) Coopers light malt syrup**
> **2 lb. (.9 kg) M&F extra-light DME**
> **1 lb. (.45 kg) cane sugar**
> **½ oz. (14 g) @ 12% AA (6 HBU) Pride of Ringwood (bittering hop)**

Add water until total volume in the brew pot is 2.5 gallons (9 L). Boil for 45 minutes then add:

> **¼ oz. (7 g) German Hallertau Hersbrucker (flavor hop)**
> **1 tsp. (5 ml) Irish moss**

Boil for 13 minutes then add:

> **1 oz. (28 g) Styrian Goldings (aroma hop)**

Boil for 2 minutes, remove pot from the stove, and cool for 15 minutes. Strain the cooled wort into the primary fermenter and add cold water to obtain 5 gallons (18.9 L). When the wort temperature is under 80°F (26.6°C), pitch your yeast.

> **1st choice: Wyeast's 2035 American lager yeast (Ferment at 42–52°F [6–11°C])**
> **2nd choice: Wyeast's 2007 Pilsen lager yeast (Ferment at 42–52°F [6–11°C])**

Ferment in the primary fermenter 5–7 days or until fermentation slows, then siphon into the secondary fermenter. After fermentation is complete, bottle with:

> **¾ cup (180 ml) corn sugar**

 Serve at 45°F (7°C) in a chilled hefty pewter mug.

Alternate Methods

Mini-mash Method: Mash 2.75 lb. (1.25 kg) 2-row Pilsner malt and the specialty grains at 150°F (65.5°C) for 90 minutes. Then follow the extract recipe omitting the 2 lb. (.9 kg) DME at the beginning of the boil.

All-grain Method: Mash 7.5 lb. (3.4 kg) 2-row Pilsner malt and the specialty grain for 30 minutes at 122°F (50°C) and 60 minutes at 150°F (65.5°C). Add 4.5 HBU (25% less than the extract recipe) of bittering hops and the cane sugar for 60 minutes of the boil. Add the flavor hops and Irish moss for the last 15 minutes of the boil and the aroma hops for the last 2 minutes.

West End Export Lager

South Australian Brewing Co., Thebarton, SA, Australia

This medium-bodied, deep-golden lager displays a tight-knit white head. It is malty in flavor with a hint of roasted malt. There is a whiff of spicy hops in the nose followed by a dry aftertaste. A clean, well-balanced brew that is universally appreciated.

Yield: 5 gallons (18.9 L)   Final gravity: 1.012–1.015   SRM 9
Original gravity: 1.058–1.060   IBU 24   5.7% alcohol by volume

Crush and steep in ½ gallon (1.9 L) 150°F (65.5°C) water for 20 minutes:
- **6 oz. (.17 kg) 10°L crystal malt**
- **1 oz. (28 g) chocolate malt**

Strain the grain water into your brew pot. Sparge the grains with ½ gallon (1.9 L) water at 150°F (65.5°C). Add water to the brew pot for 1.5 gallons (5.7 L) total volume. Bring the water to a boil, remove the pot from the stove, and add:
- **3.3 lb. (1.5 kg) Coopers light malt syrup**
- **4 lb. (1.8 kg) M&F extra-light DME**
- **⅔ oz. (19 g) @ 10.5% AA (7 HBU) Pride of Ringwood (bittering hop)**

Add water until total volume in brew pot is 2.5 gallons (9 L). Boil for 45 minutes then add:
- **½ oz. (14 g) German Hallertau Hersbrucker (flavor hop)**
- **1 tsp. (5 ml) Irish moss**

Boil for 13 minutes then add:
- **¼ oz. (7 g) Czech Saaz (aroma hop)**

Boil for 2 minutes, remove pot from the stove, and cool for 15 minutes. Strain the cooled wort into the primary fermenter and add cold water to obtain 5 gallons (18.9 L). When the wort temperature is under 80°F (26.6°C), pitch your yeast.
- **1st choice: Wyeast's 2206 Bavarian lager yeast (Ferment at 42–52°F [6–11°C])**
- **2nd choice: Wyeast's 2278 Czech Pilsner lager yeast (Ferment at 42–52°F [6–11°C])**

Ferment in the primary fermenter 5–7 days or until fermentation slows, then siphon into the secondary fermenter. After fermentation is complete, bottle with:
- **¾ cup (180 ml) corn sugar**

 Serve this smooth lager in a Pilsner glass at 45°F (7°C).

Alternate Methods

Mini-mash Method: Mash 2.25 lb. (1 kg) 2-row German Pilsner malt and the specialty grains at 150°F (65.5°C) for 90 minutes. Then follow the extract recipe omitting 1.5 lb. (.68 kg) DME at the beginning of the boil.

All-grain Method: Mash 11 lb. (5 kg) German 2-row Pilsner malt and the specialty grains at 150°F (65.5°C) for 90 minutes. Add 5.5 HBU (21% less than the extract recipe) of bittering hops for 60 minutes of the boil. Add the flavor hop and Irish moss for the last 15 minutes of the boil and the aroma hops for the last 2 minutes.

Steinlager

New Zealand Breweries Ltd., Auckland, New Zealand

Light golden Steinlager Pilsner was voted number one in its class by the Brewing Industry Awards in 1985. It has a bright, white head full of small bubbles, pleasant bitterness, balanced hop flavor finishing with a dry aftertaste. This medium-bodied lager leaves you with fruit and New Zealand–grown hops in the nose.

Yield: 5 gallons (18.9 L)	Final gravity: 1.010–1.013	SRM 3–4
Original gravity: 1.048–1.051	IBU 24	4.8% alcohol by volume

Crush and steep in ½ gallon (1.9 L) 150°F (65.5°C) water for 20 minutes:

⅓ lb. (.15 kg) 2.5°L German light crystal malt

Strain the grain water into your brew pot. Sparge the grains with ½ gallon (1.9 L) water at 150°F (65.5°C). Add water to the brew pot for 1.5 gallons (5.7 L) total volume. Bring the water to a boil, remove the pot from the stove, and add:

3.3 lb. (1.5 kg) Black Rock light malt syrup
3 lb. (1.4 kg) M&F extra-light DME
1 oz. (28 g) @ 6% AA (6 HBU) Sticklebrict (bittering hop) (Substitute Pride of Ringwood if not available)

Add water until the total volume in the brew pot is 2.5 gallons (9 L). Boil for 45 minutes then add:

½ oz. (14 g) Tettnanger (flavor hop)
1 tsp. (5 ml) Irish moss

Boil for 13 minutes then add:

¼ oz. (7 g) Styrian Goldings (aroma hop)

Boil for 2 minutes, remove pot from the stove, and cool for 15 minutes. Strain the cooled wort into the primary fermenter and add cold water to obtain 5 gallons (18.9 L). When the wort temperature is under 80°F (26.6°C), pitch your yeast.

> **1st choice: Wyeast's 2206 Bavarian lager yeast**
> **(Ferment at 38–45°F [3–7°C])**
> **2nd choice: Wyeast's 2124 Bohemian lager yeast**
> **(Ferment at 40–45°F [4–7°C])**

Ferment in the primary 5–7 days or until fermentation slows, then siphon into secondary fermenter. After fermentation is complete, bottle with:

¾ cup (180 ml) corn sugar

 Serve this satisfying lager in a pewter mug at 45°F (7°C).

 **Alternate Methods**

Mini-mash Method: Mash 2.5 lb. (1.1 kg) German 2-row Pilsner malt and the specialty grain at 150°F (65.5°C) for 90 minutes. Then follow the extract recipe omitting 1.75 lb. (.8 kg) DME at the beginning of the boil.

All-grain Method: Mash 9 lb. (4.1 kg) German 2-row Pilsner malt and the specialty grain at 122°F (50°C) for 30 minutes and 150°F (65.5°C) for 60 minutes. Add 4.5 HBU (25% less than the extract recipe) of bittering hops for 60 minutes of the boil. Add the flavor hops and Irish moss for the last 15 minutes of the boil and the aroma hops for the last 2 minutes.

Wilde Hogge Amber Ale

Bermuda Triangle Brewing Ltd., Southampton, Bermuda

Straight from the British island of Bermuda, this satisfying, thirst-quenching light amber ale has a caramel, malty, hoppy nose and flavor. The aftertaste of this full-bodied alt beer is smooth and slightly sweet.

Yield: 5 gallons (19 L)
Original gravity: 1.056–1.060

Final gravity: 1.014–1.017
IBU 28

SRM 21
5.4% alcohol

Crush and steep in ½ gallon (1.9 L) 150°F (65.5°C) water for 20 minutes:

11 oz. (.3 kg) 60°L US crystal malt
4 oz. (113 g) US Vienna malt
2 oz. (57 g) US chocolate malt

Strain the grain water into your brew pot. Sparge the grains with ½ gallon (1.9 L) water at 150°F (65.5°C). Add water to the brew pot for 1.5 gallons (5.7 L) total volume. Bring the water to a boil, remove the pot from the stove, and add:

6.5 lb. (3 kg) M&F light malt
6 oz. (.17 kg) Malto-dextrin
¾ oz. (21 g) Northern Brewer @ 8% AA (6 HBU)
(bittering hop)

Add water until total volume in the brew pot is 2.5 gallons (9 L). Boil for 45 minutes then add:

1 oz. (28 g) Styrian Goldings (flavor hop)
1 tsp. (5 ml) Irish moss

Boil for 13 minutes then add:

½ oz. (14 g) Tettnanger (aroma hop)

Boil for 2 minutes, remove pot from the stove, and cool for 15 minutes. Strain the cooled wort into the primary fermenter and add cold water to obtain 5 gallons (18.9 L). When the wort temperature is under 80°F (26.6°C), pitch your yeast.

1st choice: Wyeast's 1007 German ale yeast
(Ferment at 66–70°F [17–21°C])
2nd choice: Wyeast's 1338 European ale yeast
(Ferment at 66–70°F [17–21°C])

Ferment in the primary fermenter 5–7 days or until fermentation slows, then siphon into the secondary fermenter. Bottle when fermentation is complete with:

1¼ cup (300 ml) M&F extra-light DME

 Serve in a pewter mug at cellar temperature 55°F (13°C).

Alternate Methods

Mini-mash Method: Mash 2 lb. (.9 kg) British 2-row pale malt and the specialty grains at 150°F (65.5°C) for 90 minutes. Then follow the extract recipe omitting 2 lb. (.9 kg) DME at the beginning of the boil.
All-grain Method: Mash 9.25 lb. (4.2 kg) British 2-row pale malt, ½ lb. (.23 kg) dextrin malt and the specialty grains at 150°F (65.5°C) for 90 minutes. Add 4 HBU (33% less than the extract recipe) of bittering hops for 90 minutes of the boil. Add the flavor hops and Irish moss for the last 15 minutes of the boil and the aroma hops for the last 2 minutes.

Dragon Stout

Desnoes & Geddes Ltd., Kingston, Jamaica

This bottom-fermented brew is a creamy, tropical stout with a blend of well-balanced fruity and mildly bitter flavors. Bold and rich, it has a dense creamy brown head sitting on deep brown to black beer. It is medium-bodied, with sweet malt in the nose, a hint of sweet chocolate in the taste, and an ultra-smooth finish.

Yield: 5 gallons (18.9 L)   Final gravity: 1.014–1.015   SRM 122
Original gravity: 1.073–1.075   IBU 14   7.5% alcohol by volume

Crush and steep in 1 gallon (3.8 L) 150°F (65.5°C) water for 20 minutes:

- **1 lb. (.45 kg) 120°L crystal malt**
- **½ lb. (.23 kg) chocolate malt**
- **⅓ lb. (.15 kg) black malt**
- **2 oz. (57 g) roasted barley**

Strain the grain water into your brew pot. Sparge the grains with ½ gallon (1.9 L) water at 150°F (65.5°C). Add water to the brew pot for 1.5 gallons (5.7 L) total volume. Bring the water to a boil, remove the pot from the stove, and add:

- **6.75 lb. (3.1 kg) M&F light DME**
- **½ lb. (.23 kg) dark brown sugar**
- **1.5 lb. (.68 kg) corn sugar**
- **½ oz. (14 g) Yakima Magnum @ 10% AA (5 HBU) (bittering hop)**

Add water until the total volume in the brew pot is 2.5 gallons (9 L). Boil for 50 minutes then add:

- **1 tsp. (5 ml) Irish moss**

Boil for 10 minutes, remove pot from the stove, and cool for 15 minutes. Strain the cooled wort into the primary fermenter and add cold water to obtain 5 gallons (18.9 L). When the wort temperature is under 80°F (26.6°C), pitch your yeast.

> **1st choice: Wyeast's 2308 Munich lager yeast (Ferment for 2 weeks at 42–52°F (6–11°C), ferment until finished at 57–62° [14–17°C])**
> **2nd choice: Wyeast's 2112 California lager yeast (Ferment at 50–62°F [10–17°C])**

Ferment in the primary fermenter 5–7 days or until fermentation slows, then siphon into the secondary fermenter. Bottle when fermentation is complete with:

- **1¼ cups (300 ml) wheat DME (55% wheat, 45% barley)**

 Serve at 55°F (13°C) in a goblet or pint glass.

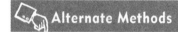 **Alternate Methods**

Mini-mash Method: Mash 1 lb. (.45 kg) US 6-row pale malt with the specialty grains at 122°F (50°C) for 30 minutes and 150°F (65.5°C) for 60 minutes. Then follow the extract recipe but omit 1.75 lb. (.8 kg) DME at the beginning of the boil.

All-grain Method: Mash 9.75 lb. (4.4 kg) 6-row lager malt, 2.25 lb. (1 kg) flaked maize, and 1 lb. (.45 kg) rice hulls with the specialty grains at 122°F (50°C) for 30 minutes and 150°F (65.5°C) for 60 minutes. Add 3.5 HBU (30% less than the extract recipe) bittering hops and the brown sugar for 90 minutes of the boil. Add the Irish moss for the last 15 minutes of the boil.

Medalla Light Cerveza

Medalla Inc., San Juan, Puerto Rico

This American light-style lager has a tight, white head and an extremely pale straw color. Highly carbonated, Medalla Light is bottle-conditioned. There is little aroma, just a faint hint of fruit and malt. Very neutral in flavor, there is a suggestion of hop bitterness that nicely balances out the light malt sweetness.

Yield: 5 gallons (18.9 L)   Final gravity: 1.006–1.008   SRM 2–2.5
Original gravity: 1.039–1.040   IBU 13.5   4.2% alcohol by volume

Crush and steep ½ gallon (1.9 L) in 150°F (65.5°C) water for 20 minutes:

4 oz. (113 g) 10°L crystal malt

Strain the grain water into your brew pot. Sparge the grains with ½ gallon (1.9 L) water at 150°F (65.5°C). Add water to the brew pot for 1.5 gallons (5.7 L) total volume. Bring the water to a boil, remove the pot from the stove, and add:

2.75 lb. (1.25 kg) M&F extra-light DME
1 lb. (.45 kg) rice solids
1 lb. (.45 kg) corn sugar
1 oz. (28 g) German Hallertau Hersbrucker @ 3.5% AA (3.5 HBU) (bittering hop)

Add water until total volume in brew pot is 2.5 gallons (9 L). Boil for 45 minutes then add:

1 tsp. (5 ml) Irish moss

Boil for 15 minutes, remove pot from the stove, and cool for 15 minutes. Strain the cooled wort into the primary fermenter and add cold water to obtain 5 gallons (18.9 L). When the wort temperature is under 80°F (26.6°C), pitch your yeast.

> **1st choice: Wyeast's 2035 American lager yeast (Ferment at 42–52°F [6–11°C])**
> **2nd choice: Wyeast's 2007 Pilsen lager yeast (Ferment at 42–52°F [6–11°C])**

Ferment in the primary fermenter 5–7 days or until fermentation slows, then siphon into the secondary fermenter. Bottle when fermentation is complete with:

¾ cup (180 ml) corn sugar

 Serve in a Pilsner glass at 45°F (7°C).

Alternate Methods

Mini-mash Method: Mash 2.25 lb. (1 kg) British 2-row lager malt with the specialty grains at 150°F (65.5°C) for 90 minutes. Then follow the extract recipe but omit 1.75 lb. (.8 kg) DME at the beginning of the boil.

All-grain Method: Grind 1.5 lb. (.68 kg) rice, then boil for 20 minutes until soft. Mash 4.75 lb. (2.2 kg) US 6-row pale malt, the rice, 1.5 lb. (.68 kg) flaked maize, and 1 lb. (.45 kg) rice hulls with the specialty grains at 122°F (50°C) for 30 minutes and 150°F (65.5°C) for 60 minutes. Use 3 HBU (15% less than the extract recipe) bittering hops for 90 minutes of the boil. Add the Irish moss for the last 15 minutes of the boil.

Carib Shandy Lager Flavored with Ginger

Carib Brewery, Champos Fleurs, Trinidad

This interesting and refreshing lager tastes very much like ginger ale. It is golden in color and has a creamy white head and low carbonation. The refreshing aroma reminds us of pickled ginger. The flavor has a heavy ginger ale taste with a sweet aftertaste. At only 1.3% alcohol, this brew is much lighter than most beers, but bolder than a soft drink. Carib Shandy with ginger is a unique thirst-quenching summer brew.

Yield: 5 gallons (18.9 L)	Final gravity: 1.003–1.004	SRM 1
Original gravity: 1.014	IBU 0	1.3% alcohol by volume

Crush and steep in ½ gallon (1.9 L) 150°F (65.5°C) water for 20 minutes:

> **1 oz. (28 g) 20°L crystal malt**

Strain the grain water into your brew pot. Sparge the grains with ½ gallon (1.9 L) water at 150°F (65.5°C). Add water to the brew pot for 1.5 gallons (5.7 L) total volume. Bring the water to a boil, remove the pot from the stove, and add:

> **1 lb. (.46 kg) corn sugar**
> **½ lb. (.23 kg) M&F extra-light DME**
> **8 oz. (226 g) lactose**

Add water until total volume in brew pot is 2.5 gallons (9 L). Boil for 45 minutes then add:

> **2 oz. (57 g) peeled, chopped fresh ginger**
> **1 tsp. (5 ml) Irish moss**

Boil for 15 minutes, remove pot from the stove, and cool for 15 minutes. Strain the cooled wort into the primary fermenter and add cold water to obtain 5 gallons (18.9 L). When the wort temperature is under 80°F (26.6°C), pitch your yeast.

> **1st choice: Wyeast's 2007 Pilsen lager yeast**
> **(Ferment at 42–52°F [6–11°C])**
> **2nd choice: Wyeast's 2035 American lager yeast**
> **(Ferment at 42–52°F [6–11°C])**

Ferment in the primary fermenter 5–7 days or until fermentation slows, then siphon into the secondary fermenter. In the second stage fermentation, add:

> **3 oz. (45 ml) natural ginger flavoring**

Bottle when fermentation is complete with:

> **1 cup (240 ml) corn sugar**

 Serve at 45°F (7°C) in a champagne flute.

 **Alternate Methods**

Mini-mash Method: Mash ¾ lb. (.34 kg) British 2-row lager malt with the specialty grain at 150°F (65.5°C) for 90 minutes. Then follow the extract recipe but omit the DME at the beginning of the boil.

All-grain Method: Mash 1 lb. (.45 kg) US 6-row pale malt, ½ lb. (.23 kg) flaked maize, and ½ lb. (.23 kg) rice hulls with the specialty grain at 122°F (50°C) for 30 minutes and 150°F (65.5°C) for 60 minutes. Add ½ lb. (.23 kg) corn sugar and ¼ lb. (113 g) lactose at the beginning of the boil. Add the ginger and Irish moss for the last 15 minutes of the boil.

Cerveza Imperial

Cerveceria Costa Rica S.A., Heredia, Costa Rica

This crisp Costa Rican lager has a tightly beaded, snow-white head and light straw color. Its sweet malt nose leads into a faint malt and hops flavor. Cerveza Imperial is a light-bodied, easy-drinking brew.

Yield: 5 gallons (18.9 L) Final gravity: 1.011–1.012 SRM 3–4
Original gravity: 1.051–1.052 IBU 18 5.1% alcohol by volume

Crush and steep in ½ gallon (1.9 L) 150°F (65.5°C) water for 20 minutes:

10 oz. (.28 kg) 10°L crystal malt

Strain the grain water into your brew pot. Sparge the grains with ½ gallon (1.9 L) water at 150°F (65.5°C). Add water to the brew pot for 1.5 gallons (5.7 L) total volume. Bring the water to a boil, remove the pot from the stove, and add:

5.5 lb. (2.5 kg) M&F extra-light DME
½ lb. (.23 kg) corn sugar
1 oz. (28 g) Tettnanger @ 5% AA (5 HBU)
(bittering hop)

Add water until total volume in brew pot is 2.5 gallons (9 L). Boil for 50 minutes then add:

½ oz. (14 g) Czech Saaz (flavor hop)
1 tsp. (5 ml) Irish moss

Boil for 10 minutes, remove pot from the stove, and cool for 15 minutes. Strain the cooled wort into the primary fermenter and add cold water to obtain 5 gallons (18.9 L). When the wort temperature is under 80°F (26.6°C), pitch your yeast.

1st choice: Wyeast's 2035 American lager yeast
(Ferment at 42–52°F [6–11°C])
2nd choice: Wyeast's 2007 Pilsen lager yeast
(Ferment at 42–52°F [6–11°C])

Ferment in the primary fermenter 5–7 days or until fermentation slows, then siphon into the secondary fermenter. Bottle when fermentation is complete with:

1¼ cups (300 ml) M&F extra-light DME.

 Serve in a Pilsner glass at 45°F (7°C).

 **Alternate Methods**

Mini-mash Method: Mash 2.75 lb. (1.25 kg) British 2-row lager malt with the specialty grain at 150°F (65.5°C) for 90 minutes. Then follow the extract recipe but omit 2 lb. (.9 kg) DME at the beginning of the boil.

All-grain Method: Mash 8.25 lb. (3.75 kg) British 2-row lager malt, ¾ lb. (.34 kg) flaked maize, and ½ lb. (.23 kg) rice hulls with the specialty grain at 122°F (50°C) for 30 minutes and 150°F (65.5°C) for 60 minutes. Use 4 HBU (20% less than the extract recipe) bittering hops for 90 minutes of the boil. Add the flavor hops and Irish moss for the last 10 minutes of the boil.

Pilsener of El Salvador Lager Bier

Cerveceria La Constacia, S. A., San Salvador, El Salvador

This soft, pale golden lager has a frothy white head with lace that lasts to the last sip. The complex, spicy hop nose is followed by a zesty, refreshing flavor with nuances of toasted grain, mild malt, and subtle herbs. With lively and sprightly carbonation, this smooth pilsner has a medium body and a dry, mild malt finish that just hints at hops.

Yield: 5 gallons (18.9 L)	Final gravity: 1.010–1.011	SRM 3–4
Original gravity: 1.047–1.048	IBU 18.5	4.7% alcohol by volume

Crush and steep ½ gallon (1.9 L) in 150°F (65.5°C) water for 20 minutes:

> **4 oz. (113 g) 10°L crystal malt**
> **3 oz. (85 g) German Vienna malt**
> **2 oz. (57 g) Belgian aromatic malt**

Strain the grain water into your brew pot. Sparge the grains with ½ gallon (1.9 L) water at 150°F (65.5°C). Add water to the brew pot for 1.5 gallons (5.7 L) total volume. Bring the water to a boil, remove the pot from the stove, and add:

> **5 lb. (2.3 kg) M&F extra-light DME**
> **½ lb. (.23 kg) rice syrup solids**
> **⅘ oz. (23 g) Czech Saaz @ 2.5% AA (2 HBU)**
> **(bittering hop)**
> **1 oz. (28 g) German Hallertau Hersbrucker @ 2.5% AA**
> **(2.5 HBU) (bittering hop)**

Add water until total volume in brew pot is 2.5 gallons (9 L). Boil for 45 minutes then add:

> **½ oz. (14 g) Styrian Goldings (flavor hop)**
> **1 tsp. (5 ml) Irish moss**

Boil for 15 minutes, remove pot from the stove, and cool for 15 minutes. Strain the cooled wort into the primary fermenter and add cold water to obtain 5 gallons (18.9 L). When the wort temperature is under 80°F (26.6°C), pitch your yeast.

> **1st choice: Wyeast's 2035 American lager yeast**
> **(Ferment at 42–52°F [6–11°C])**
> **2nd choice: Wyeast's 2007 Pilsen lager yeast**
> **(Ferment at 42–52°F [6–11°C])**

Ferment in the primary fermenter 5–7 days or until fermentation slows, then siphon into the secondary fermenter. Bottle when fermentation is complete with:

> **¼ cups (300 ml) M&F extra-light DME**

 Serve at 45°F (7°C) in a Pilsner glass.

 **Alternate Methods**

Mini-mash Method: Mash 2.75 lb. (1.25 kg) British 2-row lager malt with the specialty grains at 150°F (65.5°C) for 90 minutes. Then follow the extract recipe but omit 2 lb. (.9 kg) DME at the beginning of the boil.

All-grain Method: Grind 12 oz. (.34 kg) rice, then boil for 20 minutes until soft. Mash 7.5 lb. (3.4 kg) British 2-row lager malt, the rice, and ½ lb. (.23 kg) rice hulls with the specialty grains at 122°F (50°C) for 30 minutes and 150°F (65.5°C) for 60 minutes. Use 3.5 HBU (22% less than the extract recipe) bittering hops for 90 minutes of the boil. Add the flavor hop and Irish moss for the last 15 minutes of the boil.

Famosa Lager

Cerveceria Centro, Guatemala City, Guatemala

Cerveceria Nacional brewery has been in operation since 1895. This offering from the brewery displays a dense, snow-white head and a lovely light gold color. It introduces itself with a nose that is more malt than hops. This is followed by a smooth interplay of flavor between sweet malt and hops. It leaves you with a remembrance of hops.

Yield: 5 gallons (18.9 L)
Original gravity: 1.040–1.041

Final gravity: 1.009–1.010
IBU 17

SRM 4
3.9% alcohol by volume

Crush and steep in ½ gallon (1.9 L) 150°F (65.5°C) water for 20 minutes:

½ lb. (.23 kg) 20°L crystal malt

Strain the grain water into your brew pot. Sparge the grains with ½ gallon (1.9 L) water at 150°F (65.5°C). Add water to the brew pot for 1.5 gallons (5.7 L) total volume. Bring the water to a boil, remove the pot from the stove, and add:

4 lb. (1.8 kg) Alexander's pale malt syrup
1.5 lb. (.68 kg) M&F extra-light DME
1 oz. (28 g) Tettnanger @ 4.5% AA (4.5 HBU)
(bittering hop)

Add water until the total volume is 2.5 gallons (9 L). Boil for 45 minutes then add:

¼ oz. (7 g) Czech Saaz (flavor hop)
1 tsp. (5 ml) Irish moss

Boil for 15 minutes, remove pot from the stove, and cool for 15 minutes. Strain the cooled wort into the primary fermenter and add cold water to obtain 5 gallons (18.9 L). When the wort temperature is under 80°F (26.6°C), pitch your yeast.

1st choice: Wyeast's 2035 American lager yeast
(Ferment at 42–52°F [6–11°C])
2nd choice: Wyeast's 2007 Pilsen lager yeast
(Ferment at 42–52°F [6–11°C])

Ferment in the primary fermenter 5–7 days or until fermentation slows, then siphon into the secondary fermenter. Bottle when fermentation is complete with:

¾ cup (180 ml) corn sugar

 Serve in a Pilsner glass at 45°F (7°C).

Alternate Methods

Mini-mash Method: Mash 1.75 lb. (.8 kg) British 2-row lager malt with the specialty grain at 150°F (65.5°C) for 90 minutes. Then follow the extract recipe but omit the DME at the beginning of the boil.

All-grain Method: Mash 7 lb. (3.2 kg) British 2-row lager malt with the specialty grain at 122°F (50°C) for 30 minutes and 150°F (65.5°C) for 60 minutes. Use 3.5 HBU (22% less than the extract recipe) bittering hops for 90 minutes of the boil. Add the flavor hops and Irish moss for the last 15 minutes of the boil.

Cerveza Panama Lager Alemania style

Cerveceria Del Baru, S.A., Panama

This Panamanian lager has a creamy, tightly beaded, snow-white head and a pale golden color. It captures your attention with its sharp hop aroma blended with light malt. The feathery-bodied lager has a dry, crisp, mild flavor and ends with a dry aftertaste.

Yield: 5 gallons (18.9 L) **Final gravity: 1.010–1.011** **SRM 4**
Original gravity: 1.048–1.049 **IBU 21** **4.8% alcohol by volume**

Crush and steep in ½ gallon (1.9 L) 150°F (65.5°C) water for 20 minutes:

> **6 oz. (170 g) 20°L crystal malt**

Strain the grain water into your brew pot. Sparge the grains with ½ gallon (1.9 L) water at 150°F (65.5°C). Add water to the brew pot for 1.5 gallons (5.7 L) total volume. Bring the water to a boil, remove the pot from the stove, and add:

> **5 lb. (2.3 kg) M&F extra-light DME**
> **⅔ lb. (.3 kg) corn sugar**
> **1 oz. (28 g) Czech Saaz @ 2.5% AA (2.5 HBU)**
> **(bittering hop)**
> **⅔ oz. Tettnanger @ 4.5% AA (3 HBU) (bittering hop)**

Add water until total volume in brew pot is 2.5 gallons (9 L). Boil for 45 minutes then add:

> **½ oz. (14 g) Czech Saaz (flavor hop)**
> **1 tsp. (5 ml) Irish moss**

Boil for 10 minutes then add:

> **¼ oz. (7 g) Czech Saaz (aroma hop)**

Boil for 5 minutes, remove pot from the stove, and cool for 15 minutes. Strain the cooled wort into the primary fermenter and add cold water to obtain 5 gallons (18.9 L). When the wort temperature is under 80°F (26.6°C), pitch your yeast.

> **1st choice: Wyeast's 2007 Pilsen lager yeast**
> **(Ferment at 42–52°F [6–11°C])**
> **2nd choice: Wyeast's 2278 Czech Pilsner lager yeast**
> **(Ferment at 42–52°F [6–11°C])**

Ferment in the primary fermenter 5–7 days or until fermentation slows, then siphon into the secondary fermenter. Bottle when fermentation is complete with:

> **¾ cup (180 ml) corn sugar**

 Serve this lager at 45°F (7°C) in a Pilsner glass.

 **Alternate Methods**

Mini-mash Method: Mash 2.75 lb. (1.25 kg) British 2-row lager malt with the specialty grain at 122°F (50°C) for 30 minutes and 150°F (65.5°C) for 60 minutes. Then follow the extract recipe but omit 2 lb. (.9 kg) DME at the beginning of the boil.

All-grain Method: Mash 7.75 lb. (3.5 kg) British 2-row lager malt, 1 lb. (.45 kg) flaked maize, and ½ lb. (.23 kg) rice hulls with the specialty grain at 122°F (50°C) for 30 minutes and 150°F (65.5°C) for 60 minutes. Use 4 HBU (27% less than the extract recipe) bittering hops for 90 minutes of the boil. Add the flavor hops and Irish moss for the last 15 minutes of the boil and the aroma hops for the last 5 minutes.

Edelweiss Dunkel Weissbier

Hofbrau Kaltenhausen, Salzburg, Austria

This Austrian weissbier has a creamy, off-white head and is hazy amber in color. Enticing you with an aroma that is redolent of fruit, clove, and banana, this wheat beer lives up to its promise. It finishes with a dry aftertaste.

Yield: 5 gallons (18.9 L)　　Final gravity: 1.010–1.012　　SRM 10–11
Original gravity: 1.051–1.053　　IBU 12　　5.2% alcohol by volume

Crush and steep in ½ gallon (1.9 L) 150°F (65.5°C) water for 20 minutes:

6 oz. (.17 kg) 65°L German dark crystal malt
4 oz. (113 g) Belgian Cara-Vienne malt
2 oz. (57 g) Gambrinus honey malt

Strain the grain water into your brew pot. Sparge the grains with ½ gallon (1.9 L) water at 150°F (65.5°C). Add water to the brew pot for 1.5 gallons (5.7 L) total volume. Bring the water to a boil, remove the pot from the stove, and add:

5.75 lb. (2.6 kg) M&F wheat DME (55% wheat, 45% barley)
1 oz. (28 g) German Hallertau Hersbrucker @ 3.5% AA (3.5 HBU) (bittering hop)

Add water until total volume in the brew pot is 2.5 gallons (9 L). Boil for 60 minutes, remove pot from the stove, and cool for 15 minutes. Strain the cooled wort into the primary fermenter and add cold water to obtain 5 gallons (18.9 L). When the wort temperature is under 80°F (26.6°C), pitch your yeast.

1st choice: Wyeast's 3068 Weihenstephan wheat yeast (Ferment at 67–73°F [19–23°C])
2nd choice: Wyeast's 3333 German wheat yeast (Ferment at 67–73°F [19–23°C])

Ferment in the primary fermenter 5–7 days or until fermentation slows, then siphon into the secondary fermenter. Bottle when fermentation is complete with:

1¼ cup (300 mg) M&F wheat DME

 Serve in a wheat beer glass at 50°F (10°C).

Alternate Methods

Mini-mash Method: Mash 1.5 lb. (.68 kg) Belgian 2-row pale malt, 1.25 lb. (.57 kg) German wheat malt and the specialty grains at 150°F (65.5°C) for 90 minutes. Then follow the extract recipe omitting 2 lb. (.9 kg) wheat DME at the beginning of the boil.

All-grain Method: Mash 5 lb. (2.3 kg) Belgian 2-row pale malt, 4.25 lb. (1.9 kg) German wheat malt, and the specialty grains at 150°F (65.5°C) for 90 minutes. Add 2.5 HBU (29% less than the extract recipe) of bittering hops for 90 minutes of the boil.

MacQueen's Nessie, Original Red Ale

Eggenberg Castle, Vorchdorf, Austria

This very drinkable, light amber ale is named after Scotland's legendary monster. Nessie has an off-white, dense head and imparts a complex, malty, earthy, rich aroma. Also complex in flavor, this impressive brew hints of dryness, hops, malt, alcohol, smoke, and whiskey ending with a malty aftertaste. This red ale is aged six months in the bottle before being released for sale.

Yield: 5 gallons (18.9 L)	Final gravity: 1.016–1.020	SRM 10–11
Original gravity: 1.075–1.080	IBU 25	7.5% alcohol by volume

Crush and steep in ½ gallon (1.9 L) 150°F (65.5°C) water for 20 minutes:

> **6 oz. (.17 kg) 55°L British crystal malt**
> **6 oz. (.17 kg) German Vienna malt**
> **4 oz. (113 g) Belgian aromatic malt**
> **4 oz. (113 g) whiskey malt (Use 2 oz. [57 g] peat-smoked malt as an alternate)**

Strain the grain water into your brew pot. Sparge the grains with ½ gallon (1.9 L) water at 150°F (65.5°C). Add water to the brew pot for 1.5 gallons (5.7 L) total volume. Bring the water to a boil, remove the pot from the stove, and add:

> **6.6 lb. (3 kg) John Bull light malt syrup**
> **3.5 lb. (1.6 kg) M&F light DME**
> **2.75 oz. (78 g) German Hallertau Hersbrucker @ 3% AA (8.5 HBU) (bittering hop)**

Add water until total volume in the brew pot is 2.5 gallons (9 L). Boil for 45 minutes then add:

> **½ oz. (14 g) Styrian Goldings (flavor hop)**
> **1 tsp. (5 ml) Irish moss**

Boil for 15 minutes, remove pot from the stove, and cool for 15 minutes. Strain the cooled wort into the primary fermenter and add cold water to obtain 5 gallons (18.9 L). When the wort temperature is under 80°F (26.6°C), pitch your yeast.

> **1st choice: Wyeast's 1728 Scottish ale yeast (Ferment at 66–72°F [19–22°C])**
> **2nd choice: Wyeast's 1084 Irish ale yeast (Ferment at 66–72°F [19–22°C])**

Ferment in the primary fermenter 5–7 days or until fermentation slows, then siphon into the secondary fermenter. Bottle when fermentation is complete with:

> **1¼ cup (300 mg) M&F extra-light DME**

 Pour into a large goblet and enjoy at 55°F (13°C).

 **Alternate Methods**

Mini-mash Method: Mash 2 lb. (.9 kg) British 2-row pale malt and the specialty grains at 150°F (65.5°C) for 90 minutes. Then follow the extract recipe omitting 2 lb. (.9 kg) DME at the beginning of the boil.

All-grain Method: Mash 13 lb. (5.9 kg) British 2-row pale malt with the specialty grains at 150°F (65.5°C) for 90 minutes. Add 5 HBU (35% less than the extract recipe) of bittering hops for 90 minutes of the boil. Add the flavor hops and Irish moss for the last 15 minutes of the boil.

Affligem Abbey Tripel

Brouwerij De Smedt, Opwijk, Belgium

Affligem is finely carbonated and displays a large, white, creamy, dense head with a bright golden-amber color. This tripel has an aroma full of malt, fruit, and honey notes followed by a sweet, complex flavor of malt, spicy hops, and alcohol.

Yield: 5 gallons (18.9 L)	Final gravity: 1.016–1.019	SRM 5–6
Original gravity: 1.083–1.086	IBU 25	8.5% alcohol by volume

Crush and steep in ½ gallon (1.9 L) 150°F (65.5°C) water for 20 minutes:

6 oz. (.17 kg) Belgian aromatic malt

Strain the grain water into your brew pot. Sparge the grains with ½ gallon (1.9 L) water at 150°F (65.5°C). Add water to the brew pot for 3.5 gallons total volume. Bring the water to a boil, remove the pot from the stove, and add:

8.5 lb. (3.9 kg) M&F extra-light DME
1.5 lb. (.68 kg) Belgian clear candi sugar
½ oz. (14 g) Styrian Goldings @ 6% AA (3 HBU) (bittering hop)
½ oz. (14 g) Challenger @ 8% AA (4 HBU) (bittering hop)

Add water until total volume in the brew pot is 3 gallons (13.25 L). Boil for 45 minutes then add:

½ oz. (14 g) Styrian Goldings (flavor hop)
¼ oz. (7 g) sweet orange peel
1 tsp. (5 ml) Irish moss

Boil for 12 minutes then add:

¼ oz. (7 g) Styrian Goldings (aroma hop)

Boil for 3 minutes, remove pot from the stove, and cool for 15 minutes. Strain the cooled wort into the primary fermenter and add cold water to obtain 5 gallons (18.9 L). When the wort temperature is under 80°F (26.6°C), pitch your yeast.

> **1st choice: Wyeast's 1214 Belgian Abbey ale yeast (Ferment at 70–75°F [21–24°C])**
> **2nd choice: Wyeast's 1762 Belgian Abbey ale II yeast (Ferment at 70–75°F [21–24°C])**

Ferment in the primary fermenter 5–7 days or until fermentation slows, then siphon into the secondary fermenter. Bottle when fermentation is complete with:

⅜ cup (85 ml) corn sugar
⅜ cup (85 ml) cane sugar

 Serve in a wide-mouthed glass at 44–48°F (7–9°C).

 **Alternate Methods**

Mini-mash Method: Mash 3.5 lb. (1.6 kg) Belgian 2-row Pilsner malt and the specialty grains at 150°F (65.5°C) for 90 minutes. Then follow the extract recipe omitting 2.5 lb. (1.1 kg) DME at the beginning of the boil.

All-grain Method: Mash 13.5 lb. (6.1 kg) Belgian 2-row Pilsner malt with the specialty grain at 150°F (65.5°C) for 90 minutes. Add 5 HBU (28% less than the extract recipe) of bittering hops and the candi for 90 minutes of the boil. Add the flavor hops and Irish moss for the last 15 minutes of the boil and the aroma hops for the last 3 minutes.

Barbar Belgian Honey Ale

Lefèbvre Brewery, Quenast, Belgium

This golden honey ale is derived from mead. It has a creamy white head and a full mouthfeel. The flavor is complex with orange and fruit and a hint of honey.

Yield: 5 gallons (18.9 L)	Final gravity:1.014–1.017	SRM 7–8
Original gravity:1.079–1.083	IBU 17.5	8.3% alcohol by volume

Crush and steep in ½ gallon (1.9 L) 150°F (65.5°C) water for 20 minutes:

½ lb. (.23 kg) Belgian Cara-Vienne malt
⅓ lb. (.15 kg) Gambrinus honey malt

Strain the grain water into your brew pot. Sparge the grains with ½ gallon (1.9 L) water at 150°F (65.5°C). Add water to the brew pot for 1.5 gallons (5.7 L) total volume. Bring the water to a boil and add:

5.5 lb. (2.5 kg) M&F extra-light DME
2 lb. (.9 kg) wheat DME
1 lb. (.45 kg) clover honey
1 lb. (.45 kg) Belgian clear candi sugar
2 oz. (58 g) German Hallertau Hersbrucker @ 2.5% AA

Add water until total volume in the brew pot is 2.5 gallons (9 L). Boil for 45 minutes then add:

½ oz. (14 g) Styrian Goldings (flavor hop)
½ oz. (14 g) Curacao bitter orange peel
½ tsp. (2 ml) coriander
½ lb. (.23 kg) clover honey
1 tsp. (5 ml) Irish moss

Boil for 10 minutes then add:

½ tsp. (2 ml) coriander
¼ oz. (7 g) Curacao bitter orange peel

Boil for 5 minutes. Cool for 15 minutes. Strain the cooled wort into the primary fermenter and add cold water to obtain 5 gallons (18.9 L). When the wort temperature is under 80°F (26.6°C), pitch yeast.

Wyeast's 1214 Belgian Abbey ale yeast
(Ferment at 70–73°F [21–23°C]) Ferments to 12% ABV.

Ferment in the primary fermenter 5–7 days or until fermentation slows, then siphon into the secondary fermenter. Bottle when fermentation is complete with:

⅞ cup (210 ml) orange blossom honey

 Serve in a Belgian mug at 55°F (13°C).

 **Alternate Methods**

Mini-mash Method: Mash 3 lb. (1.36 kg) Belgian 2-row Pilsner malt and the specialty grains at 150°F (65.5°C) for 90 minutes. Then follow the extract recipe omitting 2.5 lb. (1.1 kg) DME at the beginning of the boil.

All-grain Method: Mash 10.25 lb. (4.6 kg) Belgian 2-row Pilsner malt, 1 lb. (.45 kg) German wheat malt, and the specialty grains at 150°F (65.5°C) for 90 minutes. Add 3 HBU (40% less than the extract recipe) of bittering hops, the honey, and the candi sugar for 90 minutes of the boil. Add the flavor hops and Irish moss for the last 15 minutes of the boil and the aroma hops for the last 3 minutes.

Blanche de Bruges

Brasserie de Gouden Boom, Bruges, Belgium

The refreshing white beer is less tart and citrusy than some of the other whites. It is subtly spiced with apple and orange notes and has a long, dry, finish.

Yield: 5 gallons (18.9 L)	Final gravity: 1.009–1.010	SRM 4
Original gravity: 1.048–1.049	IBU 20	5% alcohol by volume

Crush and steep in ½ gallon (1.9 L) 150°F (65.5°C) water for 20 minutes:

> **4 oz. (113 g) flaked oats**
> **3 oz. (85 g) Belgian biscuit malt**

Strain the grain water into your brew pot. Sparge the grains with ½ gallon (1.9 L) water at 150°F (65.5°C). Add water to the brew pot for 1.5 gallons (5.7 L) total volume. Bring the water to a boil and add:

> **4 lb. (1.8 kg) Alexander's wheat malt syrup (60% wheat, 40% barley)**
> **2 lb. (.9 kg) M&F wheat DME (55% wheat, 45% barley)**
> **½ lb. (.23 kg) Belgian clear candi sugar**
> **1 oz. (28 g) Styrian Goldings @ 5% AA (5 HBU)**

Add water until total volume in the brew pot is 2.5 gallons (9 L). Boil for 45 minutes then add:

> **½ oz. (14 g) Czech Saaz (flavor hop)**
> **½ oz. (14 g) Curacao bitter orange peel**
> **1 tsp. (5 ml) ground coriander**
> **¼ tsp. (1 ml) crushed cumin seeds**
> **1 tsp. (5 ml) crushed grains of paradise**
> **1 tsp. (5 ml) Irish moss**

Boil for 12 minutes then add:

> **¼ oz. (7 g) Curacao bitter orange peel**
> **½ tsp. (2 ml) coriander**

Boil for 3 minutes. Cool for 15 minutes. Strain the cooled wort into the primary fermenter and add cold water to obtain 5 gallons (18.9 L). When the wort temperature is under 80°F (26.6°C), pitch yeast.

> **Wyeast's 3944 Belgian White Beer yeast**
> **(Ferment at 70–73°F [21–23°C])**

Ferment in the primary fermenter 5–7 days or until fermentation slows, then siphon into the secondary fermenter. Bottle when fermentation is complete with:

> **½ cup (120 ml) clover or orange blossom honey**
> **⅜ cup (85 ml) corn sugar**

 Serve at 50°F (10°C) in a footed heavy goblet.

 **Alternate Methods**

Mini-mash Method: Mash 1.5 lb. (.68 kg) Belgian 2-row Pilsner malt, 1.25 lb. (.57 kg) flaked wheat, ½ lb. (.23 kg) oat hulls, and the specialty grains at 150°F (65.5°C) for 90 minutes. Then follow the extract recipe omitting 2 lb. (.9 kg) DME at the beginning of the boil.

All-grain Method: Mash 4.5 lb. (2 kg) Belgian 2-row Pilsner malt, 4 lb. (1.8 kg) flaked wheat, 1 lb. (.45 kg) oat hulls, and the specialty grains at 150°F (65.5°C) for 90 minutes. Add 4 HBU (20% less than the extract recipe) of bittering hops and the candi sugar for 90 minutes of the boil. Add the flavor hops, spices, and Irish moss for the last 15 minutes of the boil and the aroma spices for the last 3 minutes.

Boskeun

De Dolle Brouwers, Esen, Belgium

Boskeun (Easter Bunny) is a seasonal beer with a fine, white head and a hazy orange color. The aroma includes fruit, bubblegum, light malt, and honey leading to a sweet, fruity palate.

Yield: 5 gallons (18.9 L)	Final gravity: 1.015–1.017	SRM 10–11
Original gravity: 1.078–1.081	IBU 20	8.1% alcohol by volume

Crush and steep in ½ gallon (1.9 L) 150°F (65.5°C) water for 20 minutes:

> **½ lb. (.23 kg) 40°L crystal malt**
> **4 oz. (113 g) Belgian aromatic malt**

Strain the grain water into your brew pot. Sparge the grains with ½ gallon (1.9 L) water at 150°F (65.5°C). Add water to the brew pot for 1.5 gallons (5.7 L) total volume. Bring the water to a boil, remove the pot from the stove, and add:

> **7.5 lb. (3.4 kg) M&F light DME**
> **1 lb. (.46 kg) corn sugar**
> **1 lb. (.46 kg) Belgian clear candi sugar**
> **1.4 oz. (40 g) Kent Goldings @ 5% AA (7 HBU)**
> **(bittering hop)**

Add water until total volume in the brew pot is 2.5 gallons (9 L). Boil for 45 minutes then add:

> **½ oz. (14 g) Czech Saaz (flavor hop)**
> **½ oz. (14 g) sweet orange peel**
> **1 tsp. (5 ml) Irish moss**

Boil for 12 minutes then add:

> **½ oz. (14 g) sweet orange peel**
> **¼ tsp. (1 ml) crushed grains of paradise**

Boil for 3 minutes, remove pot from the stove, and cool for 15 minutes. Strain the cooled wort into the primary fermenter and add cold water to obtain 5 gallons (18.9 L). When the wort temperature is under 80°F (26.6°C), pitch your yeast.

> **Wyeast's 3944 Belgian White Beer yeast**
> **(Ferment at 70–73°F [21–23°C])**

Ferment in the primary fermenter 5–7 days or until fermentation slows, then siphon into the secondary fermenter. Bottle when fermentation is complete with:

> **½ cup (120 ml) clover or orange blossom honey**
> **⅜ cup (85 ml) corn sugar**

 Serve Boskeun in a goblet at 60°F (16°C).

Alternate Methods

Mini-mash Method: Mash 3 lb. (1.36 kg) Belgian 2-row pale malt and the specialty grains at 150°F (65.5°C) for 90 minutes. Then follow the extract recipe omitting 2.25 lb. (1 kg) DME at the beginning of the boil.

All-grain Method: Mash 11.5 lb. (5.2 kg) Belgian 2-row pale malt with the specialty grain at 150°F (65.5°C) for 90 minutes. Add 4.5 HBU (35% less than the extract recipe) of bittering hops, the candi sugar, and the corn sugar at the beginning of the boil. Add the flavor hops, spices, and Irish moss for the last 15 minutes of the boil and the aroma spices for the last 3 minutes.

Chimay Red

Bières de Chimay, Chimay, Belgium

This ale comes from the largest monastery brewery in Belgium, where the monks began brewing 130 years ago. Chimay Red has a copper color and an off-white, tightly beaded head. The aroma is sweet and fruity, and the flavor is sweet, with traces of black currants. It is brewed with winter barley.

Yield: 5 gallons (18.9 L)	Final gravity: 1.012–1.015	SRM 18–19
Original gravity: 1.068–1.071	IBU 25	7.1% alcohol by volume

Crush and steep in ½ gallon (1.9 L) 150°F (65.5°C) water for 20 minutes:

4 oz. (113 g) Belgian aromatic malt
½ lb. (.23 kg) Belgian Cara-Munich malt
1 oz. (28 g) chocolate malt

Strain the grain water into your brew pot. Sparge the grains with ½ gallon (1.9 L) water at 150°F (65.5°C). Add water to the brew pot for 1.5 gallons (5.7 L) total volume. Bring the water to a boil, remove the pot from the stove, and add:

1.25 lb. (.56 kg) M&F light DME
6.6 lb. (3 kg) Maris Otter light malt extract syrup
1.5 lb. (.68 kg) Belgian clear candi sugar
2 oz. (57 g) Tettnanger @ 4% AA (8 HBU) (bittering hop)

Add water until total volume in the brew pot is 2.5 gallons (9 L). Boil for 45 minutes then add:

¼ oz. (7 g) Styrian Goldings (flavor hop)
¼ oz. (7 g) German Hallertau Hersbrucker (flavor hop)
1 tsp. (5 ml) Irish moss

Boil for 15 minutes, remove pot from the stove, and cool for 15 minutes. Strain the cooled wort into the primary fermenter and add cold water to obtain 5 gallons (18.9 L). When the wort temperature is under 80°F (26.6°C), pitch your yeast.

1st choice: Recultured yeast from bottle of Chimay Cinq Red (Ferment at 68–75°F [20–24°C])
2nd choice: Wyeast's 1214 Belgian Abbey ale yeast (Ferment at 68–75°F [20–24°C])

Ferment in the primary fermenter 5–7 days or until fermentation slows, then siphon into the secondary fermenter. Bottle when fermentation is complete with:

1¼ cup (300 ml) M&F wheat malt

 Serve at 55°F (13°C) in a goblet.

Alternate Methods

Mini-mash Method: Mash 3 lb. (1.36 kg) Maris Otter 2-row pale malt (winter barley) and the specialty grains at 150°F (65.5°C) for 90 minutes. Then follow the extract recipe omitting 3.3 lb. (1.5 kg) Maris Otter malt syrup and adding an additional ½ lb. (.23 kg) M&F light DME at the beginning of the boil.

All-grain Method: Mash 10 lb. (4.5 kg) Maris Otter 2-row pale malt (winter barley) with the specialty grains at 150°F (65.5°C) for 90 minutes. Add 5.5 HBU (31% less than the extract recipe) of bittering hops and the candi sugar for 90 minutes of the boil. Add the flavor hops and Irish moss for the last 15 minutes of the boil.

Double Enghien Blonde Ale

Brouwerij de Silly, Silly, Belgium

This lovely bottle-conditioned ale is pronounced "double engine." It has a creamy, white head, a bright gold color, and a full, round body and mouthfeel. The aroma is a combination of sweet malt, light fruit, and spice. The flavor is well balanced with malt and spicy hops followed by a long-lasting complex aftertaste. This ale is traced back to a local chateau and park built and occupied for several centuries by German nobility.

Yield: 5 gallons (18.9 L)	Final gravity: 1.015–1.019	SRM 6.5
Original gravity: 1.073–1.078	IBU 26	7.5% alcohol by volume

Crush and steep in ½ gallon (1.9 L) 150°F (65.5°C) water for 20 minutes:

> **4 oz. (113 g) Belgian aromatic malt**
> **4 oz. (113 g) Belgian biscuit malt**
> **4 oz. (113 g) German Vienna malt**

Strain the grain water into your brew pot. Sparge the grains with ½ gallon (1.9 L) water at 150°F (65.5°C). Add water to the brew pot for 1.5 gallons (5.7 L) total volume. Bring the water to a boil, remove the pot from the stove, and add:

> **8.5 lb. (3.9 kg) M&F extra-light DME**
> **½ lb. (.23 kg) Belgian clear candi sugar**
> **2 oz. (57 g) Styrian Goldings @ 4.5% AA (9 HBU)**
> **(bittering hop)**

Add water until total volume in the brew pot is 2.5 gallons (9 L). Boil for 45 minutes then add:

> **½ oz. (14 g) Styrian Goldings (flavor hop)**
> **1 tsp. (5 ml) Irish moss**

Boil for 15 minutes, remove pot from the stove, and cool for 15 minutes. Strain the cooled wort into the primary fermenter and add cold water to obtain 5 gallons (18.9 L). When the wort temperature is under 80°F (26.6°C), pitch your yeast.

> **1st choice: Wyeast's 1214 Belgian Abbey ale yeast**
> **(Ferment at 68–72°F [20–22°C])**
> **2nd choice: Wyeast's 1762 Belgian Abbey ale II yeast**
> **(Ferment at 68–72°F [20–22°C])**

Ferment in the primary fermenter 5–7 days or until fermentation slows, then siphon into the secondary fermenter. Bottle when fermentation is complete with:

> **1¼ cup (300 ml) M&F wheat DME**

 Serve in a footed goblet at 55°F (13°C).

 **Alternate Methods**

Mini-mash Method: Mash 2.5 lb. (1.13 kg) Belgian 2-row Pilsner malt and the specialty grains at 150°F (65.5°C) for 90 minutes. Then follow the extract recipe omitting 2 lb. (.9 kg) DME at the beginning of the boil.

All-grain Method: Mash 12.75 lb. (4.5 kg) Belgian 2-row Pilsner malt with the specialty grains at 150°F (65.5°C) for 90 minutes. Add 5.5 HBU (39% less than the extract recipe) of bittering hops and the candi sugar for 90 minutes of the boil. Add the flavor hops and Irish moss for the last 15 minutes of the boil.

Duvel

Moortgat Brewery, Village of Breendonk in Flanders, Belgium

Duvel (Devil) is Belgium's best selling beer. It has a yeast and pear aroma with a complex flavor of malt and hops. This pale colored classic finishes dry and aromatic.

Yield: 5 gallons (18.9 L) Final gravity: 1.012–1.015 SRM 5
Original gravity: 1.079–1.082 IBU 31 8.5% alcohol by volume

Crush and steep in 150°F (65.5°C) water for 20 minutes:

> ½ lb. (.23 kg) 2.5°L German light crystal malt
> 4 oz. (113 g) Belgian aromatic malt

Strain the grain water into your brew pot. Sparge the grains with ½ gallon (1.9 L) water at 150°F (65.5°C). Add water to the brew pot for 1.5 gallons (5.7 L) total volume. Bring the water to a boil and add:

> 6.5 lb. (3 kg) M&F extra-light DME
> 1 lb. (.45 kg) Belgian clear candi sugar
> 1.33 lb. (.7 kg) corn sugar
> 2 oz. (57 g) Styrian Goldings @ 5% AA (10 HBU)
> (bittering hop)

Add water until total volume in the brew pot is 2.5 gallons (9 L). Boil for 45 minutes then add:

> ½ oz. (14 g) Styrian Goldings (flavor hop)
> ½ oz. Czech Saaz (flavor hop)
> 1 tsp. (5 ml) Irish moss

Boil for 12 minutes then add:

> ½ oz. (14 g) Styrian Goldings (aroma hop)

Boil for 3 minutes. Cool for 15 minutes. Strain the cooled wort into the primary fermenter and add cold water to obtain 5 gallons (18.9 L). When the wort temperature is under 80°F (26.6°C), pitch yeast.

> Recultured yeast from Duvel bottle
> (Ferment at 70–75°F [21–24°C])

Ferment in the primary fermenter 5–7 days, then siphon into the secondary fermenter. Add:

> 1 lb. (.45 kg) corn sugar boiled in 1 pint (460 ml) water
> 1 oz. (28 g) of pear flavoring

When fermentation is complete cold condition at 35°F (1.6°C) for 4 weeks then bottle with:

> ¾ cup (180 ml) corn sugar

Mature in bottles for 5 weeks at about 70°F (21.1°C).

 Serve at 45°F (7°C) in a chilled Duvel or burgundy glass.

 **Alternate Methods**

Mini-mash Method: Mash 3.25 lb. (1.5 kg) Belgian 2-row Pilsner malt and the specialty grains at 150°F (65.5°C) for 90 minutes. Then follow the extract recipe omitting 2.5 lb. (1.1 kg) DME at the beginning of the boil.

All-grain Method: Mash 9.75 lb. (4.4 kg) Belgian 2-row Pilsner malt with the specialty grains at 150°F (65.5°C) for 90 minutes. Add 6 HBU (40% less than the extract recipe) of bittering hops, the candi sugar, and the corn sugar for 90 minutes of the boil. Add the flavor hops and Irish moss for the last 15 minutes of the boil and the aroma hops for the last 3 minutes.

Gulden Draak

Van Steenberge, Ertvelde, Belgium

Gulden Draak (Golden Dragon) is an amber tripel ale that displays a big, light beige, creamy head. The round, sweet aroma imparts whiffs of caramel and toffee blended with malt and light alcohol. This chewy, full-bodied beer has a complex and well-balanced palate of sweet malt and toffee with alcohol highlights and a mild hop accent.

Yield: 5 gallons (18.9 L)	Final gravity: 1.020–1.026	SRM 21
Original gravity: 1.104–1.109	IBU 26	10.5% alcohol by volume

Crush and steep in ½ gallon (1.9 L) 150°F (65.5°C) water for 20 minutes:

> **14 oz. (.4 kg) 65°L German crystal malt**
> **4 oz. (113 g) Belgian aromatic malt**
> **3 oz. (85 g) Belgian Cara-Munich malt**
> **2 oz. (57 g) Belgian biscuit malt**

Strain the grain water into your brew pot. Sparge the grains with ½ gallon (1.9 L) water at 150°F (65.5°C). Add water to the brew pot for 1.5 gallons (5.7 L) total volume. Bring the water to a boil, remove the pot from the stove, and add:

> **11 lb. (5 kg) M&F extra-light DME**
> **1 lb. (.45 kg) M&F wheat DME (55% wheat, 45% barley)**
> **½ lb. (.23 kg) Belgian clear candi sugar**
> **1 oz. (28 g) Brewers Gold @ 9.0% AA (9 HBU) (bittering hop)**

Add water until total volume in the brew pot is 3.5 gallons (13 L). Boil for 45 minutes then add:

> **¼ oz. (7 g) Styrian Goldings (flavor hop)**
> **1 tsp. (5 ml) Irish moss**

Boil for 15 minutes, remove pot from the stove, and cool for 15 minutes. Strain the cooled wort into the primary fermenter and add cold water to obtain 5 gallons (18.9 L). When the wort temperature is under 80°F (26.6°C), pitch your yeast.

> **1st choice: Wyeast's 1388 Belgian strong ale yeast (Ferment at 70–73°F [21–23°C])**
> **2nd choice: Wyeast's 3787 Trappist high gravity yeast (Ferment at 70–73°F [21–23°C])**

Ferment in the primary fermenter 5–7 days or until fermentation slows, then siphon into the secondary fermenter. Bottle when fermentation is complete with:

> **1¼ cup (300 ml) M&F extra-light DME**

 Serve in a wide-mouthed goblet at 60°F (16°C).

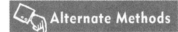 **Alternate Methods**

Mini-mash Method: Mash 2.5 lb. (1.1 kg) Belgian 2-row pale malt and the specialty grains at 150°F (65.5°C) for 90 minutes. Then follow the extract recipe omitting 2.5 lb. (1.1 kg) DME at the beginning of the boil.

All-grain Method: Mash 9 lb. (4.1 kg) Belgian 2-row Pilsner malt, 4 lb. (1.8 kg) Belgian 2-row pale malt, and 1 lb. (.45 kg) German wheat malt with the specialty grains at 150°F (65.5°C) for 90 minutes. Add 6.5 HBU (28% less than the extract recipe) of bittering hops and the candi sugar for 90 minutes of the boil. Add the flavor hops and Irish moss for the last 15 minutes of the boil.

Kwak Pauwel Belgian Ale

Bosteels Brewery, Buggenhout, East Flanders, Belgium

Tawny amber Kwak sports a creamy off-white head and starts off with a down-to-earth, mildly spicy, malt aroma. Smooth, rich, and full-bodied, it entices with a malty, slightly sweet, alcoholic taste on the palate before finishing with a warm, dry aftertaste.

Yield: 5 gallons (18.9 L)   Final gravity: 1.015–1.019   SRM 15
Original gravity: 1.081–1.086   IBU 18–20   8.5% alcohol by volume

Crush and steep in ½ gallon (1.9 L) 150°F (65.5°C) water for 20 minutes:
> **½ lb. (.23 kg) German Munich malt**
> **5 oz. (.14 kg) Special B malt**

Strain the grain water into your brew pot. Sparge the grains with ½ gallon (1.9 L) water at 150°F (65.5°C). Add water to the brew pot for 1.5 gallons (5.7 L) total volume. Bring the water to a boil, remove the pot from the stove, and add:
> **8.5 lb. (3.9 kg) M&F light DME**
> **1.5 lb. (.68 kg) Belgian clear candi sugar**
> **⅔ oz. (19 g) Challenger @ 7.5 % AA (5 HBU)**
> **(bittering hop)**

Add water until total volume in the brew pot is 2.5 gallons (9 L). Boil for 45 minutes then add:
> **1 oz. (28 g) Styrian Goldings (flavor hop)**
> **1 tsp. (5 ml) Irish moss**

Boil for 12 minutes then add:
> **¼ oz. (7 g) Challenger (aroma hop)**
> **¼ oz. (7 g) Czech Saaz (aroma hop)**

Boil for 3 minutes, remove pot from the stove, and cool for 15 minutes. Strain the cooled wort into the primary fermenter and add cold water to obtain 5 gallons (18.9 L). When the wort temperature is under 80°F (26.6°C), pitch your yeast.
> **1st choice: Wyeast's 1762 Belgian Abbey ale II yeast**
> **(Ferment at 70–73°F [21–23°C])**
> **2nd choice: Wyeast's 1214 Belgian Abbey ale yeast**
> **(Ferment at 70–73°F [21–23°C])**

Ferment in the primary fermenter 5–7 days or until fermentation slows, then siphon into the secondary fermenter.

Bottle when fermentation is complete with:
> **1¼ cup (300 ml) M&F extra-light DME**

 Serve at 55°F (13°C) in a foot, ½-yard or yard glass.

 **Alternate Methods**

Mini-mash Method: Mash 3.25 lb. (1.5 kg) Belgian 2-row Pilsner malt and the specialty grains at 150°F (65.5°C) for 90 minutes. Then follow the extract recipe omitting 2.5 lb. (1.1 kg) DME at the beginning of the boil.

All-grain Method: Mash 11 lb. (5 kg) Belgian 2-row Pilsner malt, the specialty grains, and 2 lb. (.9 kg) additional German Munich malt at 150°F (65.5°C) for 90 minutes. Add 3 HBU (40% less than the extract recipe) of bittering hops and the candi sugar for 90 minutes of the boil. Add the flavor hops and Irish moss for the last 15 minutes of the boil and the aroma hops for the last 3 minutes.

Lindeman's Framboise

Brouwerij Lindemans, Vlezenbeek, Belgium

This classic lambic fermented with wild yeasts has an off-white head and light ruby color. The intense berry aroma and dry fruit-acid flavor remind us of a "raspberry champagne."
Note: Do not use your lambic equipment (plastic fermenter, tubing, air-lock, stopper, racking cane, or bottle filler) for any other beer. The bacteria and yeasts in these beers are so strong that it is extremely difficult to sanitize effectively to kill them and they will infect other beers.

Yield: 5 gallons (18.9 L)	Final gravity: 1.010–1.011	SRM 22
Original gravity: 1.061–1.063	IBU 13	6.5% alcohol by volume

Crush and steep in ½ gallon (1.9 L) 150°F (65.5°C) water for 20 minutes:

> **½ lb. (.23 kg) Gambrinus honey malt**

Strain the grain water into your brew pot. Sparge the grains with ½ gallon (1.9 L) water at 150°F (65.5°C). Add water to the brew pot for 1.5 gallons (5.7 L) total volume. Bring the water to a boil and add:

> **2.5 lb. (1.1 kg) M&F wheat DME (55% wheat, 45% barley)**
> **1.5 lb. (.68 kg) M&F extra-light DME**
> **2 oz. (57 g) Old (2 years old) Czech Saaz @ 2% AA (4 HBU)**
> **(bittering hop)**

Add water until total volume in the brew pot is 2.5 gallons (9 L). Boil for 45 minutes then add:

> **1 tsp. (5 ml) Irish moss**
> **½ tsp. (2.5 ml) elderberries (for color, optional)**

Boil for 15 minutes, remove pot from the stove, and cool for 15 minutes. Strain the cooled wort into the primary fermenter and add cold water to obtain 5 gallons (18.9 L). When the wort temperature is under 80°F (26.6°C), pitch your yeast.

> **Wyeast's 1056 American ale yeast**
> **(Ferment at 68–75°F [20–24°C])**

Ferment in the primary fermenter 5–7 days or until fermentation slows. Into a separate secondary fermenter add:

> **1 46-oz. can Oregon Seedless Raspberry Concentrate**
> **20 drops pectic enzyme**
> **Wyeast's 3278 lambic blend yeast**
> **(Ferment at 68–75°F [20–24°C])**

Rack the beer on top of fruit. Let ferment in secondary fermenter for 6 months. Then bottle with:

> **1¼ cup (300 ml) M&F wheat DME**
> **12 oz. (340 g) natural raspberry beer flavoring**

 Serve at 45°F (7°C) in flute glasses.

Alternate Methods

Mini-mash Method: Mash 18 oz. (.5 kg) Belgian 2-row Pilsner malt, 12 oz. (.34 kg) Belgian wheat, 8 oz. (.23 kg) flaked wheat, ½ lb. (.23 kg) rice hulls, and the specialty grain at 150°F (65.5°C) for 90 minutes. Then follow the extract recipe omitting 2.5 lb. (1.1 kg) wheat DME at the beginning of the boil.

All-grain Method: Mash 4.5 lb. (2 kg) Belgian 2-row Pilsner malt, 1.5 lb. (.68 kg) Belgian wheat malt, ½ lb. (.23 kg) flaked wheat malt, 1 lb. (.45 kg) rice hulls, and the specialty grain at 150°F (65.5°C) for 90 minutes. Add 3 HBU (25% less than the extract recipe) of bittering hops for 90 minutes of the boil. Add the elderberries and Irish moss for the last 15 minutes.

Orval

Brasserie d'Orval, Orval, Belgium

Orval has a huge off-white, whipped-cream head with Belgian lace. This classic has firm body and finishes long and dry.

Yield: 5 gallons (18.9 L)	Final gravity: 1.010–1.013
Original gravity: 1.059–1.062	IBU 33

SRM 10–11
6.2% alcohol by volume

Crush and steep in ½ gallon (1.9 L) 150°F (65.5°C) water for 20 minutes:
½ lb. (.23 kg) 40°L crystal malt
6 oz. (.17 kg) Belgian Cara-Vienne malt

Strain the grain water into your brew pot. Sparge the grains with ½ gallon (1.9 L) water at 150°F (65.5°C). Add water to the brew pot for 1.5 gallons (5.7 L) total volume. Bring the water to a boil and add:
3.3 lb. (1.5 kg) Bierkeller light malt extract syrup
3 lb. (1.35 kg) M&F extra-light DME
1.5 lb. (.68 kg) Belgian clear candi sugar
1 oz. (28 g) Styrian Goldings @ 5% AA
1 oz. (28 g) German Hallertau Hersbrucker @ 3.5% AA

Add water until total volume in the brew pot is 2.5 gallons (9 L). Boil for 45 minutes then add:
1 oz. (28 g) Styrian Goldings (flavor hop)
½ oz. (14 g) Curacao bitter orange peel
1 tsp. (5 ml) ground coriander
1 tsp. (5 ml) Irish moss

Boil for 12 minutes then add:
½ oz. (14 g) Styrian Goldings (aroma hop)
½ oz. (14 g) Curacao bitter orange peel
½ tsp. (2 ml) ground coriander

Boil for 3 minutes. Cool for 15 minutes. Strain the cooled wort into the primary fermenter and add cold water to obtain 5 gallons (18.9 L). When the wort temperature is under 80°F (26.6°C), pitch yeast.
Recultured orval yeast from the bottle
(Ferment at 70–73°F [21–23°C])

Ferment in the primary fermenter 5–7 days or until fermentation slows, then siphon into the secondary fermenter. Add:
½ oz. (14 g) Styrian Goldings (dry hop)

Keep in the secondary fermenter for 3 to 4 weeks. Then bottle with:
¾ cup (180 ml) Belgian clear candi sugar

 Pour gently into a balloon glass and serve at 53°F (12°C).

 **Alternate Methods**

Mini-mash Method: Mash 2.25 lb. (1 kg) Belgian 2-row pale malt and the specialty grains at 150°F (65.5°C) for 90 minutes. Then follow the extract recipe omitting 2 lb. (.9 kg) DME at the beginning of the boil.

All-grain Method: Mash 8.5 lb. (3.9 kg) Belgian 2-row pale malt with the specialty grains at 150°F (65.5°C) for 90 minutes. Add 6 HBU (30% less than the extract recipe) of bittering hops and the candi sugar for 90 minutes of the boil. Add the flavor hops, spices, and Irish moss for the last 15 minutes of the boil and the aroma hops and spices for the last 3 minutes.

Petrus Tripel

Bavik de Brabandere Brewery, Bavikhove, Belgium

Gold-orange Petrus has a stark white creamy head. The nose has elements of malt and citrus, leading to a mildly, sweet orange citrus flavor.

Yield: 5 gallons (18.9 L)	Final gravity: 1.014–1.016	SRM 8
Original gravity: 1.073–1.075	IBU 27–28	7.5% alcohol by volume

Crush and steep in ½ gallon (1.9 L) 150°F (65.5°C) water for 20 minutes:

> **½ lb. (.23 kg) Belgian Cara-Vienne malt**
> **4 oz. (113 g) Belgian aromatic malt**

Strain the grain water into your brew pot. Sparge the grains with ½ gallon (1.9 L) water at 150°F (65.5°C). Add water to the brew pot for 1.5 gallons (5.7 L) total volume. Bring the water to a boil, remove the pot from the stove, and add:

> **4.5 lb. (2 kg) M&F extra-light DME**
> **3.3 lb. (1.5 kg) Maris Otter light malt syrup**
> **1.5 lb. (.68 kg) Belgian clear candi sugar**
> **1.5 oz (42 g) Styrian Goldings @ 5% AA (7.5 HBU)**
> **   (bittering hop)**

Add water until total volume in the brew pot is 2.5 gallons (9 L). Boil for 45 minutes then add:

> **1 oz. (28 g) Styrian Goldings (flavor hop)**
> **½ oz. (14 g) sweet orange peel**
> **1 tsp. (5 ml) Irish moss**

Boil for 12 minutes then add:

> **½ oz. (14 g) Willamette (aroma hop)**
> **½ oz. (14 g) sweet orange peel**

Boil for 3 minutes, remove pot from the stove, and cool for 15 minutes. Strain the cooled wort into the primary fermenter and add cold water to obtain 5 gallons (18.9 L). When the wort temperature is under 80°F (26.6°C), pitch your yeast.

> **Wyeast's 3787 Trappist high gravity yeast**
> **(Ferment at 70–73°F [21–23°C])**

Ferment in the primary fermenter 5–7 days or until fermentation slows, then siphon into the secondary fermenter. Into the secondary add:

> **¼ oz. (7 g) steamed oak chips**

Bottle when fermentation is complete with:

> **1¼ cup (300 ml) M&F wheat DME**

 Serve at 55°F (13°C) in a goblet.

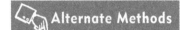
Alternate Methods

Mini-mash Method: Mash 3.25 lb. (1.5 kg) Maris Otter 2-row pale malt and the specialty grains at 150°F (65.5°C) for 90 minutes. Then follow the extract recipe omitting 2.5 lb. (1.1 kg) DME at the beginning of the boil.

All-grain Method: Mash 11 lb. (5 kg) Maris Otter 2-row pale malt with the specialty grains at 150°F (65.5°C) for 90 minutes. Add 5 HBU (33% less than the extract recipe) of bittering hops and the candi sugar for 90 minutes of the boil. Add the flavor hops, spices, and Irish moss for the last 15 minutes of the boil and the aroma hops and spices for the last 3 minutes.

Piraat Ale IPA

Brewery Van Steenberge, Ertvelde, Belgium

More of a tripel than an IPA. The flavor ia a complex medley of spice, malt, mild bubblegum sweetness and tropical fruit.

Yield: 5 gallons (18.9 L)	Final gravity: 1.020–1.024	SRM 9–10
Original gravity: 1.103–1.106	IBU 23	10.5% alcohol by volume

Crush and steep in ½ gallon (1.9 L) 150°F (65.5°C) water for 20 minutes:

> ½ lb. (.23 kg) 20°L crystal malt
> 4 oz. (113 g) Belgian Cara-Vienne malt
> 4 oz. (113 g) Belgian aromatic malt

Strain the grain water into your brew pot. Sparge the grains with ½ gallon (1.9 L) water at 150°F (65.5°C). Add water to the brew pot for 1.5 gallons (5.7 L) total volume. Bring the water to a boil, remove the pot from the stove, and add:

> 11 lb. (5 kg) M&F extra-light DME
> 1.33 lb. (.6 kg) Belgian clear candi sugar
> 1 oz. (28 g) Brewers Gold @ 7% AA (7 HBU)
> (bittering hop)

Add water until total volume in the brew pot is 3.5 gallons (13.25 L). Boil for 45 minutes then add:

> 1 oz. (28 g) Styrian Goldings (flavor hop)
> ½ tsp. (2 ml) ground coriander
> 1 tsp. (5 ml) Irish moss

Boil for 10 minutes then add:

> ½ oz. (14 g) Styrian Goldings (aroma hop)
> ½ tsp. (2 ml) ground coriander
> 1 tsp. (5 ml) sweet orange peel

Boil for 5 minutes, remove pot from the stove, and cool for 15 minutes. Strain the cooled wort into the primary fermenter and add cold water to obtain 5 gallons (18.9 L). When the wort temperature is under 80°F (26.6°C), pitch your yeast.

> Wyeast's 3787 Trappist high gravity yeast
> (Ferment at 68–73°F [20–23°C])

Ferment in the primary fermenter 5–7 days or until fermentation slows, then siphon into the secondary fermenter. Bottle when fermentation is complete with:

> 1½ cup (350 ml) M&F wheat DME

 Serve at 55°F (13°C) in a footed goblet.

 **Alternate Methods**

Mini-mash Method: Mash 3 lb. (1.36 kg) Belgian 2-row pale malt and the specialty grains at 150°F (65.5°C) for 90 minutes. Then follow the extract recipe omitting 2.5 lb. (1.1 kg) DME at the beginning of the boil.

All-grain Method: Mash 17 lb. (7.7 kg) Belgian 2-row Pilsner malt with the specialty grains at 150°F (65.5°C) for 90 minutes. Add 5 HBU (33% less than the extract recipe) of bittering hops and the candi sugar for 90 minutes of the boil. Add the flavor hops, spices, and Irish moss for the last 15 minutes of the boil and the aroma hops and spices for the last 5 minutes.

Rodenbach Grand Cru

Brasserie Rodenbach, Roeselare, Belgium

This classic Belgian Red Ale is aged for two years in Slovenian oak barrels and then bottled. It is the wood's tannins and color that gives the character and color to this exquisite beer. Grand Cru has a dark amber to deep ruby color, a sweet tangy, fruity aroma, and a very tart, complex taste.

Yield: 5 gallons (18.9 L)   Final gravity: 1.011–1.013   SRM 24

Original gravity: 1.053–1.055   IBU 15   5.3% alcohol by volume

Crush and steep in ½ gallon (1.9 L) 150°F (65.5°C) water for 20 minutes:

> **10 oz. (.28 kg) German Vienna malt**
> **8 oz. (.23 kg) Belgian Cara-Vienne malt**
> **4 oz. (113 g) acid malt**
> **3 oz. (87 g) chocolate malt**

Strain the grain water into your brew pot. Sparge the grains with ½ gallon (1.9 L) water at 150°F (65.5°C). Add water to the brew pot for 1.5 gallons (5.7 L) total volume. Bring the water to a boil, remove the pot from the stove, and add:

> **5.25 lb. (2.4 kg) M&F light DME**
> **1 lb. (.45 kg) corn sugar**
> **2 oz. (57 g) lactose**
> **½ oz. (14 g) Styrian Goldings @ 6% AA (3 HBU)**
> **(bittering hop)**

Add water until total volume in the brew pot is 2.5 gallons (9 L). Boil for 45 minutes then add:

> **½ oz. (14 g) Brewers Gold (flavor hop)**
> **1 tsp. (5 ml) Irish moss**

Boil for 12 minutes then add:

> **½ oz. (14 g) Kent Goldings (aroma hop)**

Boil for 3 minutes. Cool for 15 minutes. Strain the cooled wort into the primary fermenter and add cold water to obtain 5 gallons (18.9 L). When the wort temperature is under 80°F (26.6°C), pitch yeast.

> **Wyeast's 3278 lambic blend yeast**
> **(Ferment at 70–75°F [21–24°C])**

Ferment in the primary fermenter 5–7 days or until fermentation slows, then siphon into the secondary fermenter. Into the secondary, add:

> **¼ oz. (7 g) steamed oak chips**

Bottle when fermentation is complete with:

> **1¼ cup (300 ml) M&F wheat DME**

 Serve in a footed goblet at 55°F (13°C).

 **Alternate Methods**

Mini-mash Method: Mash 2 lb. (.9 kg) Belgian 2-row pale malt and the specialty grains at 150°F (65.5°C) for 90 minutes. Then follow the extract recipe omitting 2.25 lb. (1 kg) DME at the beginning of the boil.

All-grain Method: Mash 7 lb. (3.2 kg) Belgian 2-row pale malt, 1.5 lb. (.68 kg) flaked maize, 1 lb. (.45 kg) rice hulls, and the specialty grains at 122°F (50°C) for 30 minutes and 150°F (65.5°C) for 60 minutes. Add 2 HBU (33% less than the extract recipe) and the lactose for 90 minutes of the boil. Add the flavor hop and Irish moss for the last 15 minutes of the boil and the aroma hop for the last 3 minutes.

Saison Dupont

Brasserie Dupont, Tourpes, Belgium

This classic example of the saison style is made in a farmhouse brewery in the Hainault province of Belgium. The highly carbonated, golden-orange saison bursts forth with a huge, rocky white head of Belgian lace. The fruity and sweet aroma is followed by a complex, fruity sharp flavor and a lingering dry finish and aftertaste.

Yield: 5 gallons (18.9 L)	Final gravity: 1.013–1.014	SRM 3.5
Original gravity: 1.064–1.067	IBU 25	6.5% alcohol by volume

Crush and steep in ½ gallon (1.9 L) 150°F (65.5°C) water for 20 minutes:

½ lb. (.23 kg) German Vienna malt

Strain the grain water into your brew pot. Sparge the grains with ½ gallon (1.9 L) water at 150°F (65.5°C). Add water to the brew pot for 1.5 gallons (5.7 L) total volume. Bring the water to a boil, remove the pot from the stove, and add:

5.75 lb. (2.6 kg) M&F extra-light DME
1 lb. (.45 kg) M&F wheat DME
1 lb. (.45 kg) Belgian clear candi sugar
1.4 oz. (40 g) Styrian Goldings @ 5% AA (7 HBU)
(bittering hop)

Add water until total volume in the brew pot is 2.5 gallons (9 L). Boil for 45 minutes then add:

½ oz. (14 g) East Kent Goldings (flavor hop)
½ oz. (14 g) Curacao bitter orange peel
1 tsp. (5 ml) Irish moss

Boil for 10 minutes then add:

¼ oz. (7 g) East Kent Goldings (aroma hop)

Boil for 5 minutes, remove pot from the stove, and cool for 15 minutes. Strain the cooled wort into the primary fermenter and add cold water to obtain 5 gallons (18.9 L). When the wort temperature is under 80°F (26.6°C), pitch your yeast.

1st choice: Recultured yeast from a bottle of Saison Dupont (Ferment at 70–75°F [21–24°C])
2nd choice: Wyeast's 1214 Belgian Abbey ale yeast (Ferment at 70–75°F [21–24°C])

Ferment in the primary fermenter 5–7 days or until fermentation slows, then siphon into the secondary fermenter. Bottle when fermentation is complete with:

1¼ cup (300 ml) M&F extra-light DME

 Serve at 45°F (7°C) in a footed goblet.

Alternate Methods

Mini-mash Method: Mash 3 lb. (1.36 kg) Belgian 2-row Pilsner malt and the specialty grain at 150°F (65.5°C) for 90 minutes. Then follow the extract recipe omitting 2.25 lb. (1 kg) DME at the beginning of the boil.

All-grain Method: Mash 9.5 lb. (4.3 kg) Belgian 2-row Pilsner malt, 1 lb. (.45 kg) Belgian wheat malt, and the specialty grain at 150°F (65.5°C) for 90 minutes. Add 5 HBU (29% less than the extract recipe) of bittering hops and the candi sugar for 90 minutes of the boil. Add the flavor hops and Irish moss for the last 15 minutes of the boil and the aroma hops for the last 5 minutes.

Scaldis Noel

Brasserie Dubuisson, Pipaux, Hainauet, Belgium
The tripel is the holiday version of Scaldis. The amber colored winter warmer has a creamy, beige head and a balanced aroma. The flavor is a malty, nutty complex blend with a warming, dry finish.

Yield: 5 gallons (18.9 L)   Final gravity: 1.022–1.027   SRM 20
Original gravity: 1.116–1.120   IBU 25.5   12% alcohol by volume

Crush and steep in ½ gallon (1.9 L) 150°F (65.5°C) water for 20 minutes:

> **12 oz. (.34 kg) 60°L crystal malt**
> **4 oz. (113 g) toasted 2-row pale malt**

Strain the grain water into your brew pot. Sparge the grains with ½ gallon (1.9 L) water at 150°F (65.5°C). Remove 4 cups of the wort and caramelize in a separate pan before returning to the brew pot. Add water to the brew pot for 1.5 gallons (5.7 L) total volume. Bring the water to a boil, remove the pot from the stove, and add:

> **6.6 lb. (3 kg) Maris Otter light malt syrup**
> **6.5 lb. (2.95 kg) M&F light DME**
> **2 lb. (.9 kg) Belgian clear candi sugar**
> **2 oz. (57 g) Kent Goldings @ 4% AA (8 HBU)**
> **(bittering hop)**

Add water until total volume in the brew pot is 4 gallons (15.25 L). Boil for 45 minutes then add:

> **½ oz. (14 g) Styrian Goldings (flavor hop)**
> **1 tsp. (5 ml) Irish moss**

Boil for 10 minutes then add:

> **½ oz. (14 g) East Kent Goldings (aroma hop)**

Boil for 5 minutes, remove pot from the stove, and cool for 15 minutes. Strain the cooled wort into the primary fermenter and add cold water to obtain 5 gallons (18.9 L). When the wort temperature is under 80°F (26.6°C), pitch your yeast.

> **Wyeast's 1388 Belgian strong ale yeast**
> **(Ferment at 75°F–77°F [24–25°C])**

Ferment in the primary fermenter 5–7 days or until fermentation slows, then siphon into the secondary fermenter. To the secondary add:

> **¼ oz. (7 g) Kent Goldings (dry hop)**

Bottle when fermentation is complete with:

> **1¼ cup (300 ml) M&F wheat DME**

Age at least 6 months in the bottle before drinking.

 Serve at 68–70°F (20–21°C) in a brandy snifter.

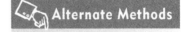 **Alternate Methods**

Mini-mash Method: Mash 4 lb. (1.8 kg) Belgian 2-row pale malt and the specialty grains at 150°F (65.5°C) for 90 minutes. Then follow the extract recipe omitting 3 lb. (1.36 kg) DME at the beginning of the boil.

All-grain Method: Mash 9.5 lb. (4.3 kg) Maris Otter 2-row pale malt, 9 lb. (4.1 kg) Belgian 2-row pale malt, and the specialty grains at 150°F (65.5°C) for 90 minutes. Add 6 HBU (33% less than the extract recipe) of bittering hops and the candi sugar for 90 minutes of the boil. Add the flavor hops and Irish moss for the last 15 minutes of the boil and the aroma hops for the last 5 minutes.

Scotch Silly

Brasserie de Silly, Silly, Belgium

This Belgian version of a Scottish ale is brewed with English malt and hops. Reddish-brown in color, it is not as dark as other Scottish ales. Its full, light beige head gives way to an aroma that is a pleasant blend of sweetness, caramel, alcohol, and light, toasted malt. The flavor is malty, smooth, and velvety with a slight hop bitterness.

Yield: 5 gallons (18.9 L) Final gravity: 1.016–1.020 SRM 18–19
Original gravity: 1.078–1.082 IBU 25 8% alcohol by volume

Crush and steep in 1 gallon (3.8 L) 150°F (65.5°C) water for 20 minutes:

14 oz. (.4 kg) 55°L British crystal malt
6 oz. (.17 kg) Belgian aromatic malt
4 oz. (113 g) whiskey malt or 2 oz. (57 g) peated malt

Strain the grain water into your brew pot. Sparge the grains with ½ gallon (1.9 L) water at 150°F (65.5°C). Add water to the brew pot for 1.5 gallons (5.7 L) total volume. Remove 4 cups of the wort and caramelize in a separate pan before returning back to the brew pot. Bring the water to a boil, remove the pot from the stove, and add:

9 lb. (4.1 kg) M&F light DME
⅓ lb. (.15 kg) Belgian clear candi sugar
2 oz. (57 g) glucose syrup
1.5 oz. (42 g) East Kent Golding @ 5.3% AA (8 HBU)
(bittering hop)

Add water until total volume in the brew pot is 2.5 gallons (9 L). Boil for 45 minutes then add:

½ oz. (14 g) East Kent Goldings (flavor hop)
1 tsp. (5 ml) Irish moss

Boil for 15 minutes, remove pot from the stove, and cool for 15 minutes. Strain the cooled wort into the primary fermenter and add cold water to obtain 5 gallons (18.9 L). When the wort temperature is under 80°F (26.6°C), pitch your yeast.

1st choice: Wyeast's 1084 Irish ale yeast
(Ferment at 68–72°F [20–22°C])
2nd choice: Wyeast's 1728 Scottish ale yeast
(Ferment at 68–72°F [20–22°C])

Ferment in the primary fermenter 5–7 days or until fermentation slows, then siphon into the secondary fermenter. Bottle when fermentation is complete with:

1¼ cup (300 ml) M&F extra-light DME

 Serve in a goblet or thistle glass at 55°F (13°C).

Alternate Methods

Mini-mash Method: Mash 1.75 lb. (.8 kg) British 2-row pale malt and the specialty grains at 150°F (65.5°C) for 90 minutes. Then follow the extract recipe omitting 2 lb. (.9 kg) DME at the beginning of the boil.

All-grain Method: Mash 12.75 lb. (5.8 kg) British 2-row pale malt with the specialty grains, and 2 oz. (57 g) additional 55°L crystal malt at 150°F (65.5°C) for 90 minutes. Add 5.5 HBU (39% less than the extract recipe) of bittering hops, the candi sugar, and the glucose syrup for 90 minutes of the boil. Add the flavor hops and Irish moss for the last 15 minutes of the boil.

St. Feuillien Abbey Ale

Brasserie Friart, Roeulx, Belgium

This refreshing Belgian blonde ale displays a big, snow-white Belgian lace head and has a burnished gold color. The palate brims with spice, malt, hops, and hints of orange.

Yield: 5 gallons (18.9 L)	Final gravity: 1.013–1.016	SRM 4.5
Original gravity: 1.068–1.071	IBU 24	7% alcohol by volume

Crush and steep in ½ gallon (1.9 L) 150°F (65.5°C) water for 20 minutes:

> **4 oz. (113 g) 2.5°L German light crystal malt**
> **4 oz. (113 g) Belgian aromatic malt**

Strain the grain water into your brew pot. Sparge the grains with ½ gallon (1.9 L) water at 150°F (65.5°C). Add water to the brew pot for 1.5 gallons (5.7 L) total volume. Bring the water to a boil, remove the pot from the stove, and add:

> **7.25 lb. (3.3 kg) M&F extra-light DME**
> **1 lb. (.45 kg) Belgian clear candi sugar**
> **1.5 oz. (43 g) Styrian Goldings @ 5% AA (7.5 HBU)**
> **(bittering hop)**

Add water until total volume in the brew pot is 2.5 gallons (9 L). Boil for 45 minutes then add:

> **1 tsp. (5 ml) Curacao bitter orange peel**
> **1 tsp. (5 ml) sweet orange peel**
> **¼ tsp. (1 ml) crushed juniper berries**
> **½ oz. (14 g) Styrian Goldings (flavor hop)**
> **1 tsp. (5 ml) Irish moss**

Boil for 10 minutes then add:

> **1 tsp. (5 ml) Curacao bitter orange peel**
> **1 tsp. (5 ml) sweet orange peel**
> **½ tsp. (2 ml) ground coriander**

Boil for 5 minutes, remove pot from the stove, and cool for 15 minutes. Strain the cooled wort into the primary fermenter and add cold water to obtain 5 gallons (18.9 L). When the wort temperature is under 80°F (26.6°C), pitch your yeast.

> **Wyeast's 1762 Belgian Abbey ale II yeast**
> **(Ferment at 70–73°F [21–23°C])**

Ferment in the primary fermenter 5–7 days or until fermentation slows, then siphon into the secondary fermenter. Bottle when fermentation is complete with:

> **1¼ cup (300 ml) M&F extra-light DME**

 Serve in a goblet at 50°F (10°C).

Alternate Methods

Mini-mash Method: Mash 3.5 lb. (1.6 kg) Belgian 2-row Pilsner malt and the specialty grains at 150°F (65.5°C) for 90 minutes. Then follow the extract recipe omitting 2.5 lb. (1.1 kg) DME at the beginning of the boil.

All-grain Method: Mash 11.25 lb. (5.1 kg) Belgian 2-row Pilsner malt with the specialty grains at 150°F (65.5°C) for 90 minutes. Add 5 HBU (33% less than the extract recipe) of bittering hops and the candi sugar for 90 minutes of the boil. Add the flavor hops, spices, and Irish moss for the last 15 minutes of the boil and the aroma spices for the last 5 minutes.

St. Hermes Ale

Brewery Clarysee NV, Krekelput-Oudenaarde, Belgium

Saint Hermes is the patron saint of the nearby town of Ronse where he was known to cure mental illness. The beer named in his honor has an off-white head and golden color. It is full-bodied. The aroma is malty and nutty, with a faint trace of hazelnut and smoke. The flavor mimics the aroma before finishing with a hoppy, bitter aftertaste.

Yield: 5 gallons (18.9 L)   Final gravity: 1.014–1.018   SRM 7
Original gravity: 1.072–1.078   IBU 22   7.5% alcohol by volume

Crush and steep in ½ gallon (1.9 L) 150°F (65.5°C) water for 20 minutes:

- **½ lb. (.23 kg) German Vienna malt**
- **4 oz. (113 g) Belgian aromatic malt**
- **4 oz. (113 g) Belgian biscuit malt**
- **3 oz. (85 g) German smoked malt**

Strain the grain water into your brew pot. Sparge the grains with ½ gallon (1.9 L) water at 150°F (65.5°C). Add water to the brew pot for 1.5 gallons (5.7 L) total volume. Bring the water to a boil, remove the pot from the stove, and add:

- **8 lb. (3.6 kg) M&F extra-light DME**
- **1 lb. (.45 kg) Belgian clear candi sugar**
- **1.5 oz. (42 g) Styrian Goldings @ 4.7% AA (7 HBU) (bittering hop)**

Add water until total volume in the brew pot is 2.5 gallons (9 L). Boil for 45 minutes then add:

- **½ oz. (14 g) Styrian Goldings (flavor hop)**
- **1 tsp. (5 ml) Irish moss**

Boil for 15 minutes, remove pot from the stove, and cool for 15 minutes. Strain the cooled wort into the primary fermenter and add cold water to obtain 5 gallons (18.9 L). When the wort temperature is under 80°F (26.6°C), pitch your yeast.

> **1st choice: Wyeast's 1762 Belgian Abbey ale II yeast (Ferment at 70–73°F [21–23°C])**
> **2nd choice: Wyeast's 3787 Trappist high gravity yeast (Ferment at 70–73°F [21–23°C])**

Ferment in the primary fermenter 5–7 days or until fermentation slows, then siphon into the secondary fermenter. Bottle when fermentation is complete with:

- **1¼ cup (300 ml) M&F extra-light DME**

 Serve at 45°F (7°C) in a footed goblet.

Alternate Methods

Mini-mash Method: Mash 2.5 lb. (1.1 kg) Belgian 2-row Pilsner malt and the specialty grains at 150°F (65.5°C) for 90 minutes. Then follow the extract recipe omitting 2.5 lb. (1.1 kg) DME at the beginning of the boil.

All-grain Method: Mash 11.25 lb. (5.1 kg) Belgian 2-row Pilsner malt with the specialty grains at 150°F (65.5°C) for 90 minutes. Add 4.5 HBU (36% less than the extract recipe) of bittering hops and the candi sugar for 90 minutes of the boil. Add the flavor hops and Irish moss for the last 15 minutes of the boil.

Trois Monts Flanders Golden Ale

Brasserie De Saint Sylvestre, Belgium

This bière de garde is named after the three hills in the area of the brewery. Trois Monts has a white head of fine lace and a rich golden color. Full-bodied Trois Monts is brewed with Pilsner malts from England and France. The aroma is dry and slightly sour leading to well-balanced and complex flavor with some winelike qualities. The aftertaste is dry and slightly bitter. A classic beer from this classic, artisan, farmhouse brewery.

Yield: 5 gallons (18.9 L)	Final gravity: 1.017–1.020	SRM 5–6
Original gravity: 1.084–1.087	IBU 25	8.5% alcohol by volume

Crush and steep in ½ gallon (1.9 L) 150°F (65.5°C) water for 20 minutes:

4 oz. (113 g) Belgian Cara-Munich malt

Strain the grain water into your brew pot. Sparge the grains with ½ gallon (1.9 L) water at 150°F (65.5°C). Add water to the brew pot for 1.5 gallons (5.7 L) total volume. Bring the water to a boil, remove the pot from the stove, and add:

9.25 lb. (4.2 kg) M&F extra-light DME
12 oz. (.34 kg) Belgian clear candi sugar
1 oz. (28 g) Brewers Gold @ 9.5% AA (9.5 HBU)
(bittering hop)

Add water until total volume in the brew pot is 2.5 gallons (9 L). Boil for 45 minutes then add:

½ oz. (7 g) Tettnanger (flavor hop)
1 tsp. (5 ml) Irish moss

Boil for 15 minutes, remove pot from the stove, and cool for 15 minutes. Strain the cooled wort into the primary fermenter and add cold water to obtain 5 gallons (18.9 L). When the wort temperature is under 80°F (26.6°C), pitch your yeast.

1st choice: Wyeast's 1762 Belgian Abbey ale II yeast
(Ferment at 68–72°F [20–22°C])
2nd choice: Wyeast's 1214 Belgian Abbey ale yeast
(Ferment at 68–72°F [20–22°C])

Ferment in the primary fermenter 5–7 days or until fermentation slows, then siphon into the secondary fermenter. Bottle when fermentation is complete with:

1¼ cup (300 ml) extra-light DME

 Serve at 45°F (7°C) in a flute glass.

 **Alternate Methods**

Mini-mash Method: Mash 3.25 lb. (1.5 kg) British 2-row lager malt and the specialty grain at 150°F (65.5°C) for 90 minutes. Then follow the extract recipe omitting 2.25 lb. (1 kg) DME at the beginning of the boil.

All-grain Method: Mash 7.75 lb. (3.5 kg) British 2-row lager malt, 7 lb. (3.2 kg) Belgian 2-row Pilsner malt, and the specialty grain at 150°F (65.5°C) for 90 minutes. Add 5.5 HBU (42% less than the extract recipe) of bittering hops and the candi sugar for 90 minutes of the boil. Add the flavor hops and Irish moss for the last 15 minutes of the boil.

Westmalle Tripel

Westmalle Trappist Monastery, Westmalle, Belgium

Bright gold Westmalle Tripel, the palest of the Trappist monastery beers, has a smooth, creamy palate, complex with flavors of crisp hops, fruit, orange, alcohol, and slight toffee hints. The aromatic nose is one of orange, toffee, and malt.

Yield: 5 gallons (18.9 L)   Final gravity: 1.018–1.020   SRM 5–6
Original gravity: 1.088–1.090   IBU 26   9% alcohol by volume

Crush and steep in ½ gallon (1.9 L) 150°F (65.5°C) water for 20 minutes:

4 oz. (113 g) Belgian aromatic malt

Strain the grain water into your brew pot. Sparge the grains with ½ gallon (1.9 L) water at 150°F (65.5°C). Add water to the brew pot for 1.5 gallons (5.7 L) total volume. Bring the water to a boil and add:

9 lb. (4.1 kg) M&F extra-light DME
1.5 lb. (.68 kg) Belgian clear candi sugar
1.5 oz. (42 g) Styrian Goldings @ 5% ▲▲ (7.5 HBU)
  (bittering hop)

Remove 4 cups of wort and caramelize it in a separate pan. Then add it back to the original wort to achieve the toffee taste and aroma. Add water until total volume in the brew pot is 3.5 gallons (13 L). Boil for 45 minutes then add:

¼ oz. (7 g) German Hallertau Hersbrucker (flavor hop)
¼ oz. (7 g) Tettnanger (flavor hop)
1 tsp. (5 ml) Irish moss

Boil for 10 minutes then add:

½ oz. (14 g) Czech Saaz (aroma hop)

Boil for 5 minutes. Cool for 15 minutes. Strain the cooled wort into the primary fermenter and add cold water to obtain 5 gallons (18.9 L). When the wort temperature is under 80°F (26.6°C), pitch yeast.

1st choice: Recultured yeast from the Westmalle Tripel (Ferment at 70–73°F [21–23°C])
2nd choice: Wyeast's 1214 Belgian Abbey ale yeast (Ferment at 70–73°F [21–23°C])

Ferment in the primary fermenter 5–7 days or until fermentation slows, then siphon into the secondary fermenter. Bottle when fermentation is complete with:

½ cup (120 ml) corn sugar
⅓ cup (80 ml) white rock candi

Age in bottle for 6 months.

 Serve at 55°F (13°C) in a goblet.

 **Alternate Methods**

Mini-mash Method: Mash 3.75 lb. (1.7 kg) German 2-row Pilsner malt and the specialty grain at 150°F (65.5°C) for 90 minutes. Then follow the extract recipe omitting 2.5 lb. (1.1 kg) DME at the beginning of the boil.

All-grain Method: Mash 14.75 lb. (6.7 kg) German 2-row Pilsner malt with the specialty grain at 150°F (65.5°C) for 90 minutes. Add 5 HBU (33% less than the extract recipe) of bittering hops and the candi sugar for 90 minutes of the boil. Add the flavor hops and Irish moss for the last 15 minutes of the boil and the aroma hops for the last 5 minutes.

Witkap-Pater Abbey Single Ale

Brouwerij Slaghmuylder, Ninove, Belgium

This bottle-conditioned Belgian single (known in Belgium as Stimulo) has a billowy, white head, champagne-like effervarance, and a light straw color. The aroma and flavor are well-balanced with nuances of fruit and malt.

Yield: 5 gallons (18.9 L)
Original gravity: 1.059–1.062

Final gravity: 1.012–1.015
IBU 21

SRM 3.5
6.1% alcohol by volume

Crush and steep in ½ gallon (1.9 L) 150°F (65.5°C) water for 20 minutes:

½ lb. (.23 kg) 2.5°L German light crystal malt

Strain the grain water into your brew pot. Sparge the grains with ½ gallon (1.9 L) water at 150°F (65.5°C). Add water to the brew pot for 1.5 gallons (5.7 L) total volume. Bring the water to a boil and add:

4 lb. (1.8 kg) Alexander's pale malt syrup
3.5 lb. (1.6 kg) M&F extra-light DME
1.5 oz. (42 g) Styrian Goldings @ 4.3% AA (6.5 HBU)
(bittering hop)

Add water until total volume in the brew pot is 2.5 gallons (9 L). Boil for 45 minutes then add:

¼ oz. (7 g) Czech Saaz (flavor hop)
½ oz. (14 g) sweet orange peel
½ tsp. (2 ml) ground coriander
1 tsp. (5 ml) lemon peel
1 tsp. (5 ml) Irish moss

Boil for 10 minutes then add:

½ oz. (14 g) sweet orange peel

Boil for 5 minutes, remove pot from the stove, and cool for 15 minutes. Strain the cooled wort into the primary fermenter and add cold water to obtain 5 gallons (18.9 L). When the wort temperature is under 80°F (26.6°C), pitch your yeast.

Wyeast's 1762 Belgian Abbey ale II yeast
(Ferment at 70–73°F [21–23°C])

Ferment in the primary fermenter 5–7 days or until fermentation slows, then siphon into the secondary fermenter. Bottle when fermentation is complete with:

½ cup (120 ml) corn sugar
⅓ cup (80 ml) clear rock candi

Bottle-condition for 1 month at 41°F (5°C).

 Serve at 55°F (13°C) in a champagne tulip glass.

 **Alternate Methods**

Mini-mash Method: Mash 3.5 lb. (1.6 kg) Belgian 2-row Pilsner malt and the specialty grain at 150°F (65.5°C) for 90 minutes. Then follow the extract recipe omitting 2.5 lb. (1.1 kg) DME at the beginning of the boil.

All-grain Method: Mash 10.25 lb. (4.6 kg) Belgian 2-row Pilsner malt with the specialty grain at 150°F (65.5°C) for 90 minutes. Add 4.5 HBU (30% less than the extract recipe) of bittering hops and the candi sugar for 90 minutes of the boil. Add the flavor hops, spices, and Irish moss for the last 15 minutes of the boil and the aroma spices for the last 5 minutes.

Pilsner Urquell

Pilsner Urquell-Plzen, Czech Republic

This classic Pilsner has a thick white head, a bright gold color, and a wonderfully floral bouquet of Saaz hops in the nose. Only whole Czech Saaz hops which are grown in Zatec, a town in the heart of the Czech hop-growing region, are used in this beer. This Pilsner is extremely well-balanced with hop bitterness and malt sweetness. Drinking this delicate-bodied Pilsner when it is fresh is as close to beer heaven as you can get.

Yield: 5 gallons (18.9 L)   Final gravity: 1.011–1.013   SRM 3.5
Original gravity: 1.050–1.053   IBU 43   5% alcohol by volume

Crush and steep in ½ gallon (1.9 L) 150°F (65.5°C) water for 20 minutes:

> **½ lb. 2.5°L German light crystal malt**
> **2 oz. (57 g) German Munich malt**

Strain the grain water into your brew pot. Sparge the grains with ½ gallon (1.9 L) water at 150°F (65.5°C). Add water to the brew pot for 1.5 gallons (5.7 L) total volume. Bring the water to a boil, remove the pot from the stove, and add:

> **6 lb. (2.7 kg) M&F extra-light DME**
> **3.67 oz. (104 g) Czech Saaz @ 3% AA (11 HBU)**
>   **(bittering hop)**

Add water until total volume in the brew pot is 2.5 gallons (9 L). Boil for 45 minutes then add:

> **1 oz. (28 g) Czech Saaz (flavor hop)**
> **1 tsp. (5 ml) Irish moss**

Boil for 12 minutes then add:

> **1 oz. (28 g) Czech Saaz (aroma hop)**

Boil for 3 minutes, remove pot from the stove, and cool for 15 minutes. Strain the cooled wort into the primary fermenter and add cold water to obtain 5 gallons (18.9 L). When the wort temperature is under 80°F (26.6°C), pitch your yeast.

> **1st choice: Wyeast's 2278 Czech Pilsner lager yeast**
> **(Ferment at 42–52°F [6–11°C])**
> **2nd choice: Wyeast's 2007 Pilsen lager yeast**
> **(Ferment at 42–52°F [6–11°C])**

Ferment in the primary fermenter 5–7 days or until fermentation slows, then siphon into the secondary fermenter and add:

> **½ oz. (14 g) Czech Saaz (dry hop)**

Bottle when fermentation is complete with:

> **1¼ cup (300 ml) M&F extra-light DME**

 Serve at 45°F (7°C) in a Pilsner glass.

 **Alternate Methods**

Mini-mash Method: Mash 3.25 lb. (1.5 kg) German 2-row Pilsner malt and the specialty grains at 150°F (65.5°C) for 90 minutes. Then follow the extract recipe omitting 2.5 lb. (1.1 kg) DME at the beginning of the boil.

All-grain Method: Mash 9 lb. (4.1 kg) German 2-row Pilsner malt with the specialty grain at 150°F (65.5°C) for 90 minutes. Add 8 HBU (27% less than the extract recipe) of bittering hops for 90 minutes of the boil. Add the flavor hops and Irish moss for the last 15 minutes of the boil and the aroma hops for the last 3 minutes.

Kumburak Bohemian Pilsner

Nova Paka Brewery, Nova Paka, Czech Republic

Kumburak is deep golden in color and has a white frothy head. It is medium-bodied and has an aroma that is a blend of sharp, spicy hops and heavy malt. The malty flavor is laced with hop spiciness followed by a dry, bitter finish and long aftertaste.

Yield: 5 gallons (18.9 L)   Final gravity: 1.013–1.015   SRM 4–5.5
Original gravity: 1.051–1.053   IBU 36–37   4.9% alcohol by volume

Crush and steep in ½ gallon (1.9 L) 150°F (65.5°C) water for 20 minutes:

> **6 oz. (.17 kg) 2.5°L German light crystal malt**
> **6 oz. (.17 kg) German Vienna malt**

Strain the grain water into your brew pot. Sparge the grains with ½ gallon (1.9 L) water at 150°F (65.5°C). Add water to the brew pot for 1.5 gallons (5.7 L) total volume. Bring the water to a boil, remove the pot from the stove, and add:

> **3.3 lb. (1.5 kg) Bierkeller light malt syrup**
> **3 lb. (1.36 kg) M&F extra-light DME**
> **4 oz. (113 g) Malto-dextrin**
> **3 oz. (85 g) Czech Saaz @ 3.0% AA (9 HBU)**
> **(bittering hop)**

Add water until total volume in the brew pot is 2.5 gallons (9 L). Boil for 45 minutes then add:

> **1 oz. (28 g) Czech Saaz (flavor hop)**
> **1 tsp. (5 ml) Irish moss**

Boil for 12 minutes then add:

> **1 oz. (28 g) Czech Saaz (aroma hop)**

Boil for 3 minutes, remove pot from the stove, and cool for 15 minutes. Strain the cooled wort into the primary fermenter and add cold water to obtain 5 gallons (18.9 L). When the wort temperature is under 80°F (26.6°C), pitch your yeast.

> **1st choice: Wyeast's 2124 Bohemian lager yeast**
> **(Ferment at 42–52°F [6–11°C])**
> **2nd choice: Wyeast's 2308 Munich lager yeast**
> **(Ferment at 42–52°F [6–11°C])**

Ferment in the primary fermenter 5–7 days or until fermentation slows, then siphon into the secondary fermenter. Bottle when fermentation is complete with:

> **1¼ cup (300 ml) M&F extra-light DME**

 Serve at 45°F (7°C) in a Pilsner glass.

 **Alternate Methods**

Mini-mash Method: Mash 2.5 lb. (1.1 kg) German 2-row Pilsner malt, 6 oz. (.17 kg) dextrin malt and the specialty grains at 150°F (65.5°C) for 90 minutes. Then follow the extract recipe omitting 2 lb. (.9 kg) DME at the beginning of the boil.

All-grain Method: Mash 8.75 lb. (4 kg) German 2-row Pilsner malt, ½ lb. (.23 kg) dextrin malt and the specialty grains at 150°F (65.5°C) for 90 minutes. Add 7 HBU (22% less than the extract recipe) of bittering hops for 90 minutes of the boil. Add the flavor hops and Irish moss for the last 15 minutes of the boil and the aroma hops for the last 3 minutes.

Elephant Malt Liquor

Carlsberg Breweries, Copenhagen, Denmark

Dark straw in color with a tightly beaded white head, Elephant Malt Liquor starts off with a light, fruity, malt aroma and hints of alcohol. This medium-bodied, well-balanced lager has a caramel and Saaz hop palate and a big malt aftertaste balanced with hops.

Yield: 5 gallons (18.9 L)	Final gravity: 1.013–1.016	SRM 4
Original gravity: 1.069–1.070	IBU 37	7.1% alcohol by volume

Crush and steep in ½ gallon (1.9 L) 150°F (65.5°C) water for 20 minutes:

> ½ lb. (.23 kg) 2.5°L German light crystal malt

Strain the grain water into your brew pot. Sparge the grains with ½ gallon (1.9 L) water at 150°F (65.5°C). Add water to the brew pot for 1.5 gallons (5.7 L) total volume. Bring the water to a boil, remove the pot from the stove, and add:

> 7.25 lb. (3.3 kg) M&F extra-light DME
> 1.25 lb. (.57 kg) corn sugar
> 4 oz. (113 g) German Hallertau Hersbrucker @ 3% AA (12 HBU) (bittering hop)

Add water until total volume in the brew pot is 2.5 gallons (9 L). After 48 minutes of the boil, add:

> ½ oz. (14 g) German Hallertau Hersbrucker (flavor hop)
> 1 tsp. (5 ml) Irish moss

Boil for 13 minutes then add:

> ½ oz. (14 g) Czech Saaz (aroma hop)

Boil for 2 minutes, remove pot from the stove, and cool for 15 minutes. Strain the cooled wort into the primary fermenter and add cold water to obtain 5 gallons (18.9 L). When the wort temperature is under 80°F (26.6°C), pitch your yeast.

> 1st choice: Wyeast's 2042 Danish lager yeast
> (Ferment at 42–52°F [6–11°C])
> 2nd choice: Wyeast's 2247 Danish II lager yeast
> (Ferment at 42–52°F [6–11°C])

Ferment in the primary fermenter 5–7 days or until fermentation slows, then siphon into the secondary fermenter. Bottle when fermentation is complete with:

> ¾ cup (180 ml) corn sugar

 Serve in a goblet at 55°F (13°C).

 **Alternate Methods**

Mini-mash Method: Mash 2.75 lb. (1.25 kg) 2-row lager malt and the specialty grain at 150°F (65.5°C) for 90 minutes. Then follow the extract recipe omitting 2.25 lb. (1 kg) DME at the beginning of the boil.

All-grain Method: Mash 10.75 lb. (4.9 kg) 2-row lager malt with the specialty grain at 150°F (65.5°C) for 90 minutes. Add 8 HBU (33% less than the extract recipe) of bittering hops and the corn sugar for 90 minutes of the boil. Add the flavor hops and Irish moss for the last 15 minutes of the boil and the aroma hops for the last 2 minutes.

Saku Estonian Porter

Saku Brewery, Saku, Estonia

This bottom-fermented porter has a creamy, tan head and is dark-amber in color. It's medium-bodied and has a caramel, buttery flavor intertwined with some roasted malt.

Yield: 5 gallons (18.9 L) Final gravity: 1.016–1.020 SRM 30
Original gravity: 1.076–1.079 IBU 36 7.5% alcohol by volume

Crush and steep in 1 gallon (3.8 L) 150°F (65.5°C) water for 20 minutes:

10 oz. (.28 kg) 65°L German dark crystal malt
½ lb. (.23 kg) German Munich malt
2 oz. (57 g) chocolate malt

Strain the grain water into your brew pot. Sparge the grains with ½ gallon (1.9 L) water at 150°F (65.5°C). Add water to the brew pot for 1.5 gallons (5.7 L) total volume. Bring the water to a boil, remove the pot from the stove, and add:

6.6 lb. (3 kg) Ireks light malt syrup
3.3 lb. (1.5 kg) Bierkeller light malt syrup
½ lb. (.23 kg) M&F light DME
1.3 oz. (37 g) Northern Brewer @ 10% AA (13 HBU)
(bittering hop)

Add water until total volume in the brew pot is 2.5 gallons (9 L). Boil for 45 minutes then add:

½ oz. (14 g) German Hallertau Hersbrucker (flavor hop)
1 tsp. (5 ml) Irish moss

Boil for 10 minutes then add:

½ oz. (14 g) German Hallertau Hersbrucker (aroma hop)

Boil for 5 minutes, remove pot from the stove, and cool for 15 minutes. Strain the cooled wort into the primary fermenter and add cold water to obtain 5 gallons (18.9 L). When the wort temperature is under 80°F (26.6°C), pitch your yeast.

1st choice: Wyeast's 2308 Munich yeast
(Ferment at 42–52°F [6–11°C])
2nd choice: Wyeast's 2206 Bavarian lager yeast
(Ferment at 42–52°F [6–11°C])

Ferment in the primary fermenter 5–7 days or until fermentation slows, then siphon into the secondary fermenter. Bottle when fermentation is complete with:

1¼ cup (300 ml) M&F extra-light DME

 Serve in a pint glass or dimpled mug at 60°F (16°C).

 **Alternate Methods**

Mini-mash Method: Mash 2.5 lb. (1.13 kg) British 2-row pale malt and the specialty grains at 150°F (65.5°C) for 90 minutes. Then follow the extract recipe omitting 3.3 lb. (1.5 kg) Bierkeller light malt syrup and adding an additional ½ lb. (.23 kg) M&F light DME at the beginning of the boil.

All-grain Method: Mash 13 lb. (5.9 kg) 2-row Lager malt with the specialty grains and an additional 1 oz. (28 g) chocolate malt at 150°F for 90 minutes. Add 8 HBU (38% less than the extract recipe) of bittering hops for 90 minutes of the boil. Add the flavor hops and Irish moss for the last 15 minutes of the boil and the aroma hops for the last 5 minutes.

Sinebrychoff Porter

Oy Sinebrychoff Brewery, Helsinki, Finland

This bottle-conditioned, intense porter has a deep tan head and a rich, dark brown color. The aroma is malty and fruity, almost citrusy. The big flavor has fruit, bitter roasted grains, and an assertive zing of hops.

Yield: 5 gallons (18.9 L)	Final gravity: 1.017–1.019	SRM 62
Original gravity: 1.074–1.077	IBU 44	7.2% alcohol by volume

Crush and steep in 1 gallon (3.8 L) 150°F (65.5°C) water for 20 minutes:

> **6 oz. (.17 kg) German Vienna malt**
> **6 oz. (.17 kg) German Munich malt**
> **½ lb. (.23 kg) chocolate malt**
> **½ lb. (.23 kg) 55°L crystal malt**

Strain the grain water into your brew pot. Sparge the grains with ½ gallon (1.9 L) water at 150°F (65.5°C). Add water to the brew pot for 1.5 gallons (5.7 L) total volume. Bring the water to a boil, remove the pot from the stove, and add:

> **6.6 lb. (3 kg) Ireks light malt syrup**
> **3 lb. (1.36 kg) M&F light DME**
> **2 oz. (57 g) German Hallertau Northern Brewer**
> **   @ 7.5% AA (15 HBU) (bittering hop)**

Add water until total volume in the brew pot is 2.5 gallons (9 L). Boil for 45 minutes then add:

> **½ oz. (14 g) German Hallertau Hersbrucker (flavor hop)**
> **1 tsp. (5 ml) Irish moss**

Boil for 10 minutes then add:

> **½ oz. (14 g) Czech Saaz (aroma hop)**

Boil for 5 minutes, remove pot from the stove, and cool for 15 minutes. Strain the cooled wort into the primary fermenter and add cold water to obtain 5 gallons (18.9 L). When the wort temperature is under 80°F (26.6°C), pitch your yeast.

> **1st choice: Wyeast's 1742 Swedish ale yeast**
> **(Ferment at 68–70°F [20–21°C])**
> **2nd choice: Wyeast's 1084 Irish ale yeast**
> **(Ferment at 68–70°F [20–21°C])**

Ferment in the primary fermenter 5–7 days or until fermentation slows, then siphon into the secondary fermenter. Bottle when fermentation is complete with:

> **1¼ cup (300 ml) M&F extra-light DME**

 Serve this porter at 55°F (13°C) in a pint glass.

 **Alternate Methods**

Mini-mash Method: Mash 2 lb. (.9 kg) British 2-row pale malt and the specialty grain at 150°F (65.5°C) for 90 minutes. Then follow the extract recipe omitting 2.5 lb. (1.1 kg) DME at the beginning of the boil.

All-grain Method: Mash 12 lb. (5.4 kg) British 2-row pale malt with the specialty grain and ½ lb. (.23 kg) dextrin malt at 150°F (65.5°C) for 90 minutes. Add 10 HBU (33% less than the extract recipe) of bittering hops for 90 minutes of the boil. Add the flavor hops and Irish moss for the last 15 minutes of the boil and the aroma hops for the last 5 minutes.

Castelain Blond Bière de Garde

Brasserie Castelain, Benifontaine, France

This classic blond Bière de Garde (French country ale) from northern France has a spicy aroma, an alcoholic, winey, malty nose, and a sweet palate full of fruit and malt. It finishes smooth and long.

Yield: 5 gallons (18.9 L)	Final gravity: 1.015–1.017	SRM 6
Original gravity: 1.066–1.068	IBU 26	6.5% alcohol by volume

Crush and steep in ½ gallon (1.9 L) 150°F (65.5°C) water for 20 minutes:

½ lb. (.23 kg) Belgian Cara-Vienne malt

Strain the grain water into your brew pot. Sparge the grains with ½ gallon (1.9 L) water at 150°F (65.5°C). Add water to the brew pot for 1.5 gallons (5.7 L) total volume. Bring the water to a boil, remove the pot from the stove, and add:

7.75 lb. (3.5 kg) M&F extra-light DME
1 oz. (28 g) Brewers Gold @ 8% AA (8 HBU)
  (bittering hop)

Add water until total volume in the brew pot is 2.5 gallons (9 L). Boil for 45 minutes then add:

¼ oz. (7 g) Tettnanger (flavor hop)
¼ oz. (7 g) German Hallertau Hersbrucker (flavor hop)
1 tsp. (5 ml) Irish moss

Boil for 15 minutes, remove pot from the stove, and cool for 15 minutes. Strain the cooled wort into the primary fermenter and add cold water to obtain 5 gallons (18.9 L). When the wort temperature is under 80°F (26.6°C), pitch your yeast.

1st choice: Recultured yeast from bottle of Jenlain
  (Ferment at 70–73°F [21–23°C])
2nd choice: Wyeast's 1338 European ale yeast
  (Ferment at 70–73°F [21–23°C]

Ferment in the primary fermenter 5–7 days or until fermentation slows, then siphon into the secondary fermenter. Bottle when fermentation is complete with:

¾ cup (180 ml) corn sugar

 Serve at 50°F (10°C) in a footed Pilsner glass.

Alternate Methods

Mini-mash Method: Mash 3 lb. (1.36 kg) Belgian 2-row Pilsner malt and the specialty grain at 150°F (65.5°C) for 90 minutes. Then follow the extract recipe omitting 2.25 lb. (1 kg) DME at the beginning of the boil.

All-grain Method: Mash 12.25 lb. (5.5 kg) Belgian 2-row Pilsner malt with the specialty grain at 150°F (65.5°C) for 90 minutes. Add 5.5 HBU (31% less than the extract recipe) of bittering hops for 90 minutes of the boil. Add the flavor hops and Irish moss for the last 15 minutes of the boil.

Jenlain Bière de Garde

Brasserie Duyck, Jenlain, France

Jenlain is a classic Bière de Garde or French country ale. Deep amber in color, it has a full, white head with Belgian lace, leading to a complex nose of malt and fruit. The flavor is also complex with hints of malt, citrus fruit, and vanilla. Full-bodied and smooth, it is an all-malt, top-fermenting brew that is filtered but not pasteurized.

Yield: 5 gallons (18.9 L)	Final gravity: 1.014–1.017	SRM 15
Original gravity: 1.065–1.068	IBU 26	6.5% alcohol by volume

Crush and steep in ½ gallon (1.9 L) 150°F (65.5°C) water for 20 minutes:

> **5 oz. (.14 kg) Belgian Cara-Munich malt**
> **6 oz. (.17 kg) 60°L crystal malt**

Strain the grain water into your brew pot. Sparge the grains with ½ gallon (1.9 L) water at 150°F (65.5°C). Add water to the brew pot for 1.5 gallons (5.7 L) total volume. Bring the water to a boil, remove the pot from the stove, and add.

> **7.75 lb. (3.5 kg) M&F light DME**
> **1 oz. (28 g) Brewers Gold @ 8.5% AA (8.5 HBU)**
> **(bittering hop)**

Add water until total volume in the brew pot is 2.5 gallons (9 L). Boil for 45 minutes then add:

> **¼ oz. (7 g) Czech Saaz (flavor hop)**
> **1 tsp. (5 ml) Irish moss**

Boil for 15 minutes, remove pot from the stove, and cool for 15 minutes. Strain the cooled wort into the primary fermenter and add cold water to obtain 5 gallons (18.9 L). When the wort temperature is under 80°F (26.6°C), pitch your yeast.

> **1st choice: Recultured yeast from bottle of Jenlain**
> **(Ferment at 70–73°F [21–23°C])**
> **2nd choice: Wyeast's 3944 White Beer yeast**
> **(Ferment at 70–73°F [21–23°C])**

Ferment in the primary fermenter 5–7 days or until fermentation slows, then siphon into the secondary fermenter. Bottle when fermentation is complete with:

> **1¼ cup (300 ml) M&F wheat DME**

 Serve in a goblet at 55°F (13°C).

Alternate Methods

Mini-mash Method: Mash 3 lb. (1.36 kg) Belgian 2-row Pilsner malt and the specialty grains at 150°F (65.5°C) for 90 minutes. Then follow the extract recipe omitting 2.25 lb. (1 kg) DME at the beginning of the boil.

All-grain Method: Mash 12 lb. (5.4 kg) Belgian 2-row Pilsner malt and the specialty grains at 150°F (65.5°C) for 90 minutes. Add 5.5 HBU (35% less than the extract recipe) of bittering hops for 90 minutes of the boil. Add the flavor hops and Irish moss for the last 15 minutes of the boil.

Aventinus Wheat-Doppelbock

Privatbrauerei Georg Schneider & Sohn, Bavaria, Germany

Aventinus, the world's oldest top-fermenting wheat doppelbock, was created in 1907. This beer has received commendations for its perfect balance of two complex flavor profiles — fruity spiciness from the top-fermenting yeast and the nuances of chocolate created by brewing with crystal and dark malts. It enters with a huge tan head, a rich copper-ruby color, and a nose full of malt, cloves, and fruit. The complex palate combines sweet malt, spice, and fruit, with a hint of chocolate. Big in body, it finishes very long with the same qualities of the palate.

Yield: 5 gallons (18.9 L)	Final gravity: 1.015–1.016	SRM 17–18
Original gravity: 1.075–1.076	IBU 11	7.7% alcohol by volume

Crush and steep in ½ gallon (1.9 L) 150°F (65.5°C) water for 20 minutes:

> **9 oz. (.26 kg) 40°L crystal malt**
> **1 oz. (28 g) chocolate malt**
> **4 oz. (113 g) German melanoidin malt**
> **8 oz. (.23 kg) German Munich malt**

Strain the grain water into your brew pot. Sparge the grains with ½ gallon (1.9 L) water at 150°F (65.5°C). Add water to the brew pot for 1.5 gallons (5.7 L) total volume. Bring the water to a boil, remove the pot from the stove, and add:

> **8.5 lb. (3.9 kg) M&F wheat DME (55% wheat, 45% barley)**
> **1 oz. (28 g) German Hallertau Hersbrucker @ 3.5% AA (3.5 HBU) (bittering hop)**

Add water until total volume in the brew pot is 2.5 gallons (9 L). Boil for 45 minutes then add:

> **½ oz. (14 g) German Hallertau Hersbrucker (flavor hop)**
> **1 tsp. (5 ml) Irish moss**

Boil for 15 minutes, remove pot from the stove, and cool for 15 minutes. Strain the cooled wort into the primary fermenter and add cold water to obtain 5 gallons (18.9 L). When the wort temperature is under 80°F (26.6°C), pitch your yeast.

> **1st choice: Wyeast's 3333 German wheat yeast (Ferment at 68–72°F [20–22°C])**
> **2nd choice: Wyeast's 3056 Bavarian wheat yeast (Ferment at 68–72°F [20–22°C])**

Ferment in the primary fermenter 5–7 days or until fermentation slows, then siphon into the secondary fermenter. Bottle when fermentation is complete with:

> **1¼ cup (300 ml) M&F wheat DME**

 Serve in a classic Aventinus or wheat beer glass at 55°F (13°C).

 **Alternate Methods**

Mini-mash Method: Mash ¾ lb. (.34 kg) Belgian 2-row pale malt, 2 lb. (.9 kg) German wheat malt, the specialty grain, and an additional ½ lb. (.23 kg) German Munich malt at 150°F (65.5°C) for 90 minutes. Then follow the extract recipe omitting 2.5 lb. (1.1 kg) wheat DME at the beginning of the boil.

All-grain Method: Mash 8.5 lb. (3.9 kg) German wheat malt, 5 lb. (2.3 kg) Belgian 2-row pale malt, and an additional 1 lb. (.45 kg) German Munich malt the specialty grains at 150°F (65.5°C) for 90 minutes. Add 2.5 HBU (29% less than the extract recipe) of bittering hops for 90 minutes of the boil. Add the flavor hops and Irish moss for the last 15 minutes of the boil.

Ayinger Maibock

Brauerui Ayinger, Aying, Germany

Bock beer was first brewed in Einbeck, northern Germany, to be served in May as a celebration of springtime. This light May bock, also called a helles bock, displays a deep-gold color topped with a creamy off-white head. The enticingly sweet aroma is very malty, almost buttery. The smooth, soft palate is a complex blend of malt and spice before finishing with a sweet-fruit hop aroma.

Yield: 5 gallons (18.9 L)	**Final gravity: 1.018–1.019**	**SRM 5–7**
Original gravity: 1.070–1.072	**IBU 25**	**6.7% alcohol by volume**

Crush and steep in ½ gallon (1.9 L) 150°F (65.5°C) water for 20 minutes:

- **4 oz. (113 g) German Munich malt**
- **4 oz. (113 g) 2.5°L German light crystal malt**
- **2 oz. (57 g) Belgian aromatic malt**

Strain the grain water into your brew pot. Sparge the grains with ½ gallon (1.9 L) water at 150°F (65.5°C). Add water to the brew pot for 1.5 gallons (5.7 L) total volume. Bring the water to a boil, remove the pot from the stove, and add:

- **6.6 lb. (3 kg) Ireks light malt syrup**
- **2.25 lb. (1 kg) M&F extra-light DME**
- **4 oz. (113 g) Malto-dextrin**
- **2.67 oz. (76 g) German Hallertau Hersbrucker @ 3% AA (8 HBU) (bittering hop)**

Add water until total volume in the brew pot is 2.5 gallons (9 L). Boil for 45 minutes then add:

- **½ oz. (14 g) German Hallertau Hersbrucker (flavor hop)**
- **1 tsp. (5 ml) Irish moss**

Boil for 15 minutes, remove pot from the stove, and cool for 15 minutes. Strain the cooled wort into the primary fermenter and add cold water to obtain 5 gallons (18.9 L). When the wort temperature is under 80°F (26.6°C), pitch your yeast.

> **1st choice: Wyeast's 2308 Munich lager yeast (Ferment at 47–52° [8–11°C])**
> **2nd choice: Wyeast's 2206 Bavarian lager yeast (Ferment at 42–52°F [6–11°C])**

Ferment in the primary fermenter 5–7 days or until fermentation slows, then siphon into the secondary fermenter. Bottle when fermentation is complete with:

- **1¼ cup (300 ml) M&F extra-light DME**

 Serve in a stemmed tumbler at 45°F (7°C).

 **Alternate Methods**

Mini-mash Method: Mash 2.75 lb. (1.25 kg) German 2-row lager malt and the specialty grains at 150°F (65.5°C) for 90 minutes. Then follow the extract recipe omitting the 2.25 lb. (1 kg) DME at the beginning of the boil.

All-grain Method: Mash 12 lb. (5.4 kg) German 2-row lager malt, ½ lb. (.23 kg) dextrin malt, and the specialty grains at 150°F (65.5°C) for 90 minutes. Add 5.5 HBU (31% less than the extract recipe) of bittering hops for 90 minutes of the boil. Add the flavor hops and Irish moss for the last 15 minutes of the boil.

Ayinger Oktober Fest-Märzen

Brauerui Ayinger, Aying, Germany

Märzen (March) is brewed in March and lagered for months to be ready for the beer festivals in September and October. The body is medium to big. The aroma is rich in malty sweetness and toasted malt. The flavor is a balanced combination of malty smoothness, low hop bitterness, and soft dryness from long maturation.

Yield: 5 gallons (18.9 L)	Final gravity:1.013–1.016	SRM 10
Original gravity: 1.053–1.056	IBU 25	5.1% alcohol by volume

Crush and steep in 1 gallon (3.8 L) 150°F (65.5°C) water for 20 minutes:

- **½ lb. (.23 kg) Belgian Cara-Munich malt**
- **½ lb. (.23 kg) German Munich malt**
- **4 oz. (113 g) 40°L crystal malt**

Strain the grain water into your brew pot. Sparge the grains with ½ gallon (1.9 L) water at 150°F (65.5°C). Add water to the brew pot for 1.5 gallons (5.7 L) total volume. Bring the water to a boil, remove the pot from the stove, and add:

- **6.6 lb. (3 kg) Bierkeller light malt syrup**
- **⅓ lb. (.15 kg) M&F light DME**
- **6 oz. (.17 kg) Malto-dextrin**
- **1.4 oz. (39 g) Tettnanger @ 5% AA (7 HBU) (bittering hop)**

Add water until total volume in the brew pot is 2.5 gallons (9 L). Boil for 50 minutes then add:

- **¼ oz. (7 g) German Hallertau Hersbrucker (flavor hop)**
- **1 tsp. (5 ml) Irish moss**

Boil for 10 minutes, remove pot from the stove, and cool for 15 minutes. Strain the cooled wort into the primary fermenter and add cold water to obtain 5 gallons (18.9 L). When the wort temperature is under 80°F (26.6°C), pitch your yeast.

1st choice: Wyeast's 2308 Munich lager yeast (Ferment at 47–52° [8–11°C]). Last week of fermentation bring temperature up to 55°F (13°C).

2nd choice: Wyeast's 2206 Bavarian lager yeast (Ferment at 42–52°F [6–11°C])

Ferment in the primary fermenter 5–7 days or until fermentation slows, then siphon into the secondary fermenter. Bottle when fermentation is complete with:

- **1¼ cup (300 ml) extra-light DME**

 Serve at 50°F (10°C) in a tall earthenware or stein.

Alternate Methods

Mini-mash Method: Mash 2 lb. (.9 kg) German 2-row Pilsner malt, 9 oz. (.26 kg) dextrin malt, the specialty grains, and 1 lb. (.45 kg) additional Munich malt at 150°F (65.5°C) for 90 minutes. Then follow the extract recipe omitting 3.3 lb. (1.5 kg) Bierkeller light malt syrup and the Malto-dextrin. Use an additional ⅙ lb. (76 g) M&F light DME at the beginning of the boil.

All-grain Method: Mash 7.25 lb. (3.3 kg) German 2-row Pilsner malt, 9 oz. (.26 kg) dextrin malt, the specialty grains, an additional 4 oz. (113 g) Cara-Vienne malt, and an additional 1 lb. (.45 kg) German Munich malt at 150°F (65.5°C) for 90 minutes. Add 5 HBU (28% less than the extract recipe) of bittering hops for 90 minutes of the boil. Add the flavor hops and Irish moss for the last 15 minutes of the boil.

Bitburger Premium Pils

Bitburger Brauerei, Thomas Simon, Bitburg, Germany

Only spring barleys (Alexis, Arena, and Steiner) are used in this double decoction Pilsner, which is lagered for three months. This light- to medium-bodied Pilsner makes a lively entrance with a big, well-balanced malt and hop nose. The flavor begins with malt bursting into a hop finish, and gently lingers with a dry hop aftertaste.

Yield: 5 gallons (18.9 L)   Final gravity: 1.010–1.013   SRM 3–5
Original gravity: 1.048–1.050   IBU 36   4.8% alcohol by volume

Crush and steep in ½ gallon (1.9 L) 150°F (65.5°C) water for 20 minutes:

4 oz. (113 g) 2.5°L German light crystal malt
4 oz. (113 g) German Munich malt

Strain the grain water into your brew pot. Sparge the grains with ½ gallon (1.9 L) water at 150°F (65.5°C). Add water to the brew pot for 1.5 gallons (5.7 L) total volume. Bring the water to a boil, remove the pot from the stove, and add:

6.6 lb. (3 kg) Ireks light malt syrup
1 oz. (28 g) German Northern Brewer @ 8.5% AA
(8.5 HBU) (bittering hop)

Add water until total volume in the brew pot is 2.5 gallons (9 L). Boil for 45 minutes then add:

½ oz. (14 g) Perle (flavor hop)
1 tsp. (5 ml) Irish moss

Boil for 5 minutes then add:

¼ oz. (7 g) Hallertauer Mittelfrüh (flavor hop)

Boil for 5 minutes then add:

¼ oz. (7 g) Tettnanger (aroma hop)

Boil for 5 minutes, remove pot from the stove, and cool for 15 minutes. Strain the cooled wort into the primary fermenter and add cold water to obtain 5 gallons (18.9 L). When the wort temperature is under 80°F (26.6°C), pitch your yeast.

1st choice: Wyeast's 2278 Czech Pilsner lager yeast
(Ferment at 41–46°F [5–8°C])
2nd choice: Wyeast's 2007 Pilsen lager yeast
(Ferment at 41–46°F [5–8°C])

Ferment in the primary fermenter 5–7 days or until fermentation slows, then siphon into the secondary fermenter. Bottle when fermentation is complete with:

¾ cup (180 ml) corn sugar

 Serve in a Pilsner glass at 40°F (4°C).

Alternate Methods

Mini-mash Method: Mash 3.25 lb. (1.5 kg) German 2-row Pilsner malt and the specialty grains at 150°F (65.5°C) for 90 minutes. Then follow the extract recipe replacing the Ireks light malt syrup with 3.3 lb. (1.5 kg) Bierkeller light malt syrup and ½ lb. (.23 kg) M&F extra-light DME at the beginning of the boil.

All-grain Method: Mash 8.5 lb. (3.9 kg) German 2-row Pilsner malt with the specialty grains at 150°F (65.5°C) for 90 minutes. Add 6.5 HBU (24% less than the extract recipe) of bittering hops for 90 minutes of the boil. Add the flavor hops and Irish moss for the last 15 minutes of the boil, more flavor hops for the last 10 minutes and the aroma hops for the last 5 minutes.

Celebrator Doppelbock

Brauerui Ayinger, Aying, Germany

Sold in Germany as Fortunator, this deep black brew has a creamy, tan head. Full-bodied and velvety from six months of aging, this brew sports a big, malty nose leading into a flavor that is a smooth, well-balanced blend of maltiness, roasted malts, and hop flowers. It leaves you with a long, semi-dry, faintly smoky finish.

Yield: 5 gallons (18.9 L)	Final gravity: 1.020–1.023	SRM 43–44
Original gravity: 1.080–1.083	IBU 24	7.6% alcohol by volume

Crush and steep in 1 gallon (3.8 L) 150°F (65.5°C) water for 20 minutes:

> **12 oz. (.34 kg) German Munich malt**
> **½ lb. (.23 kg) 65°L German dark crystal malt**
> **5 oz. (142 g) chocolate malt**

Strain the grain water into your brew pot. Sparge the grains with ½ gallon (1.9 L) water at 150°F (65.5°C). Add water to the brew pot for 1.5 gallons (5.7 L) total volume. Bring the water to a boil, remove the pot from the stove, and add:

> **6.6 lb. (3 kg) Ireks light malt syrup**
> **3.3 lb. (1.5 kg) Bierkeller light malt syrup**
> **½ lb. (.23 kg) M&F light DME**
> **½ lb. (.23 kg) Malto-dextrin**
> **¾ oz. (21 g) Northern Brewer @ 7.3% AA (5.5 HBU) (bittering hop)**
> **1 oz. (28 g) German Hallertau Hersbrucker @ 3.5% AA (3.5 HBU) (bittering hop)**

Add water until total volume in the brew pot is 2.5 gallons (9 L). Boil for 45 minutes then add:

> **½ oz. (14 g) German Hallertau Hersbrucker (flavor hop)**
> **1 tsp. (5 ml) Irish moss**

Boil for 15 minutes, remove pot from the stove, and cool for 15 minutes. Strain the cooled wort into the primary fermenter and add cold water to obtain 5 gallons (18.9 L). When the wort temperature is under 80°F (26.6°C), pitch your yeast.

> **Wyeast's 2308 Munich lager yeast**
> **(Ferment at 42–52°F [6–11°C]). Last week of fermentation bring temperature up to 55°F (13°C).**

Ferment in the primary fermenter 5–7 days or until fermentation slows, then siphon into the secondary fermenter. Bottle when fermentation is complete with:

> **1¼ cup (300 ml) M&F wheat DME**

 Serve in a stemmed tumbler at 50°F (10°C).

Alternate Methods

Mini-mash Method: Mash 2.25 lb. (1 kg) German 2-row Pilsner malt and the specialty grains at 150°F (65.5°C) for 90 minutes. Then follow the extract recipe omitting 3.3 lb. (1.5 kg) Bierkeller light malt syrup and adding an additional ½ lb. (.23 kg) M&F light DME at the beginning of the boil.

All-grain Method: Mash 12 lb. (5.4 kg) German 2-row Pilsner malt, 14 oz. (.4 kg) dextrin malt, the specialty grains, and an additional 1 lb. (.45 kg) German Munich malt at 150°F (65.5°C) for 90 minutes. Add 5.5 HBU (39% less than the extract recipe) of bittering hops for 90 minutes of the boil. Add the flavor hops and Irish moss for the last 15 minutes of the boil.

Kaiserdom Rauchbier

Kaiserdom-Privatbrauerei, Bamberg, Bavaria, Germany

This unique German Rauchbier has a creamy, tan head and a burnt amber color with a delicious balance of the aromas and flavors of smoke, malt, and hops. It is lagered for 3 months.

Yield: 5 gallons (18.9 L)   Final gravity: 1.013–1.015   SRM 10–12
Original gravity: 1.052–1.054   IBU 25–26   4.9% alcohol by volume

Crush and steep in 1 gallon (3.8 L) 150°F (65.5°C) water for 20 minutes:

> **1 lb. (.45 kg) Weyermann smoked malt**
> **½ lb. (.23 kg) German Cara-Munich malt**

Strain the grain water into your brew pot. Sparge the grains with ½ gallon (1.9 L) water at 150°F (65.5°C). Add water to the brew pot for 1.5 gallons (5.7 L) total volume. Bring the water to a boil, remove the pot from the stove, and add:

> **6.6 lb. (3 kg) Ireks Munich light malt syrup**
> **4 oz. (113 g) M&F light DME**
> **¾ oz. (21 g) Tettnanger @ 4% AA (3 HBU)**
> **(bittering hop)**
> **1 oz. (28 g) German Hallertau Hersbrucker @ 3% AA**
> **(3 HBU) (bittering hop)**

Add water until total volume in the brew pot is 2.5 gallons (9 L). Boil for 45 minutes then add:

> **1 oz. (28 g) German Hallertau Hersbrucker (flavor hop)**
> **1 tsp. (5 ml) Irish moss**

Boil for 12 minutes then add:

> **1 oz. (28 g) German Hallertau Hersbrucker (aroma hop)**

Boil for 3 minutes, remove pot from the stove, and cool for 15 minutes. Strain the cooled wort into the primary fermenter and add cold water to obtain 5 gallons (18.9 L). When the wort temperature is under 80°F (26.6°C), pitch your yeast.

> **1st choice: Wyeast's 2206 Bavarian lager yeast**
> **(Ferment at 42–52°F [6–11°C])**
> **2nd choice: Wyeast's 2308 Munich lager yeast**
> **(Ferment at 42–52°F [6–11°C] for the first 2 weeks of**
> **fermentation, then at 57–62° [14–17°C] for the**
> **remainder of fermentation)**

Ferment in the primary fermenter 5–7 days or until fermentation slows, then siphon into the secondary fermenter. Bottle when fermentation is complete with:

> **¾ cup (180 ml) corn sugar**

 Serve in a dimpled mug at 45°F (7°C).

Alternate Methods

Mini-mash Method: Mash 2.5 lb. (1.1 kg) German 2-row Pilsner malt, 6 oz. (.17 kg) dextrin malt, and the specialty grains at 150°F (65.5°C) for 90 minutes. Then follow the extract recipe replacing the Ireks light malt syrup with 3.3 lb. (1.5 kg) Bierkeller light malt syrup and an additional ¼ lb. (113 g) M&F light DME at the beginning of the boil.

All-grain Method: Mash 8.25 lb. (3.7 kg) German 2-row Pilsner malt with the specialty grains at 150°F (65.5°C) for 90 minutes. Add 4.5 HBU (25% less than the extract recipe) of bittering hops for 90 minutes of the boil. Add the flavor hops and Irish moss for the last 15 minutes of the boil and the aroma hops for the last 3 minutes.

Paulaner Hefe-Weizen

Paulaner Brauerei, Munich, Germany

This Bavarian-style unfiltered hefe-weizen has an off-white head and a light golden color. The sweet malt aroma leads into a smooth blend of sweetness and wheat flavor with a semi-dry aftertaste. This highly carbonated wheat beer is crisp and refreshing.

Yield: 5 gallons (18.9 L)   Final gravity: 1.011–1.012   SRM 4–5
Original gravity: 1.053–1.054   IBU 10   5.4% alcohol by volume

Crush and steep in ½ gallon (1.9 L) 150°F (65.5°C) water for 20 minutes:

> **4 oz. (113 g) German Munich malt**

Strain the grain water into your brew pot. Sparge the grains with ½ gallon (1.9 L) water at 150°F (65.5°C). Add water to the brew pot for 1.5 gallons (5.7 L) total volume. Bring the water to a boil, remove the pot from the stove, and add:

> **6 lb. (2.7 kg) wheat DME (55% wheat, 45% barley)**
> **1 oz. (28 g) German Hallertau Hersbrucker @ 3% AA (3 HBU) (bittering hop)**

Add water until total volume in the brew pot is 2.5 gallons (9 L). Boil for 60 minutes, remove pot from the stove, and cool for 15 minutes. Strain the cooled wort into the primary fermenter and add cold water to obtain 5 gallons (18.9 L). When the wort temperature is under 80°F (26.6°C), pitch your yeast.

> **1st choice: Wyeast's 3056 Bavarian wheat yeast (Ferment at 68–72°F [20–22°C])**
> **2nd choice: Wyeast's 3333 German wheat yeast (Ferment at 68–72°F [20–22°C])**

Ferment in the primary fermenter 5–7 days or until fermentation slows, then siphon into the secondary fermenter. Bottle when fermentation is complete with:

> **1¼ cup (300 ml) M&F wheat DME**

 Serve at 40°F (4°C) in a wheat beer glass.

 **Alternate Methods**

Mini-mash Method: Mash 2 lb. (.9 kg) German wheat malt, 1.5 lb. (.68 kg) German 2-row lager malt and the specialty grain at 150°F (65.5°C) for 90 minutes. Then follow the extract recipe omitting 2.25 lb. (1 kg) wheat DME at the beginning of the boil.

All-grain Method: Mash 5.25 lb. (2.4 kg) German wheat malt and 4.75 lb. (2.2 kg) Belgian 2-row pale malt with the specialty grain at 150°F (65.5°C) for 90 minutes. Add 2 HBU (33% less than the extract recipe) of bittering hops for 90 minutes of the boil.

Pinkus Homebrew Münster Alt

Brauerei Pinkus Müller, Münster, Germany

The Pinkus brewery and restaurant was founded in 1816. Only organic malt and hops are used in this pale golden Alt which matures for six months before being distributed. Münster Alt is 40 percent wheat and has a white creamy head of small bubbles, and full mouthfeel. The aroma is a combination of fruit and herbs followed by a delicate fruit-acid palate with a long dry finish. It can be enjoyed as an aperitif with a splash of fruit-flavored syrup and a slice of fruit on the side.

Yield: 5 gallons (18.9 L)
Original gravity: 1.050–1.051

Final gravity: 1.011
IBU 17

SRM 3
5% alcohol by volume

Crush and steep in ½ gallon (1.9 L) 150°F (65.5°C) water for 20 minutes:
> **5 oz. (142 g) German Munich malt**

Strain the grain water into your brew pot. Sparge the grains with ½ gallon (1.9 L) water at 150°F (65.5°C). Add water to the brew pot for 1.5 gallons (5.7 L) total volume. Bring the water to a boil, remove the pot from the stove, and add:
> **1.5 lb. (.68 kg) M&F extra-light DME**
> **4.33 lb. (2 kg) M&F wheat DME (55% wheat, 45% barley)**
> **2 oz. (57 g) Czech Saaz @ 2.25% AA (4.5 HBU)**
> **(bittering hop)**

Add water until total volume in the brew pot is 2.5 gallons (9 L). Boil for 45 minutes then add:
> **¼ oz. (7 g) Czech Saaz (flavor hop)**
> **1 tsp. (5 ml) Irish moss**

Boil for 15 minutes, remove pot from the stove, and cool for 15 minutes. Strain the cooled wort into the primary fermenter and add cold water to obtain 5 gallons (18.9 L). When the wort temperature is under 80°F (26.6°C), pitch your yeast.
> **1st choice: Wyeast's 1007 German Alt yeast**
> **(Ferment at 65–70°F [18–21°C])**
> **2nd choice: Wyeast's 2565 Kölsch yeast**
> **(Ferment at 65–70°F [18–21°C])**

Ferment in the primary fermenter 5–7 days or until fermentation slows, then siphon into the secondary fermenter. Bottle when fermentation is complete with:
> **1¼ cup (300 ml) M&F wheat DME**

 Serve in a thin, delicate straight glass at 55°F (13°C).

 **Alternate Methods**

Mini-mash Method: Mash 1.75 lb. (.8 kg) German 2 row Pilsner malt, 1.5 lb. (.68 kg) German wheat malt, and the specialty grain at 150°F (65.5°C) for 90 minutes. Then follow the extract recipe omitting 2.33 lb. (1.1 kg) wheat DME at the beginning of the boil.

All-grain Method: Mash 5.25 lb. (2.4 kg) German 2-row lager malt, 3.75 lb. (1.7 kg) German wheat malt, and the specialty grain at 150°F (65.5°C) for 90 minutes. Add 3.5 HBU (23% less than the extract recipe) of bittering hops for 90 minutes of the boil. Add the flavor hops and Irish moss for the last 15 minutes of the boil.

St. Pauli Girl Dark

St. Pauli Brauerei, Bremen, Germany

This well-known, dark German lager has an off-white head sitting on top of a deep ruby-brown beer. The light malt and bolder hop aroma is followed by a very malty and slight hop flavor. There are hints of hops in the finish with a mild hop aftertaste.

Yield: 5 gallons (18.9 L)	Final gravity: 1.010–1.013	SRM 22
Original gravity: 1.047–1.050	IBU 29	4.7% alcohol by volume

Crush and steep in ½ gallon (1.9 L) 150°F (65.5°C) water for 20 minutes:

- **½ lb. (.23 kg) 65°L German dark crystal malt**
- **4 oz. (113 g) German Munich malt**
- **2 oz. (57 g) chocolate malt**

Strain the grain water into your brew pot. Sparge the grains with ½ gallon (1.9 L) water at 150°F (65.5°C). Add water to the brew pot for 1.5 gallons (5.7 L) total volume. Bring the water to a boil, remove the pot from the stove, and add:

- **6.6 lb. (3 kg) Bierkeller light malt syrup**
- **2 oz. (57 g) Spalt @ 3.5% AA (7 HBU) (bittering hop)**

Add water until total volume in the brew pot is 2.5 gallons (9 L). Boil for 45 minutes then add:

- **½ oz. (14 g) German Hallertau Hersbrucker (flavor hop)**
- **½ oz. (14 g) Tettnanger (flavor hop)**
- **1 tsp. (5 ml) Irish moss**

Boil for 15 minutes, remove pot from the stove, and cool for 15 minutes. Strain the cooled wort into the primary fermenter and add cold water to obtain 5 gallons (18.9 L). When the wort temperature is under 80°F (26.6°C), pitch your yeast.

> **1st choice: Wyeast's 2206 Bavarian lager yeast**
> **(Ferment at 42–52°F [6–11°C])**
> **2nd choice: Wyeast's 2038 Munich lager yeast**
> **(Ferment at 42–52°F [6–11.1°C] for the first 14 days**
> **of fermentation and at 57–62° [14–17°C] for the**
> **remainder of fermentation)**

Ferment in the primary fermenter 5–7 days or until fermentation slows, then siphon into the secondary fermenter. Bottle when fermentation is complete with:

- **¾ cup (180 ml) corn sugar**

 Serve this dark, smooth lager in a dimpled mug at 50°F (10°C).

Alternate Methods

Mini-mash Method: Mash 2 lb. (.9 kg) German 2-row Pilsner malt and the specialty grains at 150°F (65.5°C) for 90 minutes. Then follow the extract recipe omitting 3.3 lb. (1.5 kg) Bierkeller light malt syrup and adding 1 lb. (.45 kg) M&F light DME at the beginning of the boil.

All-grain Method: Mash 8 lb. (3.6 kg) German 2-row lager malt with the specialty grains at 150°F (65.5°C) for 90 minutes. Add 5 HBU (29% less than the extract recipe) of bittering hops for 90 minutes of the boil. Add the flavor hops and Irish moss for the last 15 minutes of the boil.

Warsteiner Premium Verum

Brauerei Warsteiner GEBR, Warstein, Germany

Warsteiner, which is lagered for two months, is the number-one selling beer in Germany. Golden in color with an off-white head, this Pilsner has a light, fruity, hop and toasted malt nose. It is soft and round on the palate with initial hop bitterness. This beer has a finely balanced toasted malt and hop flavor with a dry aftertaste.

Yield: 5 gallons (18.9 L)	Final gravity: 1.010–1.013	SRM 4–5.5
Original gravity: 1.048–1.050	IBU 33	4.8% alcohol by volume

Crush and steep in ½ gallon (1.9 L) 150°F (65.5°C) water for 20 minutes:

> **6 oz. (.17 kg) 2.5°L German light crystal malt**
> **½ lb. (.23 kg) German Munich malt**

Strain the grain water into your brew pot. Sparge the grains with ½ gallon (1.9 L) water at 150°F (65.5°C). Add water to the brew pot for 1.5 gallons (5.7 L) total volume. Bring the water to a boil, remove the pot from the stove, and add:

> **6.6 lb. (3 kg) Ireks Munich light malt syrup**
> **2 oz. (57 g) Tettnanger @ 4.5% AA (9 HBU)**
> **(bittering hop)**

Add water until total volume in the brew pot is 2.5 gallons (9 L). Boil for 45 minutes then add:

> **⅓ oz. (9 g) German Hallertau Hersbrucker (flavor hop)**
> **1 tsp. (5 ml) Irish moss**

Boil for 15 minutes, remove pot from the stove, and cool for 15 minutes. Strain the cooled wort into the primary fermenter and add cold water to obtain 5 gallons (18.9 L). When the wort temperature is under 80°F (26.6°C), pitch your yeast.

> **1st choice: Wyeast's 2124 Bohemian lager yeast**
> **(Ferment at 42–52°F [6–11°C])**
> **2nd choice: Wyeast's 2206 Bavarian lager yeast**
> **(Ferment at 42–52°F [6–11°C])**

Ferment in the primary fermenter 5–7 days or until fermentation slows, then siphon into the secondary fermenter. Bottle when fermentation is complete with:

> **1¼ cup (300 ml) M&F extra-light DME**

 Serve in a Pilsner glass at 40°F (4°C).

Alternate Methods

Mini-mash Method: Mash 2.5 lb. (1.1 kg) German 2-row Pilsner malt and the specialty grain at 150°F (65.5°C) for 90 minutes. Then follow the extract recipe replacing the Ireks light malt syrup with 3.3 lb. (1.5 kg) Bierkeller light malt syrup and ¾ lb. (.34 kg) M&F extra-light DME at the beginning of the boil.

All-grain Method: Mash 8.5 lb. (3.9 kg) German 2-row Pilsner malt with the specialty grains at 150°F (65.5°C) for 90 minutes. Add 6.5 HBU (28% less than the extract recipe) of bittering hops for 90 minutes of the boil. Add the flavor hops and Irish moss for the last 15 minutes of the boil.

Bass Ale

Bass Brewers Limited, Burton-on-Trent, England

Bottled Bass Ale is copper-colored with a creamy, off-white head. The splendid, estery, hop and malt aroma leads into a smooth, well-balanced flavor. Malt is on the palate followed by a dry hop aftertaste. Bass is a very popular, well-integrated brew!

Yield: 5 gallons (18.9 L)   Final gravity: 1.012–1.013   SRM 13–14
Original gravity: 1.051–1.053   IBU 37   5% alcohol by volume

Crush and steep in ½ gallon (1.9 L) 150°F (65.5°C) water for 20 minutes:

14 oz. (.4 kg) 55°L British crystal malt

Strain the grain water into your brew pot. Sparge the grains with ½ gallon (1.9 L) water at 150°F (65.5°C). Add water to the brew pot for 1.5 gallons (5.7 L) total volume. Bring the water to a boil, remove the pot from the stove, and add:

6 lb. (2.7 kg) M&F light DME
1 oz. (28 g) Northdown @ 9% AA (9 HBU)
(bittering hop)
1 tsp. (5 ml) Burton water salts

Add water until total volume in the brew pot is 2.5 gallons (9 L). Boil for 45 minutes then add:

¼ oz. (7 g) Challenger (flavor hop)
1 tsp. (5 ml) Irish moss

Boil for 5 minutes then add:

½ oz. (7 g) Northdown (flavor hop)

Boil for 9 minutes then add:

¼ oz. (14 g) Northdown (aroma hop)

Boil for 1 minute, remove pot from the stove, and cool for 15 minutes. Strain the cooled wort into the primary fermenter and add cold water to obtain 5 gallons (18.9 L). When the wort temperature is under 80°F (26.6°C), pitch your yeast.

Wyeast's 1098 British ale yeast
(Ferment at 68–72°F [20–22°C])

Ferment in the primary fermenter 4–5 days or until fermentation slows, then siphon into the secondary fermenter. Bottle when fermentation is complete with:

¾ cup (180 ml) corn sugar

 Serve at 50°F (10°C) in a mug or a pint glass.

 **Alternate Methods**

Mini-mash Method: Mash 2.5 lb. (1.1 kg) British 2-row pale malt and the specialty grain at 150°F (65.5°C) for 90 minutes. Then follow the extract recipe omitting 2 lb. (.9 kg) DME at the beginning of the boil.

All-grain Method: Mash 9 lb. (4.1 kg) British 2-row pale malt with the specialty grain at 150°F (65.5°C) for 90 minutes. Add 6.5 HBU (27% less than the extract recipe) of bittering hops for 90 minutes of the boil. Add the flavor hops and Irish moss for the last 15 minutes of the boil, the additional flavor hops for the last 10 minutes and the aroma hops for the last 1 minute.

Belhaven Scottish Ale

Belhaven Brewery, Dunbar, Scotland

This classic strong Scottish ale has an off-white head, and the color of a bright copper penny. The aroma is complex blend of malt and smoke with hints of toasted malt and hops. It finishes smooth and clean with a dry hop aftertaste. Sold as a 90 shilling ale in Great Britain, this beer has a smoky, malty flavor with a smoky, bitter aftertaste.

Yield: 5 gallons (18.9 L)   Final gravity: 1.015–1.019   SRM 18
Original gravity: 1.074–1.077   IBU 35   7.5% alcohol by volume

Crush and steep in 1 gallon (3.8 L) 150°F (65.5°C) water for 20 minutes:

12 oz. (.34 kg) 55°L British crystal malt
2 oz. (57 g) toasted 2-row pale malt
2 oz. (57 g) peat-smoked malt

Strain the grain water into your brew pot. Sparge the grains with ½ gallon (1.9 L) water at 150°F (65.5°C). Add water to the brew pot for 1.5 gallons (5.7 L) total volume. Bring the water to a boil, remove the pot from the stove, and add:

6.6 lb. (3 kg) John Bull light malt syrup
2.75 lb. (1.25 kg) M&F light DME
4 oz. (113 g) black treacle
4 oz. (113 g) cane sugar
**2 oz. (56 g) East Kent Goldings @ 6% AA (12 HBU)
(bittering hop)**

Add water until total volume in the brew pot is 2.5 gallons (9 L). Boil for 45 minutes then add:

½ oz. (14 g) East Kent Goldings (flavor hop)
1 tsp. (5 ml) Irish moss

Boil for 15 minutes, remove pot from the stove, and cool for 15 minutes. Strain the cooled wort into the primary fermenter and add cold water to obtain 5 gallons (18.9 L). When the wort temperature is under 80°F (26.6°C), pitch your yeast.

**1st choice: Wyeast's 1728 Scottish ale yeast
(Ferment at 68–72°F [20–22°C])**
**2nd choice: Wyeast's 1275 Thames Valley ale yeast
(Ferment at 68–72°F [20–22°C])**

Ferment in the primary fermenter 4–5 days or until fermentation slows, then siphon into the secondary fermenter. Bottle when fermentation is complete with:

1¼ cup (300 ml) M&F extra-light DME

Serve in a traditional thistle glass or a mug at 60°F (16°C).

Alternate Methods

Mini-mash Method: Mash 2 lb. (.9 kg) Golden Promise 2-row pale malt and the specialty grains at 150°F (65.5°C) for 90 minutes. Then follow the extract recipe omitting 1.75 lb. (.8 kg) DME at the beginning of the boil.

All-grain Method: Mash 12.25 lb. (5.6 kg) Golden Promise 2-row pale malt with the specialty grains at 150°F (65.5°C) for 90 minutes. Add 7.5 HBU (37% less than the extract recipe) of bittering hops and the black treacle and cane sugar for 90 minutes of the boil. Add the flavor hops and Irish moss for the last 15 minutes of the boil.

Bishop's Finger Kentish Ale

Shepherd Neame, Faversham, England

This light amber ale has a light tan head with a caramel and malt aroma. The flavor is smooth and malty with light smoke undertones.

Yield: 5 gallons (18.9 L)   Final gravity: 1.011–1.014   SRM 13
Original gravity: 1.052–1.055   IBU 40   5.2% alcohol by content

Crush and steep in 1 gallon (3.8 L) 150°F (65.5°C) water for 20 minutes:

> **10 oz. (.28 kg) 55°L British crystal malt**
> **12 oz. (.34 kg) torrified wheat**
> **4 oz. (113 g) British amber malt**

Strain the grain water into your brew pot. Sparge the grains with ½ gallon (1.9 L) water at 150°F (65.5°C). Add water to the brew pot for 1.5 gallons (5.7 L) total volume. Bring the water to a boil, remove the pot from the stove, and add:

> **6.25 lb. (2.8 kg) M&F light DME**
> **2 oz. (56 g) glucose syrup**
> **1 oz. (28 g) Target @ 8.5% AA (8.5 HBU)**
> **(bittering hop)**

Add water until total volume in the brew pot is 2.5 gallons (9 L). Boil for 45 minutes then add:

> **½ oz. (14 g) East Kent Goldings (flavor hop)**
> **½ oz. (14 g) Challenger (flavor hop)**
> **1 tsp. (5 ml) Irish moss**

Boil for 14 minutes then add:

> **½ oz. (14 g) East Kent Goldings (aroma hop)**
> **½ oz. (14 g) Styrian Goldings (aroma hop)**

Boil for 1 minute, remove pot from the stove and cool for 15 minutes. Strain the cooled wort into the primary fermenter and add cold water to obtain 5 gallons (18.9 L). When the wort temperature is under 80°F (26.6°C), pitch your yeast.

> **1st choice: Wyeast's 1275 Thames Valley ale yeast**
> **(Ferment at 68–72°F [20–22°C])**
> **2nd choice: Wyeast's 1968 Special London ale yeast**
> **(Ferment at 68–72°F [20–22°C])**

Ferment in the primary fermenter 4–5 days or until fermentation slows, then siphon into the secondary fermenter. Bottle when fermentation is complete with:

> **¾ cup (180 ml) corn sugar**

 Serve in a pint glass at 50°F (10°C).

 **Alternate Methods**

Mini-mash Method: Mash 2.25 lb. (1 kg) British 2-row pale malt and the specialty grains at 150°F (65.5°C) for 90 minutes. Then follow the extract recipe omitting 2.5 lb. (1.1 kg) DME at the beginning of the boil.

All-grain Method: Mash 8.25 lb. (3.7 kg) British 2-row pale malt with the specialty grains at 150°F (65.5°C) for 90 minutes. Add 6 HBU (30% less than the extract recipe) of bittering hops and 2 oz. (57 g) glucose syrup for 90 minutes of the boil. Add the flavor hops and Irish moss for the last 15 minutes of the boil and the aroma hops for the last 1 minute.

Brains Traditional Welsh Ale

Brains and Co., Cardiff, Wales

The slogan for this brewing company is, "It's Brains you need!" and if you drink this beer it will be Brains that you will get. This orange-gold ale has a tightly beaded white head of small bubbles. With light hops in the nose, the flavor is slightly bitter and dominated by hops with a big grain mouthfeel. This refreshing ale finishes dry and hoppy.

Yield: 5 gallons (18.9 L)	**Final gravity: 1.008–1.010**	**SRM 8.5**
Original gravity: 1.041–1.043	**IBU 33**	**4.2% alcohol by volume**

Crush and steep in ½ gallon (1.9 L) 150°F (65.5°C) water for 20 minutes:

½ lb. (.23 kg) 55°L British crystal malt

Strain the grain water into your brew pot. Sparge the grains with ½ gallon (1.9 L) water at 150°F (65.5°C). Add water to the brew pot for 1.5 gallons (5.7 L) total volume. Bring the water to a boil, remove the pot from the stove, and add:

4.5 lb. (2 kg) M&F light DME
4 oz. (113 g) cane sugar
2 oz. (57 g) glucose syrup
1.5 oz. (42 g) Fuggles @ 5% AA (7.5 HBU) (bittering hop)

Add water until total volume in the brew pot is 2.5 gallons (9 L). Boil for 45 minutes then add:

½ oz. (14 g) East Kent Goldings (flavor hop)
1 tsp. (5 ml) Irish moss

Boil for 13 minutes then add:

½ oz. (14 g) Fuggles (aroma hop)

Boil for 2 minutes, remove pot from the stove, and cool for 15 minutes. Strain the cooled wort into the primary fermenter and add cold water to obtain 5 gallons (18.9 L). When the wort temperature is under 80°F (26.6°C), pitch your yeast.

1st choice: Wyeast's 1028 London ale yeast
(Ferment at 68–72°F [20–22°C])
2nd choice: Wyeast's 1098 British ale yeast
(Ferment at 68–72°F [20–22°C])

Ferment in the primary fermenter 4–5 days or until fermentation slows, then siphon into the secondary fermenter. Bottle when fermentation is complete with:

¾ cup (180 ml) corn sugar

 Serve in a pint glass at 55°F (13°C).

 **Alternate Methods**

Mini-mash Method: Mash 3 lb. (1.36 kg) British 2-row pale malt and the specialty grain at 150°F (65.5°C) for 90 minutes. Then follow the extract recipe omitting 2.25 lb. (1 kg) DME at the beginning of the boil.

All-grain Method: Mash 6.75 lb. (3.1 kg) British 2-row pale malt with the specialty grain at 150°F (65.5°C) for 90 minutes. Add 6 HBU (20% less than the extract recipe) of bittering hops, the cane sugar, and glucose syrup for 90 minutes of the boil. Add the flavor hops and Irish moss for the last 15 minutes of the boil and the aroma hops for the last 2 minutes.

Courage Director's Bitter

Courage Ltd., Bristol Brewery, Counterslip, Bristol, Avon, England

This hoppy, complex bitter from John Courage is their best-known beer. It has a profound hop character with grain and fruit on the nose and palate, finishing intensely bittersweet. It is a full-bodied, excellent bitter.

Yield: 5 gallons (18.9 L)	Final gravity: 1.010–1.012	SRM 12
Original gravity: 1.047–1.051	IBU 36	4.8% alcohol by volume

Crush and steep in ½ gallon (1.9 L) 150°F (65.5°C) water for 20 minutes:

12 oz. (.34 kg) 55°L British crystal malt

Strain the grain water into your brew pot. Sparge the grains with ½ gallon (1.9 L) water at 150°F (65.5°C). Add water to the brew pot for 1.5 gallons (5.7 L) total volume. Bring the water to a boil, remove the pot from the stove, and add:

5.5 lb. (2.5 kg) M&F light DME
4 oz. (113 g) cane sugar
1 oz. (28 g) Target @ 8.5% AA (8.5 HBU)
(bittering hop)

Add water until total volume in the brew pot is 2.5 gallons (9 L). Boil for 45 minutes then add:

¼ oz. (7 g) Styrian Goldings (flavor hop)
¼ oz. (7 g) German Hallertau Hersbrucker (flavor hop)
1 tsp. (5 ml) Irish moss

Boil for 14 minutes then add:

½ oz. (28 g) Styrian Goldings (aroma hop)

Boil for 1 minute, remove pot from the stove and cool for 15 minutes. Strain the cooled wort into the primary fermenter and add cold water to obtain 5 gallons (18.9 L). When the wort temperature is under 80°F (26.6°C), pitch your yeast.

1st choice: Wyeast's 1098 British ale yeast
(Ferment at 68–72°F [20–22°C])
2nd choice: Wyeast's 1028 London ale yeast
(Ferment at 68–72°F [20–22°C])

Ferment in the primary fermenter 4–5 days or until fermentation slows, then siphon into the secondary fermenter. In the secondary fermenter add:

½ oz. (14 g) Styrian Goldings (dry hop)

Bottle when fermentation is complete with:

¾ cup (180 ml) corn sugar

 Serve in a pint glass at 55°F (13°C).

 **Alternate Methods**

Mini-mash Method: Mash 3 lb. (1.36 kg) British 2-row pale malt and the specialty grain at 150°F (65.5°C) for 90 minutes. Then follow the extract recipe omitting 2.5 lb. (1.1 kg) DME at the beginning of the boil.

All-grain Method: Mash 7.75 lb. (3.5 kg) British 2-row pale malt with the specialty grain at 150°F (65.5°C) for 90 minutes. Add 6.5 HBU (24% less than the extract recipe) of bittering hops and the cane sugar for 90 minutes of the boil. Add the flavor hops and Irish moss for the last 15 minutes of the boil and the aroma hops for the last 1 minute.

Double Diamond

Ind Coope Burton Brewery, Carlsberg-Tetley, England

This well-balanced English pale ale captures your interest, holds you with a nice balance of hops and malt, and lets you go slowly with a lingering bitterness.

Yield: 5 gallons (18.9 L)	Final gravity: 1.011–1.014	SRM 12
Original gravity: 1.054–1.057	IBU 36	5.5% alcohol by volume

Crush and steep in 1 gallon (3.8 L) 150°F (65.5°C) water for 20 minutes:

7 oz. (.2 kg) 55°L British crystal malt
6 oz. (.17 kg) toasted 2-row pale malt
3 oz. (85 g) British amber malt

Strain the grain water into your brew pot. Sparge the grains with ½ gallon (1.9 L) water at 150°F (65.5°C). Add water to the brew pot for 1.5 gallons (5.7 L) total volume. Bring the water to a boil, remove the pot from the stove, and add:

6.25 lb. (2.8 kg) M&F light DME
4 oz. (113 g) corn sugar
1.6 oz. (45 g) East Kent Goldings @ 5% AA (8 HBU)
(bittering hop)

Add water until total volume in the brew pot is 2.5 gallons (9 L). Boil for 45 minutes then add:

½ oz. (14 g) East Kent Goldings (flavor hop)
½ oz. (14 g) Challenger (flavor hop)
1 tsp. (5 ml) Irish moss

Boil for 14 minutes then add:

½ oz. (14 g) Styrian Goldings (aroma hop)
½ oz. (14 g) Fuggles (aroma hop)

Boil for 1 minute, remove pot from the stove and cool for 15 minutes. Strain the cooled wort into the primary fermenter and add cold water to obtain 5 gallons (18.9 L). When the wort temperature is under 80°F (26.6°C), pitch your yeast.

1st choice: Wyeast's 1968 Special London ale yeast
(Ferment at 68–72°F [20–22°C])
2nd choice: Wyeast's 1338 European ale yeast
(Ferment at 68–72°F [20–22°C])

Ferment in the primary fermenter 4–5 days or until fermentation slows, then siphon into the secondary fermenter. Bottle when fermentation is complete with:

¾ cup (180 ml) corn sugar

 Serve at 50°F (10°C) in a pint glass.

Alternate Methods

Mini-mash Method: Mash 2.5 lb. (1.1 kg) British 2-row pale malt, 6 oz. (.17 kg) flaked maize, and the specialty grains at 150°F (65.5°C) for 90 minutes. Then follow the extract recipe omitting 2.25 lb. (1 kg) DME at the beginning of the boil.

All-grain Method: Mash 8.75 lb. (4 kg) British 2-row pale malt, 6 oz. (.17 kg) flaked maize, and the specialty grains at 150°F (65.5°C) for 90 minutes. Add 5.5 HBU (31% less than the extract recipe) of bittering hops for 90 minutes of the boil. Add the flavor hops and Irish moss for the last 15 minutes of the boil and the aroma hops for the last 1 minute.

Flag Porter

Elgood & Sons, Wisbech, England

In the early 1990s, several bottles of porter were recovered from a ship that had sunk in the English Channel in 1825. The yeast was recultured from one of these bottles and it is now used in the second stage of this porter modeled after a Whitbread porter recipe of the early 1800s. Flag Porter sails in with a dark tan head sitting on a dark brown beer with a malty, slightly fruity aroma. Slightly sweet on the palate, it drifts away with a roasted malt bitterness in the aftertaste.

Yield: 5 gallons (18.9 L)	Final gravity: 1.012–1.013	SRM 44
Original gravity: 1.051–1.053	IBU 28	5.1% alcohol by volume

Crush and steep in 1 gallon (3.8 L) 150°F (65.5°C) water for 20 minutes:

> **½ lb. (.23 kg) 55°L British crystal malt**
> **6 oz. (.17 kg) British brown malt**
> **5 oz. (142 g) British chocolate malt**

Strain the grain water into your brew pot. Sparge the grains with ½ gallon (1.9 L) water at 150°F (65.5°C). Add water to the brew pot for 1.5 gallons (5.7 L) total volume. Bring the water to a boil, remove the pot from the stove, and add:

> **6 lb. (2.7 kg) M&F light DME**
> **1.4 oz. (40 g) East Kent Goldings @ 5% AA (7 HBU)**
> **(bittering hop)**

Add water until total volume in the brew pot is 2.5 gallons (9 L). Boil for 45 minutes then add:

> **½ oz. (14 g) Fuggles (flavor hop)**
> **1 tsp. (5 ml) Irish moss**

Boil for 15 minutes, remove pot from the stove, and cool for 15 minutes. Strain the cooled wort into the primary fermenter and add cold water to obtain 5 gallons (18.9 L). When the wort temperature is under 80°F (26.6°C), pitch your yeast.

> **1st choice: Wyeast's 1084 Irish ale yeast**
> **(Ferment at 68–72°F [20–22°C])**
> **2nd choice: Wyeast's 1098 British ale yeast**
> **(Ferment at 68–72°F [20–22°C])**

Ferment in the primary fermenter 5–7 days or until fermentation slows, then siphon into the secondary fermenter. Bottle when fermentation is complete with:

> **1¼ cup (300 ml) M&F light DME**

 Serve Flag Porter in a pint glass at 50°F (10°C).

 **Alternate Methods**

Mini-mash Method: Mash 3.25 lb. (1.5 kg) British 2-row pale malt and the specialty grains at 150°F (65.5°C) for 90 minutes. Then follow the extract recipe omitting 2.75 lb. (1.25 kg) DME at the beginning of the boil.

All-grain Method: Mash 8.75 lb. (4 kg) British 2-row malt with the specialty grains at 150°F (65.5°C) for 90 minutes. Add 5.5 HBU (31% less than the extract recipe) of bittering hops for 90 minutes of the boil. Add the flavor hops and Irish moss for the last 15 minutes of the boil.

Fraoch Heather Ale

Heather Ale Ltd., Alloa, Scotland

This legendary Pictish ale containing heather has been brewed in Scotland since before Christ was born. This ale, named after the Gaelic term for heather, imparts a light flowery aroma. The smooth malt and floral heather taste finishes with a hint of perfume.

Yield: 5 gallons (18.9 L)	Final gravity: 1.011–1.013	SRM 6.5
Original gravity: 1.050–1.053	IBU 17	5.1% alcohol by volume

Crush and steep in ½ gallon (1.9 L) 150°F (65.5°C) water for 20 minutes:

4 oz. (113 g) 55°L British crystal malt

Strain the grain water into your brew pot. Sparge the grains with ½ gallon (1.9 L) water at 150°F (65.5°C). Add water to the brew pot for 1.5 gallons (5.7 L) total volume. Bring the water to a boil, remove the pot from the stove, and add:

3.3 lb. (1.5 kg) John Bull light malt syrup
3.25 lb. (1.5 kg) M&F light DME
½ oz. (14 g) Brewers Gold @ 8% AA (4 HBU)
(bittering hop)
1 lb. (.45 kg) heather blossoms

Add water until total volume in the brew pot is 2.5 gallons (9 L). Boil for 45 minutes then add:

½ oz. (14 g) East Kent Goldings (flavor hop)
1 tsp. (5 ml) Irish moss
¼ lb. (113 g) heather blossoms (flavor)

Boil for 10 minutes then add:

¼ lb. (113 g) heather blossoms (aroma)

Boil for 5 minutes. Cool for 15 minutes. Strain the cooled wort into the primary fermenter through:

½ cup (120 ml) heather blossoms

Add cold water to obtain 5 gallons (18.9 L). When the wort temperature is under 80°F (26.6°C), pitch your yeast.

1st choice: Wyeast's 1728 Scottish ale yeast
(Ferment at 68–72°F [20–22°C])
2nd choice: Wyeast's 1084 Irish ale yeast
(Ferment at 68–72°F [20–22°C])

Ferment in the primary fermenter 4–5 days or until fermentation slows, then siphon into the secondary fermenter. Bottle when fermentation is complete with:

¾ cup (180 ml) corn sugar

 Serve in a stoneware mug at 55°F (13°C).

 **Alternate Methods**

Mini-mash Method: Mash 3 lb. (1.36kg.) Golden Promise 2-row pale malt and the specialty grain at 150°F (65.5°C) for 90 minutes. Then follow the extract recipe omitting 2 lb. (.9 kg) DME at the beginning of the boil.

All-grain Method: Mash 9.25 lb. (4.2 kg) Golden Promise 2-row pale malt with the specialty grain at 150°F (65.5°C) for 90 minutes. Add 3 HBU (25% less than the extract recipe) of bittering hops and heather for 90 minutes of the boil. Add the flavor hops, heather, and Irish moss for the last 15 minutes of the **boil and the aroma heather** for the last 5 minutes.

Fuller's ESB

Fuller, Smith & Turner, the Griffin Brewery in Chiswick, London, England

Fuller's ESB's aroma overflows with malt and hop spiciness. The flavor has malt up front, followed by a nice blend of malt sweetness and hop flavor. The aftertaste is dry, dominated by Goldings hop flavor and a big dry hop aroma.

Yield: 5 gallons (18.9 L)	Final gravity: 1.011–1.014	SRM 13
Original gravity: 1.054–1.057	IBU 44	5.5% alcohol by volume

Crush and steep in ½ gallon (1.9 L) 150°F (65.5°C) water for 20 minutes:

> **12 oz. (.34 kg) 55°L British crystal malt**
> **2 oz. (57 g) British amber malt**
> **2 oz. (57 g) aromatic malt**

Strain the grain water into your brew pot. Sparge the grains with ½ gallon (1.9 L) water at 150°F (65.5°C). Add water to the brew pot for 1.5 gallons (5.7 L) total volume. Bring the water to a boil and add:

> **6.25 lb. (2.8 kg) M&F light DME**
> **4 oz. (113 g) corn sugar**
> **1.25 oz. (35 g) Target @ 8% AA (10 HBU) (bittering hop)**

Add water until total volume in the brew pot is 2.5 gallons (9 L). Boil for 45 minutes then add:

> **½ oz. (14 g) Challenger (flavor hop)**
> **1 tsp. (5 ml) Irish moss**

Boil for 5 minutes then add:

> **½ oz. (14 g) Northdown (flavor hop)**

Boil for 9 minutes then add:

> **1 oz. (28 g) East Kent Goldings (aroma hop)**

Boil for 1 minute. Cool for 15 minutes. Strain the cooled wort into the primary fermenter and add cold water to obtain 5 gallons (18.9 L). When the wort temperature is under 80°F (26.6°C), pitch yeast.

> **1st choice: Wyeast's 1968 Special London ale yeast (Ferment at 68–72°F [20–22°C])**
> **2nd choice: Wyeast's 1028 London ale yeast (Ferment at 68–72°F [20–22°C])**

Ferment in the primary fermenter 5–7 days or until fermentation slows, then siphon into the secondary fermenter. In the secondary fermenter add:

> **½ oz. (14 g) East Kent Goldings (dry hop)**

Bottle when fermentation is complete with:

> **¾ cup (180 ml) corn sugar**

 Serve at 55°F (13°C) in a pint glass.

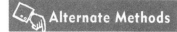 **Alternate Methods**

Mini-mash Method: Mash 2.75 lb. (1.25 kg) British 2-row pale malt and the specialty grains at 150°F (65.5°C) for 90 minutes. Then follow the extract recipe omitting 2.25 lb. (1 kg) DME at the beginning of the boil.

All-grain Method: Mash 9 lb. (4.1 kg) British 2-row pale malt, ½ lb. (.23 kg) flaked maize, and the specialty grains at 150°F (65.5°C) for 90 minutes. Add 7 HBU (30% less than the extract recipe) of bittering hops for 90 minutes of the boil. Add the flavor hops and Irish moss for the last 15 minutes of the boil, the additional flavor hops for the last 10 minutes and the aroma hops for the last 1 minute.

Harvey's Elizabethan Ale

Harvey's and Son (Lewes) Ltd., Lewes, Sussex, England

Elizabethan Ale was first produced at this Victorian-Gothic brewery in 1953 to celebrate the coronation of Queen Elizabeth II. This full-bodied barley wine has a creamy tan head and an intense amber brown color. The aroma is very fruity with a hop signature. The flavor is a well-balanced combination of fruity hops, malt, and alcohol, followed by a malt aftertaste.

Yield: 5 gallons (18.9 L)	Final gravity: 1.018–1.022	SRM 25
Original gravity: 1.083–1.087	IBU 59	8.3% alcohol by volume

Crush and steep in ½ gallon (1.9 L) 150°F (65.5°C) water for 20 minutes:

1 lb. (.45 kg) 60°L British crystal malt

Strain the grain water into your brew pot. Sparge the grains with ½ gallon (1.9 L) water at 150°F (65.5°C). Add water to the brew pot for 1.5 gallons (5.7 L) total volume. Bring the water to a boil, remove the pot from the stove, and add:

9.9 lb. (4.5 kg) Maris Otter light malt syrup
1.25 lb. (.57 kg) M&F light DME
6 oz. (.17 kg) black treacle
1.5 oz. (43 g) Progress @ 10.5% AA (16 HBU)
   (bittering hop)

Add water until total volume is 3.5 gallons (13.25 L). Boil for 45 minutes then add:

1 oz. (28 g) East Kent Goldings (flavor hop)
1 tsp. (5 ml) Irish moss

Boil for 12 minutes then add:

1 oz. (28 g) Fuggles (aroma hop)

Boil for 3 minutes, remove pot from the stove, and cool for 15 minutes. Strain the cooled wort into the primary fermenter and add cold water to obtain 5 gallons (18.9 L). When the wort temperature is under 80°F (26.6°C), pitch your yeast.

   1st choice: Wyeast's 1098 British ale yeast
   (Ferment at 68–72°F [20–22°C])
   2nd choice: Wyeast's 1335 British ale II yeast
   (Ferment at 68–72°F [20–22°C])

Ferment in the primary fermenter 5–7 days or until fermentation slows, then siphon into the secondary fermenter and add:

½ oz. (14 g) Fuggles (dry hop)

Bottle when fermentation is complete with:

1¼ cup (300 ml) M&F wheat DME

 Serve at 60°F (16°C) in a heavy goblet.

 **Alternate Methods**

Mini-mash Method: Mash 3.5 lb. (1.6 kg) Maris Otter 2-row pale malt and the specialty grain at 150°F (65.5°C) for 90 minutes. Then follow the extract recipe omitting 3.3 lb. (1.5 kg) Maris Otter light malt syrup at the beginning of the boil.

All-grain Method: Mash 14.25 lb. (6.5 kg) Maris Otter 2-row pale malt with the specialty grain at 150°F (65.5°C) for 90 minutes. Add 12 HBU (25% less than the extract recipe) of bittering hops and the black treacle for 90 minutes of the boil. Add the flavor hops and Irish moss for the last 15 minutes of the boil and the aroma hops for the last 3 minutes.

John Courage Imperial Stout

Courage Ltd., Staines, Middlesex, England

*This offering by Courage is full-bodied and portlike with a chocolate and sour fruit aroma.
The flavor is overlaid with rich malt, sharp burnt grain, currants, and an alcohol aftertaste.*

Yield: 5 gallons (18.9 L)   Final gravity: 1.022–1.024   SRM 110
Original gravity: 1.103–1.104   IBU 61   10.3% alcohol by volume

Crush and steep in 1 gallon (3.8L) 150°F (65.5°C) water for 20 minutes:

> **12 oz. (.34 kg) 55°L British crystal malt**
> **10 oz. (.28 kg) British chocolate malt**
> **3 oz. (85 g) roasted barley**
> **3 oz. (85 g) British black malt**

Strain the grain water into your brew pot. Sparge the grains with ½ gallon (1.9 L) water at 150°F (65.5°C). Add water to the brew pot for 1.5 gallons (5.7 L) total volume. Bring the water to a boil, remove the pot from the stove, and add:

> **10.5 lb. (4.8 kg) M&F light DME**
> **1 lb. (.46 kg) cane sugar**
> **⅓ lb. (149 g) black treacle**
> **2 oz. (57 g) Target @ 8.5% AA (17 HBU) (bittering hop)**

Add water until total volume in the brew pot is 4 gallons (15 L). Boil for 45 minutes then add:

> **1 oz. (28 g) Target (flavor hop)**
> **1 tsp. (5 ml) Irish moss**

Boil for 10 minutes then add:

> **½ oz. (14 g) Target (aroma hop)**

Boil for 3 minutes, remove pot from the stove, and cool for 15 minutes. Strain the cooled wort into the primary fermenter and add cold water to obtain 5 gallons (18.9 L). When the wort temperature is under 80°F (26.6°C), pitch your yeast.

> **1st choice: Wyeast's 1084 Irish ale yeast**
> **(Ferment at 68–72°F [20–22°C])**
> **2nd choice: Wyeast's 1968 Special London ale yeast**
> **(Ferment at 68–72°F [20–22°C])**

Ferment in the primary fermenter 5–7 days or until fermentation slows, then siphon into the secondary fermenter and add:

> **¼ oz. (7 g) steamed oak chips**

Bottle when fermentation is complete with:

> **1¼ cup (300 ml) M&F light DME**

 Serve in a pint glass at 60°F (16°C).

 **Alternate Methods**

Mini-mash Method: Mash 2.5 lb. (1.1 kg) British 2-row pale malt and the specialty grains at 150°F (65.5°C) for 90 minutes. Then follow the extract recipe omitting 2.5 lb. (1.1 kg) DME at the beginning of the boil.

All-grain Method: Mash 17.5 lb. (7.9 kg) British 2-row pale malt with the specialty grain at 150°F (65.5°C) for 90 minutes. Add 14 HBU (18% less than the extract recipe) of bittering hops, the cane sugar, and black treacle for 90 minutes of the boil. Add the flavor hops and Irish moss for the last 15 minutes of the boil and the aroma hops for the last 5 minutes.

J. W. Lees Harvest Ale

J. W. Lees & Co. Breweries Ltd., Greengate Brewery, Middleton Junction, England

This light orange-amber barley wine is only brewed once a year and released on December 1st. The tightly beaded, rich tawny head rests on a beer that has an intense malt and alcohol aroma. The flavor is rich and fruity, a complex blend of malt and hops. It leaves you with a lot of hoppy dryness in the finish.

Yield: 5 gallons (18.9 L)   Final gravity: 1.027–1.030   SRM 18–20
Original gravity: 1.117–1.120   IBU 70   11.5% alcohol by volume

Crush and steep in ½ gallon (1.9 L) 150°F (65.5°C) water for 20 minutes:

10 oz. (.28 kg) 55°L British crystal malt

Strain the grain water into your brew pot. Sparge the grains with ½ gallon of 150° F water. Add water to the brew pot for 1.5 gallons (5.7 L) total volume. Bring the water to a boil, remove the pot from the stove, and add:

13.2 lb. (6 kg) Maris Otter light malt syrup
⅓ lb. (.15 kg) Lyle's Golden Syrup
2.25 lb. (1 kg) M&F light DME
5 oz. (198 g) East Kent Goldings @ 5.2% AA (26 HBU) (bittering hop)

Add water until total volume in the brew pot is 3.5 gallons (13 L). Boil for 45 minutes then add:

1 oz. (28 g) East Kent Goldings (flavor hop)
1 tsp. (5 ml) Irish moss

Boil for 12 minutes then add:

1 oz. (28 g) East Kent Goldings (aroma hop)

Boil for 3 minutes, remove pot from the stove, and cool for 15 minutes. Strain the cooled wort into the primary fermenter and add cold water to obtain 5 gallons (18.9 L). When the wort temperature is under 80°F (26.6°C), pitch your yeast.

1st choice: Wyeast's 1084 Irish ale yeast (Ferment at 68–72°F [20–22°C])
2nd choice: Wyeast's 1968 Special London ale yeast (Ferment at 68–72°F [20–22°C])

Ferment in the primary fermenter 5–7 days or until fermentation slows, then siphon into the secondary fermenter and add:

1 oz. (28 g) East Kent Goldings (dry hop)

Bottle when fermentation is complete with:

1¼ cup (300 ml) M&F light DME

 Serve in a goblet glass at 60°F (16°C).

 **Alternate Methods**

Mini-mash Method: Mash 3 lb. (1.36 kg) Maris Otter 2-row pale malt and the specialty grain at 150°F (65.5°C) for 90 minutes. Then follow the extract recipe omitting 2.25 lb. (1 kg) M&F light DME at the beginning of the boil.

All-grain Method: Mash 21 lb. (9.5 kg) Maris Otter 2-row pale malt with the specialty grain at 150°F (65.5°C) for 90 minutes. Add 17.5 HBU (67% less than the extract recipe) **of bittering hops and the** golden syrup for 90 minutes of the boil. Add the flavor hops and Irish moss for the last 15 minutes of the boil and the aroma hops for the last 3 minutes.

King and Barnes Christmas Ale

King and Barnes Ltd., Horsham, England

This amber orange seasonal offering from King and Barnes displays a tan, frothy head of tiny bubbles. The fascinating aroma is a medley of malt and alcohol with an earthy, almost winelike nose. The flavors are bittersweet with strong malt and alcohol tastes. This full-bodied beer's aftertaste is dry with slight bitter notes. It's a delicious way to celebrate the holidays.

Yield: 5 gallons (18.9 L)	Final gravity: 1.020–1.023	SRM 15–17
Original gravity: 1.083–1.087	IBU 45	8% alcohol by volume

Crush and steep in ½ gallon (1.9 L) 150°F (65.5°C) water for 20 minutes:

13 oz. (.37 kg) 55°L British crystal malt

Strain the grain water into your brew pot. Sparge the grains with ½ gallon (1.9 L) water at 150°F (65.5°C). Add water to the brew pot for 1.5 gallons (5.7 L) total volume. Bring the water to a boil, remove the pot from the stove, and add:

9.9 lb. (4.5 kg) Maris Otter light malt syrup
¾ lb. (.34 kg) M&F light DME
2.5 oz. (71 g) Brambling Cross @ 6% AA (15 HBU) (bittering hop)

Add water until total volume in the brew pot is 2.5 gallons (9 L). Boil for 45 minutes then add:

1 oz. (28 g) East Kent Goldings (flavor hop)
1 tsp. (5 ml) Irish moss

Boil for 12 minutes then add:

½ oz. (14 g) Fuggles (aroma hop)
½ oz. (14 g) Progress (aroma hop)

Boil for 3 minutes, remove pot from the stove, and cool for 15 minutes. Strain the cooled wort into the primary fermenter and add cold water to obtain 5 gallons (18.9 L). When the wort temperature is under 80°F (26.6°C), pitch your yeast.

1st choice: Wyeast's 1028 London ale yeast (Ferment at 68–72°F [20–22°C])
2nd choice: Wyeast's 1318 London III yeast (Ferment at 68–72°F [20–22°C])

Ferment in the primary fermenter 5–7 days or until fermentation slows, then siphon into the secondary fermenter. Bottle when fermentation is complete with:

1¼ cup (300 ml) M&F extra-light DME

 Serve in a goblet at 55°F (13°C).

 **Alternate Methods**

Mini-mash Method: Mash 3.5 lb. (1.6 kg) Maris Otter 2-row pale malt and the specialty grain at 150°F (65.5°C) for 90 minutes. Then follow the extract recipe omitting 3.3 lb. (1.5 kg) Maris Otter light malt syrup at the beginning of the boil.

All-grain Method: Mash 13.5 lb. (6.1 kg) Maris Otter 2-row pale malt, ¾ lb. (.34 kg) flaked maize, ¾ lb. (.34 kg) dextrin malt, and ½ lb. (.23 kg) oat hulls and the specialty grain at 150°F (65.5°C) for 90 minutes. Add 8.5 HBU (43% less than the extract recipe) of bittering hops for 90 minutes of the boil. Add the flavor hops and Irish moss for the last 15 minutes of the boil and the aroma hops for the last 3 minutes.

Mackeson XXX Stout

Whitbread PLC, London, England

Since 1910 Mackeson stout has been brewed with lactose, a by-product of cheesemaking that is 95 percent milk sugar. This stout has a foamy brown head and deep black color, and gives off a slight coffee and malt aroma. The brew's sweet, coffeelike flavor with hints of mild fruit finishes with a sweet aftertaste. In the British Isles, it is 3 percent alcohol by volume and 1.042 original gravity. In the United States, it is 4.4 percent alcohol by volume with an original gravity of 1.055. This recipe is for the U.S. version.

Yield: 5 gallons (18.9 L)	Final gravity: 1.021–1.023	SRM 110
Original gravity: 1.056–1.057	IBU 26	4.4% alcohol by volume

Crush and steep in 1 gallon (3.8 L) 150°F (65.5°C) water for 20 minutes:

> **1 lb. (.45 kg) 55°L British crystal malt**
> **12 oz. (.34 kg) British chocolate malt**
> **4 oz. (113 g) British black malt**

Strain the grain water into your brew pot. Sparge the grains with ½ gallon (1.9 L) water at 150°F (65.5°C). Add water to the brew pot for 1.5 gallons (5.7 L) total volume. Bring the water to a boil, remove the pot from the stove, and add:

> **5.25 lb. (2.4 kg) M&F light DME**
> **14 oz. (.4 kg) lactose**
> **½ lb. (.23 kg) Malto-dextrin**
> **1 oz. (28 g) Target @ 8% AA (8 HBU) (bittering hop)**

Add water until total volume in the brew pot is 2.5 gallons (9 L). Boil for 50 minutes then add:

> **1 tsp. (5 ml) Irish moss**

Boil for 10 minutes, remove pot from the stove, and cool for 20 minutes. Strain the cooled wort into the primary fermenter and add cold water to obtain 5 gallons (18.9 L). When the wort temperature is under 80°F (26.6°C), pitch your yeast.

> **1st choice: Wyeast's 1028 London ale yeast**
> **(Ferment at 68–72°F [20–22°C])**
> **2nd choice: Wyeast's 1335 British ale II yeast**
> **(Ferment at 68–72°F [20–22°C])**

Ferment in the primary fermenter 5–7 days or until fermentation slows, then siphon into the secondary fermenter. Bottle when fermentation is complete with:

> **⅔ cup (155 ml) corn sugar**
> **2 oz. (57 g) lactose**

 Serve in a pint glass at 55°F (13°C).

 **Alternate Methods**

Mini-mash Method: Mash 1 lb. (.45 kg) British 2-row pale malt, 1 lb. (.45 kg) dextrin malt, and the specialty grains at 150°F (65.5°C) for 90 minutes. Then follow the extract recipe omitting 1.75 lb. (.8 kg) DME and the Malto-dextrin at the beginning of the boil.

All-grain Method: Mash 6.5 lb. (3 kg) British 2-row pale malt, 1 lb. (.45 kg) dextrin malt, and the specialty grains at 150°F for 90 minutes. Add 6 HBU (25% less than the extract recipe) of bittering hops and the lactose for 90 minutes of the boil. Add the Irish moss for the last 15 minutes of the boil.

Marston's Oyster Stout

Marston, Thompson and Evershed, Burton-on-Trent, England

The award-winning Marston's is a dark brown stout sporting a foamy, dark tan head. The smooth aroma is dominated by roasted grains and peppery hops. The roasted grain, fruit, and hop flavor finishes with a dry aftertaste.

Yield: 5 gallons (18.9 L)	Final gravity: 1.012–1.015	SRM 67
Original gravity: 1.048–1.051	IBU 32	4.6% alcohol by volume

Crush and steep in 1 gallon (3.8L) 150°F (65.5°C) water for 20 minutes:

> **6 oz. (.17 kg) 55°L British crystal malt**
> **6 oz. (.17 kg) roasted barley**
> **6 oz. (.17 kg) British chocolate malt**

Strain the grain water into your brew pot. Sparge the grains with ½ gallon (1.9 L) water at 150°F (65.5°C). Add water to the brew pot for 1.5 gallons (5.7 L) total volume. Bring the water to a boil, remove the pot from the stove, and add:

> **5.5 lb. (2.5 kg) M&F light DME**
> **6 oz. (.17 kg) Malto-dextrin**
> **1 oz. (28 g) East Kent Goldings @ 4.5% AA (4.5 HBU) (bittering hop)**
> **1 oz. (28 g) Fuggles @ 4% AA (4 HBU) (bittering hop)**

Add water until total volume in the brew pot is 2.5 gallons (9 L). Boil for 50 minutes then add:

> **½ oz. (14 g) Styrian Goldings (flavor hop)**
> **¼ oz. (7 g) German Hallertau Hersbrucker (flavor hop)**
> **1 tsp. (5 ml) Irish moss**

Boil for 10 minutes, remove pot from the stove, and cool for 15 minutes. Strain the cooled wort into the primary fermenter and add cold water to obtain 5 gallons (18.9 L). When the wort temperature is under 80°F (26.6°C), pitch your yeast.

> **1st choice: Wyeast's 1084 Irish ale yeast**
> **(Ferment at 68–72°F [20–22°C])**
> **2nd choice: Wyeast's 1968 Special London ale yeast**
> **(Ferment at 68–72°F [20–22°C])**

Ferment in the primary fermenter 5–7 days or until fermentation slows, then siphon into the secondary fermenter. Bottle when fermentation is complete with:

> **1¼ cup (300 ml) M&F light DME**

 Serve at 55°F (13°C) in a pint glass.

 Alternate Methods

Mini-mash Method: Mash 2.25 lb. (1 kg) British 2-row pale malt, ½ lb. (.23 kg) dextrin malt, and the specialty grains at 150°F (65.5°C) for 90 minutes. Then follow the extract recipe omitting 2 lb. (.9 kg) DME and the Malto-dextrin at the beginning of the boil.

All Grain Method: Mash 7.75 lb. (3.5 kg) British 2-row pale malt, ½ lb. (.23 kg) dextrin malt, and the specialty grains at 150°F (65.5°C) for 90 minutes. Add 6.5 HBU (24% less than the extract recipe) of bittering hops for 90 minutes of the boil. Add the flavor hops and Irish moss for the last 10 minutes of the boil.

McEwan's Export IPA

Scottish & Newcastle Breweries, Edinburgh, Scotland

This amber-reddish 80-shilling ale has a smell of peated malt and caramel followed with a roasted malt and caramel flavor.

Yield: 5 gallons (18.9 L)   Final gravity: 1.009–1.010   SRM 19
Original gravity: 1.045–1.046   IBU 25   4.6% alcohol by volume

Crush and steep in ½ gallon (1.9 L) 150°F (65.5°C) water for 20 minutes:

12 oz. (.34 kg) 55°L British crystal malt
2 oz. (57 g) roasted barley
2 oz. (57 g) peat-smoked malt

Strain the grain water into your brew pot. Sparge the grains with ½ gallon (1.9 L) water at 150°F (65.5°C). Add water to the brew pot for 1.5 gallons (5.7 L) total volume. Bring the water to a boil, remove the pot from the stove, and add:

3.3 lb. (1.5 kg) John Bull light malt syrup
1.75 lb. (.8 kg) M&F light DME
½ lb. (.23 kg) corn sugar
4 oz. (113 g) cane sugar
1 oz. (28 g) East Kent Goldings @ 4.5% AA (4.5 HBU) (bittering hop)

Add water until total volume in the brew pot is 2.5 gallons (9 L). Boil for 45 minutes then add:

1 oz. (28 g) East Kent Goldings (flavor hop)
1 tsp. (5 ml) Irish moss

Boil for 13 minutes then add:

½ oz. (14 g) East Kent Goldings (aroma hop)
½ oz. (14 g) Fuggles (aroma hop)

Boil for 2 minutes, remove pot from the stove, and cool for 15 minutes. Strain the cooled wort into the primary fermenter and add cold water to obtain 5 gallons (18.9 L). When the wort temperature is under 80°F (26.6°C), pitch your yeast.

1st choice: Wyeast's 1728 Scottish ale yeast (Ferment at 66–70°F [19–21°C])
2nd choice: Wyeast's 1084 Irish ale yeast (Ferment at 66–70°F [19–21°C])

Ferment in the primary fermenter 4–5 days or until fermentation slows, then siphon into the secondary fermenter. Bottle when fermentation is complete with:

1¼ cup (300 ml) M&F wheat DME (55% wheat, 45% barley)

 Serve in a pint glass at 50°F (10°C).

 **Alternate Methods**

Mini-mash Method: Mash 2 lb. (.9 kg) Golden Promise 2-row pale malt and the specialty grains at 150°F (65.5°C) for 90 minutes. Then follow the extract recipe omitting the 1.75 lb. (.8 kg) DME at the beginning of the boil.

All-grain Method: Mash 6.5 lb. (3 kg) Golden Promise 2-row pale malt, ¾ lb. (.34 kg) flaked maize, ½ lb. (.23 kg) oat hulls, and the specialty grains at 150°F (65.5°C) for 90 minutes. Add 3.5 HBU (22% less than the extract recipe) of bittering hops and the cane sugar for 90 minutes of the boil. Add the flavor hops and Irish moss for the last 15 minutes of the boil and the aroma hops for the last 2 minutes.

Newcastle Brown Ale

Scottish and Newcastle Breweries Ltd., Newcastle-on-Tyne, England

Newcastle Brown is nicknamed "the dog," from the excuse to slip out to the pub for a brew, "I'm just popping out to walk the dog." Newcastle Brown is a blend of a stronger dark ale (which is not made available), and a lighter amber ale that is sold separately as Newcastle Amber. The blending combines the fruity esters from the strong ale with the qualities acquired from the amber. This beautiful garnet-colored ale has a rocky, off-white head followed by a sweet malt aroma. The flavor is slightly nutty and sweet, balanced with the mildest hints of fruit. This classic ends with a dry aftertaste.

Yield: 5 gallons (18.9 L)	Final gravity: 1.011–1.013	SRM 23
Original gravity: 1.048–1.051	IBU 26	4.7% alcohol by volume

Crush and steep in ½ gallon (1.9 L) 150°F (65.5°C) water for 20 minutes:

> **2 oz. (57 g) 55°L British crystal malt**
> **2 oz. (57 g) British chocolate malt**
> **1 oz. (28 g) British black malt**

Strain the grain water into your brew pot. Sparge the grains with ½ gallon (1.9 L) water at 150°F (65.5°C). Add water to the brew pot for 1.5 gallons (5.7 L) total volume. Bring the water to a boil, remove the pot from the stove, and add:

> **5.75 lb. (2.6 kg) M&F light DME**
> **⅘ oz. (23 g) Target @ 8% AA (6.5 HBU) (bittering hop)**

Add water until total volume in the brew pot is 2.5 gallons (9 L). Boil for 45 minutes then add:

> **½ oz. (14 g) East Kent Goldings (flavor hop)**
> **1 tsp. (5 ml) Irish moss**

Boil for 15 minutes, remove pot from the stove, and cool for 15 minutes. Strain the cooled wort into the primary fermenter and add cold water to obtain 5 gallons (18.9 L). When the wort temperature is under 80°F (26.6°C), pitch your yeast.

> **1st choice: Wyeast's 1098 British ale yeast**
> **(Ferment at 68–72°F [20–22°C])**
> **2nd choice: Wyeast's 1028 London ale yeast**
> **(Ferment at 68–72°F [20–22°C])**

Ferment in the primary fermenter 4–5 days or until fermentation slows, then siphon into the secondary fermenter. Bottle when fermentation is complete with:

> **¾ cup (180 ml) corn sugar**

 Serve in a pint glass at 50°F (10°C).

 **Alternate Methods**

Mini-mash Method: Mash 3 lb. (1.36 kg) British 2-row pale malt and the specialty grains at 150°F (65.5°C) for 90 minutes. Then follow the extract recipe omitting 2.25 lb. (1 kg) DME at the beginning of the boil.

All-grain Method: Mash 8.75 lb. (4 kg) British 2-row pale malt with the specialty grains at 150°F (65.5°C) for 90 minutes. Add 5 HBU (23% less than the extract recipe) of bittering hops for 90 minutes of the boil. Add the flavor hops and Irish moss for the last 15 minutes of the boil.

Old Jock Ale

Broughton Ales Ltd., Broughton, Peebleshire, Scotland

Old Jock is a beautiful dark amber color with a rocky, tan head made of large bubbles. The aroma is a mixture of malt, roasted grains, and alcohol. Full-bodied Old Jock has a smooth, complex flavor of rich caramel, and toasted malt.

Yield: 5 gallons (18.9 L)	**Final gravity:** 1.017–1.019	**SRM 25**
Original gravity: 1.070–1.072	**IBU 27**	**6.8% alcohol by volume**

Crush and steep in 1 gallon (3.8 L) 150°F (65.5°C) water for 20 minutes:

> **1 lb. (.45 kg) 55°L British crystal malt**
> **4 oz. (113 g) Belgian aromatic malt**
> **2 oz. (57 g) roasted barley**

Strain the grain water into your brew pot. Sparge the grains with ½ gallon (1.9 L) water at 150°F (65.5°C). Add water to the brew pot for 1.5 gallons (5.7 L) total volume. Bring the water to a boil, remove the pot from the stove, and add:

> **6.6 lb. (3 kg) John Bull light malt syrup**
> **2.5 lb. (1.1 kg) M&F light DME**
> **4 oz. (113 g) Malto-dextrin**
> **1 oz. (28 g) East Kent Goldings (5 HBU) (bittering hop)**
> **⅔ oz. (19 g) Fuggles @ 4.5% AA (3 HBU) (bittering hop)**

Add water until total volume in the brew pot is 2.5 gallons (9 L). Boil for 45 minutes then add:

> **½ oz. (14 g) Fuggles (flavor hop)**
> **1 tsp. (5 ml) Irish moss**

Boil for 10 minutes then add:

> **½ oz. (14 g) East Kent Goldings (aroma hop)**

Boil for 5 minutes, remove pot from the stove, and cool for 15 minutes. Strain the cooled wort into the primary fermenter and add cold water to obtain 5 gallons (18.9 L). When the wort temperature is under 80°F (26.6°C), pitch your yeast.

> **1st choice: Wyeast's 1084 Irish ale yeast**
> **(Ferment at 66–70°F [19–21°C])**
> **2nd choice: Wyeast's 1028 Scottish ale yeast**
> **(Ferment at 66–70°F [19–21°C])**

Ferment in the primary fermenter 4–5 days or until fermentation slows, then siphon into the secondary fermenter. Bottle when fermentation is complete with:

> **1¼ cup (300 ml) M&F extra-light DME**

 Serve at 55°F (13°C) in a tankard or pub mug

 **Alternate Methods**

Mini-mash Method: Mash 2 lb. (.9 kg) Golden Promise 2-row pale malt and the specialty grains at 150°F (65.5°C) for 90 minutes. Then follow the extract recipe omitting 2 lb. (.9 kg) DME at the beginning of the boil.

All-grain Method: Mash 11.5 lb. (5.2 kg) Golden Promise 2-row pale malt, ½ lb. (.23 kg) dextrin malt, and the specialty grains at 150°F (65.5°C) for 90 minutes. Add 5 HBU (37% less than the extract recipe) of bittering hops for 90 minutes of the boil. Add the flavor hops and Irish moss for the last 15 minutes of the boil and the aroma hops for the last 5 minutes.

Old Speckled Hen

Morland PLC, Abingdon, Oxfordshire, England

This light amber beer arrives with an off-white, creamy head drawing you in with its malt and butterscotch aroma. The initial flavor is malty and sweet with a dry, slightly bitter aftertaste.

Yield: 5 gallons (18.9 L)   Final gravity: 1.010–1.012   SRM 12
Original gravity: 1.051–1.053   IBU 36   5.2% alcohol by volume

Crush and steep in ½ gallon (1.9 L) 150°F (65.5°C) water for 20 minutes:

> **12 oz. (.34 kg) 55°L British crystal malt**

Strain the grain water into your brew pot. Sparge the grains with ½ gallon (1.9 L) water at 150°F (65.5°C). Add water to the brew pot for 1.5 gallons (5.7 L) total volume. Bring the water to a boil, remove the pot from the stove, and add:

> **5.25 lb. (2.4 kg) M&F light DME**
> **½ lb. (.23 kg) cane sugar**
> **4 oz. (113 g) wheat DME (55% wheat, 45% barley)**
> **1 oz. (28 g) Challenger @ 8% AA (8 HBU)**
> **(bittering hop)**

Add water until total volume in the brew pot is 2.5 gallons (9 L). Boil for 45 minutes then add:

> **½ oz. (14 g) East Kent Goldings (flavor hop)**
> **½ oz. (14 g) Challenger (flavor hop)**
> **1 tsp. (5 ml) Irish moss**

Boil for 14 minutes then add:

> **1 oz. (28 g) East Kent Goldings (aroma hop)**

Boil for 1 minute, remove pot from the stove and cool for 15 minutes. Strain the cooled wort into the primary fermenter and add cold water to obtain 5 gallons (18.9 L). When the wort temperature is under 80°F (26.6°C), pitch your yeast.

> **1st choice: Wyeast's 1084 Irish ale yeast**
> **(Ferment at 68–72°F [20–22°C])**
> **2nd choice: Wyeast's 1028 London ale yeast**
> **(Ferment at 68–72°F [20–22°C])**

Ferment in the primary fermenter 5–7 days or until fermentation slows, then siphon into the secondary fermenter. Bottle when fermentation is complete with:

> **¾ cup (180 ml) corn sugar**

 Serve in a pint glass at 50°F (10°C).

 **Alternate Methods**

Mini-mash Method: Mash 3 lb. (1.36 kg) British 2-row pale malt, 4 oz. (113 g) British wheat malt, and the specialty grain at 150°F (65.5°C) for 90 minutes. Then follow the extract recipe omitting 2.25 lb. (1 kg) M&F light DME and the wheat DME at the beginning of the boil.

All-grain Method: Mash 7.75 lb. (3.5 kg) British 2-row pale malt, 4 oz. (113 g) British wheat malt, and the specialty grain at 150°F (65.5°C) for 90 minutes. Add 5.5 HBU (31% less than the extract recipe) of bittering hops and the cane sugar for 90 minutes of the boil. Add the flavor hops and Irish moss for the last 15 minutes of the boil and the aroma hops for the last 1 minute.

Samuel Smith's Taddy Porter

Samuel Smith Old Brewery, Tadcaster, England

This black, full-bodied porter, sold in England as Nourishing Strong Stout, was originally named for train porters who were its servers and consumers. It enters with a malt and molasses aroma with a hint of butterscotch followed by an intense, dry character of roasted grain packed with full-bodied flavor.

Yield: 5 gallons (18.9 L)   Final gravity: 1.011–1.013   SRM 128
Original gravity: 1.052–1.054   IBU 33   5.2% alcohol by volume

Crush and steep in 1 gallon (3.8 L) 150°F (65.5°C) water for 20 minutes:

> **1 lb. (.46 kg) 55°L British crystal malt**
> **12 oz. (.34 kg) British black malt**
> **6 oz. (.17 kg) British chocolate malt**

Strain the grain water into your brew pot. Sparge the grains with ½ gallon (1.9 L) water at 150°F (65.5°C). Add water to the brew pot for 1.5 gallons (5.7 L) total volume. Bring the water to a boil, remove the pot from the stove, and add:

> **6 lb. (2.7 kg) M&F light DME**
> **2 oz. (57 g) black treacle**
> **1.5 oz. (42 g) East Kent Goldings @ 5.7% AA (8.5 HBU)**
> **(bittering hop)**

Add water until total volume in the brew pot is 2.5 gallons (9 L). Boil for 45 minutes then add:

> **1 tsp. (5 ml) Irish moss**
> **½ oz. (14 g) Fuggles (flavor hop)**

Boil for 12 minutes then add:

> **½ oz. (14 g) East Kent Goldings (aroma hop)**

Boil for 3 minutes, remove pot from the stove, and cool for 15 minutes. Strain the cooled wort into the primary fermenter and add cold water to obtain 5 gallons (18.9 L). When the wort temperature is under 80°F (26.6°C), pitch your yeast.

> **Wyeast's 1084 Irish ale yeast**
> **(Ferment at 68–74°F [20–23°C])**

Ferment in the primary fermenter 5–7 days or until fermentation slows, then siphon into the secondary fermenter. Bottle when fermentation is complete with:

> **1¼ cup (300 ml) M&F extra-light DME**

 Serve at 55°F (13°C) in a pint glass or a tumbler.

 **Alternate Methods**

Mini-mash Method: Mash 1.5 lb. (.68 kg) British 2-row pale malt and the specialty grains at 150°F (65.5°C) for 90 minutes. Then follow the extract recipe omitting 2 lb. (.9 kg) DME at the beginning of the boil.

All-grain Method: Mash 7.75 lb. (3.5 kg) British 2-row pale malt with the specialty grains at 150°F (65.5°C) for 90 minutes. Add 6.5 HBU (24% less than the extract recipe) of bittering hops and the black treacle for 90 minutes of the boil. Add the flavor hops and Irish moss for the last 15 minutes of the boil and the aroma hops for the last 3 minutes.

Samuel Smith's Oatmeal Stout

Samuel Smith Old Brewery, Tadcaster, England

Samuel Smith Old Brewery was the first to revive the forgotten Oatmeal Stout style by bringing it back to life in the 1980s. The dense, lacy head is light brown with fine bubbles. The rich aroma is dominated by roasted malt, fruit, and butterscotch. The very smooth and silky taste balances mild hop bitterness and bittersweet malt for a complex medium dry palate.

Yield: 5 gallons (18.9 L)	Final gravity: 1.010–1.013	SRM 68
Original gravity: 1.048–1.051	IBU 30	4.8% alcohol by volume

On a cookie sheet spread out:

> **½ lb. (.23 kg) flaked oats**

Place the sheet in an oven and heat to 325°F (162.7°C). Leave the oats in the oven for 75 minutes, turning the oats every 15 minutes. Pour the oats into a brew pot and steep them in 1 gallon (3.8 L) of 150°F (65.5°C) water for 20 minutes along with:

> **½ lb. (.23 kg) 55°L British crystal malt**
> **½ lb. (.23 kg) British chocolate malt**
> **3 oz. (85 g) roasted barley**

Strain the grain water into your brew pot. Sparge the grains with ½ gallon (1.9 L) water at 150°F (65.5°C). Add water to the brew pot for 1.5 gallons (5.7 L) total volume. Bring the water to a boil, remove the pot from the stove, and add:

> **5.75 lb. (2.6 kg) M&F light DME**
> **2 oz. (57 g) East Kent Goldings @ 4.25% AA (8.5 HBU)**
> **(bittering hop)**

Add water until total volume in the brew pot is 2.5 gallons (9 L). After 50 minutes of the boil add:

> **1 tsp. (5 ml) Irish moss**

Boil for 10 minutes, remove pot from the stove, and cool for 15 minutes. Strain the cooled wort into the primary fermenter and add cold water to obtain 5 gallons (18.9 L). When the wort temperature is under 80°F (26.6°C), pitch your yeast.

> **Wyeast's 1084 Irish ale yeast**
> **(Ferment at 68–74°F [20–23°C])**

Ferment in the primary fermenter 5–7 days or until fermentation slows, then siphon into the secondary fermenter. Bottle when fermentation is complete with:

> **1¼ cup (300 ml) M&F wheat DME**

 Serve in a mug at 55°F (13°C).

Alternate Methods

Mini-mash Method: Mash 2 lb. (.9 kg) British 2-row pale malt and the specialty grains at 150°F (65.5°C) for 90 minutes. Then follow the extract recipe omitting 2.25 lb. (1 kg) DME at the beginning of the boil.

All-grain Method: Mash 7.5 lb. (3.4 kg) British 2-row pale malt with the specialty grains at 150°F (65.5°C) for 90 minutes. Add 6.5 HBU (24% less than the extract recipe) of bittering hops for 90 minutes of the boil. Add the Irish moss for the last 15 minutes of the boil.

Samuel Smith's Winter Welcome

Samuel Smith Old Brewery, Tadcaster, England

This seasonal ale from Sam Smith is vintage-dated with a special label each year. It is a festive light amber brew with a creamy beige head. The aroma is a complex blend of diacetyl, earthy Kent Goldings hops, and malt. The flavor balances malt and hops before an elegant malt finish.

Yield: 5 gallons (18.9 L)	**Final gravity: 1.016–1.018**	**SRM 15**
Original gravity: 1.068–1.070	**IBU 29**	**6.7% alcohol by volume**

Crush and steep in 1 gallon (3.8 L) 150°F (65.5°C) water for 20 minutes:

> **12 oz. (.34 kg) 55°L British crystal malt**
> **½ lb. (.23 kg) 20°L crystal malt**

Strain the grain water into your brew pot. Sparge the grains with ½ gallon (1.9 L) water at 150°F (65.5°C). Add water to the brew pot for 1.5 gallons (5.7 L) total volume. Bring the water to a boil, remove the pot from the stove, and add:

> **8 lb. (3.6 kg) M&F light DME**
> **1.5 oz. (42 g) East Kent Goldings @ 4.7% AA (7 HBU)**
> **(bittering hop)**

Add water until total volume in the brew pot is 2.5 gallons (9 L). Boil for 45 minutes then add:

> **½ oz . (14 g) Fuggles (flavor hop)**
> **½ oz. (14 g) East Kent Goldings (flavor hop)**
> **1 tsp. (5 ml) Irish moss**

Boil for 14 minutes then add:

> **1 oz. (28 g) East Kent Goldings (aroma hop)**

Boil for 1 minute, remove pot from the stove and cool for 15 minutes. Strain the cooled wort into the primary fermenter and add cold water to obtain 5 gallons (18.9 L). When the wort temperature is under 80°F (26.6°C), pitch your yeast.

> **Wyeast's 1084 Irish ale yeast**
> **(Ferment at 68–74°F [20–23°C])**

Ferment in the primary fermenter 5–7 days or until fermentation slows, then siphon into the secondary fermenter. Bottle when fermentation is complete with:

> **1¼ cup (300 ml) M&F extra-light DME**

 Serve in a traditional tankard or Yorkshire nonik pint glasses at 55°F (13°C).

 **Alternate Methods**

Mini-mash Method: Mash 2 lb. (.9 kg) British 2-row pale malt and the specialty grains at 150°F (65.5°C) for 90 minutes. Then follow the extract recipe omitting 2 lb. (.9 kg) DME at the beginning of the boil.

All-grain Method: Mash 11.75 lb. (5.3 kg) British 2-row pale malt with the specialty grains at 150°F (65.5°C) for 90 minutes. Add 5 HBU (29% less than the extract recipe) of bittering hops for 90 minutes of the boil. Add the flavor hops and Irish moss for the last 15 minutes of the boil and the aroma hops for the last minute.

Shepherd Neame IPA

Shepherd Neame Brewery, Faversham, England

This dark golden IPA has a creamy, white, tight head and a light hop aroma. Light in body, it is slightly bitter with a dry hop aftertaste. This classic IPA is made with the freshest local hops, since the brewery sits amid hop fields in the small town of Faversham.

Yield: 5 gallons (18.9 L)   Final gravity: 1.012–1.014   SRM 10.5
Original gravity: 1.055–1.057   IBU 39   5.5% alcohol by volume

Crush and steep in ½ gallon (1.9 L) 150°F (65.5°C) water for 20 minutes:

> **7 oz. (.2 kg) 55°L British crystal malt**
> **4 oz. (113 g) torrified wheat**
> **3 oz. (85 g) British amber malt**

Strain the grain water into your brew pot. Sparge the grains with ½ gallon (1.9 L) water at 150°F (65.5°C). Add water to the brew pot for 1.5 gallons (5.7 L) total volume. Bring the water to a boil, remove the pot from the stove, and add:

> **6.5 lb. (3 kg) M&F light DME**
> **1.5 oz. (42 g) Target @ 7% AA (10.5 HBU) (bittering hop)**

Add water until total volume in the brew pot is 2.5 gallons (9 L). Boil for 45 minutes then add:

> **½ oz. (14 g) East Kent Goldings (flavor hop)**
> **1 tsp. (5 ml) Irish moss**

Boil for 14 minutes then add:

> **½ oz. (14 g) East Kent Goldings (aroma hop)**

Boil for 1 minute, remove pot from the stove and cool for 15 minutes. Strain the cooled wort into the primary fermenter and add cold water to obtain 5 gallons (18.9 L). When the wort temperature is under 80°F (26.6°C), pitch your yeast.

> **1st choice: Wyeast's 1275 Thames Valley ale yeast**
> **(Ferment at 68–72°F [20–22°C])**
> **2nd choice: Wyeast's 1968 Special London ale yeast**
> **(Ferment at 68–72°F [20–22°C])**

Ferment in the primary fermenter 5–7 days or until fermentation slows, then siphon into the secondary fermenter and add:

> **½ oz. (14 g) East Kent Goldings (dry hop)**

Bottle when fermentation is complete with:

> **1¼ cup (300 ml) M&F extra-light DME**

 Serve in a pint glass at 55°F (13°C).

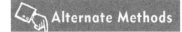 **Alternate Methods**

Mini-mash Method: Mash 3.25 lb. (1.5 kg) British 2-row pale malt and the specialty grains at 150°F (65.5°C) for 90 minutes. Then follow the extract recipe omitting 2.5 lb. (1.1 kg) DME at the beginning of the boil.

All-grain Method: Mash 9.5 lb. (4.3 kg) British 2-row pale malt with the specialty grains at 150°F (65.5°C) for 90 minutes. Add 7.5 HBU (28% less than the extract recipe) of bittering hops for 90 minutes of the boil. Add the flavor hops and Irish moss for the last 15 minutes of the boil and the aroma hops for the last 1 minute.

Skull Splitter

Orkney Brewery, Orkney, Scotland

This dark amber Scottish ale is named after Thorfinn Hausakliuf, the seventh Viking Earl of Orkney who lived around A.D. 950. Medium in body, it is deceptively light, hiding its 8.5 percent alcohol. The aroma is malty, with an almost winelike hint of alcohol. The complex flavor is winey, smooth, and malty with hints of spicy hops.

Yield: 5 gallons (18.9 L)	**Final gravity: 1.018–1.022**	**SRM 22**
Original gravity: 1.085–1.088	IBU 26	8.5% alcohol by volume

Crush and steep in ½ gallon (1.9 L) 150°F (65.5°C) water for 20 minutes:

> **10 oz. (.28 kg) 55°L British crystal malt**
> **4 oz. (113 g) Belgian aromatic malt**
> **2 oz. (57 g) roasted barley**
> **1 oz. (28 g) peat-smoked malt**

Strain the grain water into your brew pot. Sparge the grains with ½ gallon (1.9 L) water at 150°F (65.5°C). Add water to the brew pot for 1.5 gallons (5.7 L) total volume. Bring the water to a boil, remove the pot from the stove, and add:

> **4 lb. (1.8 kg) M&F light DME**
> **½ lb. (.23 kg) M&F wheat DME (55% wheat, 45% barley)**
> **6.6 lb. (3 kg) John Bull light malt syrup**
> **2 oz. (57 g) East Kent Goldings @ 4.75% AA (9.5 HBU) (bittering hop)**

Add water until total volume in the brew pot is 3 gallons (11 L). Boil for 45 minutes then add:

> **1 tsp. (5 ml) Irish moss**

Boil for 15 minutes, remove pot from the stove, and cool for 15 minutes. Strain the cooled wort into the primary fermenter and add cold water to obtain 5 gallons (18.9 L). When the wort temperature is under 80°F (26.6°C), pitch your yeast.

> **1st choice: Wyeast's 1084 Irish ale yeast**
> **(Ferment at 66–70°F [19–21°C])**
> **2nd choice: Wyeast's 1728 Scottish ale yeast**
> **(Ferment at 66–70°F [19–21°C])**

Ferment in the primary fermenter 5–7 days or until fermentation slows, then siphon into the secondary fermenter and add:

> **¼ oz. (7 g) steamed oak chips**

Bottle when fermentation is complete with:

> **1¼ cup (300 ml) M&F wheat DME**

Serve in a stoneware mug at 55°F (13°C).

Alternate Methods

Mini-mash Method: Mash 3 lb. (1.36 kg) Golden Promise 2-row pale malt and the specialty grains at 150°F (65.5°C) for 90 minutes. Then follow the extract recipe omitting 2.5 lb. (1.13 kg) DME at the beginning of the boil.

All-grain Method: Mash 14.5 lb. (6.6 kg) Golden Promise 2-row pale malt and ½ lb. (.23 kg) British wheat malt with the specialty grains at 150°F (65.5°C) for 90 minutes. Add 6.5 HBU (32% less than the extract recipe) of bittering hops for 90 minutes of the boil. Add the Irish moss for the last 15 minutes of the boil.

Spitfire Premium Ale

Shepherd Neame, Faversham, Kent, England

This bottle-conditioned, brilliant amber ale shows off in your glass with a big, rocky, off-white head. The roast malt and butterscotch aroma flows into the toasted malt and hop flavor.

Yield: 5 gallons (18.9 L)   Final gravity: 1.011–1.014   SRM 14
Original gravity: 1.052–1.055   IBU 35   5.2% alcohol by volume

Crush and steep in 1 gallon (3.8 L) 150°F (65.5°C) water for 20 minutes:

> **½ lb. (.23 kg) 55°L British crystal malt**
> **6 oz. (.17 kg) toasted 2-row pale malt**
> **6 oz. (.17 kg) British amber malt**
> **4 oz. (113 g) torrified wheat**

Strain the grain water into your brew pot. Sparge the grains with ½ gallon (1.9 L) water at 150°F (65.5°C). Add water to the brew pot for 1.5 gallons (5.7 L) total volume. Bring the water to a boil, remove the pot from the stove, and add:

> **6 lb. (2.7 kg) M&F light DME**
> **4 oz. (113 g) wheat DME**
> **1 oz. (28 g) Target @ 8.5% AA (8.5 HBU) (bittering hop)**

Add water until total volume in the brew pot is 2.5 gallons (9 L). Boil for 45 minutes then add:

> **1 oz. (28 g) East Kent Goldings (flavor hop)**
> **1 tsp. (5 ml) Irish moss**

Boil for 14 minutes then add:

> **½ oz. (14 g) East Kent Goldings (aroma hop)**

Boil for 1 minute, remove pot from the stove and cool for 15 minutes. Strain the cooled wort into the primary fermenter and add cold water to obtain 5 gallons (18.9 L). When the wort temperature is under 80°F (26.6°C), pitch your yeast.

> **Wyeast's 1084 Irish ale yeast**
> **(Ferment at 68–72°F [20–22°C])**

Ferment in the primary fermenter 5–7 days or until fermentation slows, then siphon into the secondary fermenter and add:

> **½ oz. (14 g) East Kent Goldings (dry hop)**

Bottle when fermentation is complete with:

> **1 cup (230 ml) wheat DME (55% wheat, 45% barley)**
> **¼ cup (60 ml) glucose syrup**

 Serve this ale in a pub mug at 50°F (10°C).

 **Alternate Methods**

Mini-mash Method: Mash 2.5 lb. (1.1 kg) British 2-row pale malt and the specialty grain at 150°F (65.5°C) for 90 minutes. Then follow the extract recipe omitting 2.5 lb. (1.1 kg) DME at the beginning of the boil.

All-grain Method: Mash 8.25 lb. (3.7 kg) British 2-row pale malt, ¼ lb. (113 g) British wheat malt, and the specialty grains at 150°F (65.5°C) for 90 minutes. Add 6 HBU (30% less than the extract recipe) of bittering hops for 90 minutes of the boil. Add the flavor hops and Irish moss for the last 15 minutes of the boil and the aroma hops for the last 1 minute.

Thames Welsh Bitter Ale

Felinfoel Brewery Co. Ltd., Llanelli, Wales

This Welsh ale has an off-white, creamy head, a dark gold to light amber color and a sweet malt aroma. The light-bodied ale's smooth taste finishes with a sweet, malty aftertaste. It's a very refreshing bitter.

Yield: 5 gallons (18.9 L)   Final gravity: 1.009–1.012   SRM 9

Original gravity: 1.046–1.049   IBU 29   4.7% alcohol by volume

Crush and steep in ½ gallon (1.9 L) 150°F (65.5°C) water for 20 minutes:

> **½ lb. (.23 kg) 55°L British crystal malt**
> **½ lb. (.23 kg) torrified wheat**

Strain the grain water into your brew pot. Sparge the grains with ½ gallon (1.9 L) water at 150°F (65.5°C). Add water to the brew pot for 1.5 gallons (5.7 L) total volume. Bring the water to a boil, remove the pot from the stove, and add:

> **5.25 lb. (2.4 kg) M&F light DME**
> **4 oz. (113 g) cane sugar**
> **1.3 oz. (37 g) East Kent Goldings @ 5% AA (6.5 HBU) (bittering hop)**

Add water until total volume in the brew pot is 2.5 gallons (9 L). Boil for 45 minutes then add:

> **½ oz. (14 g) Challenger (flavor hop)**
> **1 tsp. (5 ml) Irish moss**

Boil for 13 minutes then add:

> **½ oz. (14 g) Fuggles (aroma hop)**

Boil for 2 minutes, remove pot from the stove, and cool for 15 minutes. Strain the cooled wort into the primary fermenter and add cold water to obtain 5 gallons (18.9 L). When the wort temperature is under 80°F (26.6°C), pitch your yeast.

> **1st choice: Wyeast's 1028 London ale yeast (Ferment at 68–72°F [20–22°C])**
> **2nd choice: Wyeast's 1084 Irish ale yeast (Ferment at 68–72°F [20–22°C])**

Ferment in the primary fermenter 4–5 days or until fermentation slows, then siphon into the secondary fermenter. Bottle when fermentation is complete with:

> **1¼ cup (300 ml) M&F extra-light DME**

 Serve in a pint glass at 50°F (10°C).

Alternate Methods

Mini-mash Method: Mash 2.5 lb. (1.1 kg) British 2-row pale malt and the specialty grains at 150°F (65.5°C) for 90 minutes. Then follow the extract recipe omitting 2.25 lb. (1 kg) DME at the beginning of the boil.

All-grain Method: Mash 7.25 lb. (3.3 kg) British 2-row pale malt with the specialty grains at 150°F (65.5°C) for 90 minutes. Add 5 HBU (23% less than the extract recipe) of bittering hops and the cane sugar for 90 minutes of the boil. Add the flavor hops and Irish moss for the last 15 minutes of the boil and the aroma hops for the last 2 minutes.

Theakston's Old Peculiar

T&R Theakston, Wellgarth, Masham, Ripon, Yorkshire, England

This classic old ale has a creamy, tan head and a brown color with ruby tints. The bouquet of ripe fruit and malt flows into a sweet malt and hop flavor. It has a memorable bittersweet finish with a hint of hops.

Yield: 5 gallons (18.9 L)	Final gravity: 1.012–1.015	SRM 35
Original gravity: 1.061–1.064	IBU 29	6.2% alcohol by volume

Crush and steep in 1 gallon (3.8 L) 150°F (65.5°C) water for 20 minutes:

> **12 oz. (.34 kg) 55°L British crystal malt**
> **4 oz. (113 g) torrified wheat**
> **3 oz. (85 g) British chocolate malt**

Strain the grain water into your brew pot. Sparge the grains with ½ gallon (1.9 L) water at 150°F (65.5°C). Add water to the brew pot for 1.5 gallons (5.7 L) total volume. Bring the water to a boil, remove the pot from the stove, and add:

> **6.5 lb. (3 kg) M&F light DME**
> **½ lb. (.23 kg) Belgian clear candi sugar**
> **½ lb. (.23 kg) dark brown sugar**
> **4 oz. (113 g) Lyle's golden syrup**
> **1 oz. (28 g) Northern Brewer @ 8% AA (8 HBU)**
> **(bittering hop)**

Add water until total volume in the brew pot is 2.5 gallons (9 L). Boil for 45 minutes then add:

> **½ oz. (14 g) Fuggles (flavor hop)**
> **1 tsp. (5 ml) Irish moss**

Boil for 13 minutes then add:

> **½ oz. (14 g) Fuggles (aroma hop)**

Boil for 2 minutes, remove pot from the stove, and cool for 15 minutes. Strain the cooled wort into the primary fermenter and add cold water to obtain 5 gallons (18.9 L). When the wort temperature is under 80°F (26.6°C), pitch your yeast.

> **Wyeast's 1084 Irish ale yeast**
> **(Ferment at 68–72°F [20–22°C])**

Ferment in the primary fermenter 5–7 days or until fermentation slows, then siphon into the secondary fermenter and add:

> **1 oz. (28 g) Fuggles (dry hop)**

Bottle when fermentation is complete with:

> **1¼ cup (300 ml) M&F extra-light DME**

 Serve at 55°F (13°C) in a pint glass.

 **Alternate Methods**

Mini-mash Method: Mash 2.5 lb. (1.1 kg) British 2-row pale malt and the specialty grains at 150°F (65.5°C) for 90 minutes. Then follow the extract recipe omitting 2.25 lb. (1 kg) DME at the beginning of the boil.

All-grain Method: Mash 9.25 lb. (4.2 kg) British 2-row pale malt with the specialty grains at 150°F (65.5°C) for 90 minutes. Add 5.5 HBU (31% less than the extract recipe) of bittering hops, the candi sugar, brown sugar, and Lyle's golden syrup for 90 minutes of the boil. Add the flavor hops and Irish moss for the last 15 minutes of the boil and the aroma hops for the last 2 minutes.

Thomas Hardy Ale

Eldridge Pope & Co., Dorchester, England

This famous barley wine, named for poet and novelist Thomas Hardy, has a big malt nose laced with alcohol. The flavor is a complex blend of malt, fruit, and sherry with a soft, round body. It ends with sweet fruit and creamy malt. It is recommended to age for up to five years before drinking.

Yield: 5 gallons (18.9 L) Final gravity: 1.028–1.031 SRM 24
Original gravity: 1.123–1.0125 IBU 70 12% alcohol by volume

Crush and steep in 1 gallon (3.8 L) 150°F (65.5°C) water for 20 minutes:

12 oz. (.34 kg) 55°L British crystal malt
½ lb. (.23 g) British amber malt
2 oz. (57 g) British peat-smoked malt

Strain the grain water into your brew pot. Sparge the grains with ½ gallon (1.9 L) water at 150°F (65.5°C). Add water to the brew pot for 1.5 gallons (5.7 L) total volume. Bring the water to a boil and add:

16.5 lb. Maris Otter light malt syrup
⅓ lb. (15 kg) M&F wheat DME (55% wheat, 45% barley)
1 oz. (28 g) Northern Brewers @ 9% AA (9 HBU)
3 oz. (85 g) East Kent Goldings @ 5% AA (15 HBU)

Add water until total volume in the brew pot is 4 gallons (15 L). Boil for 45 minutes then add:

1 oz. (28 g) Fuggles (flavor hop)
1 tsp. (5 ml) Irish moss

Boil for 13 minutes then add:

1 oz. (28 g) East Kent Goldings (aroma hop)

Boil for 2 minutes. Cool for 15 minutes. Strain the cooled wort into the primary fermenter and add cold water to obtain 5 gallons (18.9 L). When the wort temperature is under 80°F (26.6°C), pitch yeast.

Wyeast's 1084 Irish ale yeast
(Ferment at 68–72°F [20–22°C])

Ferment in the primary fermenter 5–7 days or until fermentation slows, then siphon into the secondary fermenter and add:

½ oz. (14 g) Fuggles (dry hop)
½ oz. (14 g) East Kent Goldings (dry hop)

After 3 weeks add a champagne yeast to the secondary fermenter. Bottle when fermentation is complete with:

1¼ cup (300 ml) M&F extra-light DME

 Serve in a brandy snifter at 60°F (16°C).

 **Alternate Methods**

Mini-mash Method: Mash 3.25 lb. (1.5 kg) Maris Otter 2-row pale malt and the specialty grains at 150°F (65.5°C) for 90 minutes. Then follow the extract recipe omitting 3.3 lb. (1.5 kg) Maris Otter light malt syrup at the beginning of the boil.

All-grain Method: Mash 21.25 lb. (9.6 kg) Maris Otter 2-row pale malt, the specialty grains, and 4 oz. (113 g) additional British amber malt and ⅓ lb. (.15 kg) British wheat malt at 150°F (65.5°C) for 90 minutes. Add 18 HBU (25% less than the extract recipe) of bittering hops for 90 minutes of the boil. Add the flavor hops and Irish moss for the last 15 minutes of the boil and the aroma hops for the last 2 minutes.

Traquair House Ale

Traquair House Brewery, Innerleithen, Scotland

This classic heavy Scotch pure malt ale has a complex aroma of fruit, hops, roasted and peated malt. It is smooth and full-bodied with a flavor of grains and chocolate.

Yield: 5 gallons (18.9 L)	Final gravity: 1.020–1.022	SRM 25
Original gravity: 1.075–1.076	IBU 32	7% alcohol by volume

Crush and steep in 1 gallon (3.8 L) 150°F (65.5°C) water for 20 minutes:

> **1 lb. (.45 kg) 55°L British crystal malt**
> **3 oz. (85 g) British peat-smoked malt**
> **2 oz. (57 g) roasted barley**
> **2 oz. (57 g) Belgian aromatic malt**

Strain the grain water into your brew pot. Sparge the grains with ½ gallon (1.9 L) water at 150°F (65.5°C). Add water to the brew pot for 1.5 gallons (5.7 L) total volume. Bring the water to a boil, remove the pot from the stove, and add:

> **5.5 lb. (2.5 kg) M&F light DME**
> **3.3 lb. (1.5 kg) John Bull light malt syrup**
> **½ lb. (.23 kg) Malto-dextrin**
> **2 oz. (57 g) East Kent Goldings @ 4.5% AA (9 HBU)**
> **(bittering hop)**

Add water until total volume in the brew pot is 2.5 gallons (9 L). Boil for 45 minutes then add:

> **1 oz. (28 g) Fuggles (flavor hop)**
> **1 tsp. (5 ml) Irish moss**

Boil for 13 minutes then add:

> **1 oz. (28 g) East Kent Goldings (aroma hop)**

Boil for 2 minutes, remove pot from the stove, and cool for 15 minutes. Strain the cooled wort into the primary fermenter and add cold water to obtain 5 gallons (18.9 L). When the wort temperature is under 80°F (26.6°C), pitch your yeast.

> **Wyeast's 1084 Irish ale yeast**
> **(Ferment at 66–70°F [19–21°C])**

Ferment in the primary fermenter 5–7 days or until fermentation slows, then siphon into the secondary fermenter and add:

> **½ oz. (14 g) Fuggles (dry hop)**

Bottle when fermentation is complete with:

> **1¼ cup (300 ml) M&F extra-light DME**

 Serve this dessert beer in a balloon glass at 60°F (16°C).

 **Alternate Methods**

Mini-mash Method: Mash 2.5 lb. (1.1 kg) Golden Promise 2-row pale malt and the specialty grains at 150°F (65.5°C) for 90 minutes. Then follow the extract recipe omitting 2.25 lb. (1 kg) DME at the beginning of the boil.

All-grain Method: Mash 12.25 lb. (5.6 kg) Golden Promise 2-row pale malt, ¾ lb. (.34 kg) dextrin malt, and the specialty grains at 150°F (65.5°C) for 90 minutes. Add 5.5 HBU (39% less than the extract recipe) of bittering hops for 90 minutes of the boil. Add the flavor hops and Irish moss for the last 15 minutes of the boil and the aroma hops for the last 2 minutes.

Watney's Cream Stout

Watney Truman Ltd., London, England

This opaque black stout has a creamy, dark tan head with a sweet, roasted malt and coffee aroma. The smooth flavor is a bittersweet combination of coffee and roasted grains followed by a dry toffee aftertaste. It has a creamy mouthfeel and moderate carbonation.

Yield: 5 gallons (18.9 L)   Final gravity: 1.014–1.015   SRM 98
Original gravity: 1.047–1.048   IBU 21   4.2% alcohol by volume

Crush and steep in 1 gallon (3.8 L) 150°F (65.5°C) water for 20 minutes:

12 oz. (.34 kg) 55°L British crystal malt
12 oz. (.34 kg) British chocolate malt
4 oz. (113 g) flaked barley
4 oz. (113 g) roasted barley

Strain the grain water into your brew pot. Sparge the grains with ½ gallon (1.9 L) water at 150°F (65.5°C). Add water to the brew pot for 1.5 gallons (5.7 L) total volume. Bring the water to a boil, remove the pot from the stove, and add:

5 lb. (2.3 kg) M&F light DME
⅔ lb. (.3 kg) Malto-dextrin
1.5 oz. (42 g) Fuggles @ 4% AA (6 HBU) (bittering hop)

Add water until total volume in the brew pot is 2.5 gallons (9 L). Boil for 45 minutes then add:

1 tsp. (5 ml) Irish moss

Boil for 15 minutes, remove pot from the stove, and cool for 15 minutes. Strain the cooled wort into the primary fermenter and add cold water to obtain 5 gallons (18.9 L). When the wort temperature is under 80°F (26.6°C), pitch your yeast.

1st choice: Wyeast's 1028 London ale yeast
(Ferment at 68–72°F [20–22°C])
2nd choice: Wyeast's 1098 British ale yeast
(Ferment at 68–72°F [20–22°C])

Ferment in the primary fermenter 4–5 days or until fermentation slows, then siphon into the secondary fermenter. Bottle when fermentation is complete with:

1¼ cup (300 ml) M&F wheat DME

 Serve in a pint glass at 55°F (13°C).

Alternate Methods

Mini-mash Method: Mash 1.5 lb. (.68 kg) British 2-row pale malt and the specialty grains at 150°F (65.5°C) for 90 minutes. Then follow the extract recipe omitting 2 lb. (.9 kg) DME at the beginning of the boil.

All-grain Method: Mash 6.25 lb. (2.8 kg) British 2-row pale malt, 1 lb. (.45 kg) dextrin malt and the specialty grains at 150°F (65.5°C) for 90 minutes. Add 4.5 HBU (25% less than the extract recipe) of bittering hops for 90 minutes of the boil. Add the Irish moss for the last 15 minutes of the boil.

Marathon

Athenian Brewery S. A., Athens, Greece

Full-bodied Marathon is gold with glints of amber and shows off a creamy, white head. It has a big malt aroma, a smooth sweet malt flavor with mild bitterness, and a slightly sweet aftertaste.

Yield: 5 gallons (18.9 L)   Final gravity: 1.013–1.015   SRM 3–4
Original gravity: 1.052–1.054   IBU 17.5   5% alcohol by volume

Crush and steep in ½ gallon (1.9 L) 150°F (65.5°C) water for 20 minutes:

½ lb. (.23 kg) 2.5°L German light crystal malt

Strain the grain water into your brew pot. Sparge the grains with ½ gallon (1.9 L) water at 150°F (65.5°C). Add water to the brew pot for 1.5 gallons (5.7 L) total volume. Bring the water to a boil, remove the pot from the stove, and add:

6 lb. (2.7 kg) M&F extra-light DME
4 oz. (113 g) Malto-dextrin
**2 oz. (57 g) German Hallertau Hersbrucker @ 2.5% AA
(5 HBU) (bittering hop)**

Add water until total volume in the brew pot is 2.5 gallons (9 L). Boil for 45 minutes then add:

¼ oz. (7 g) German Hallertau Hersbrucker (flavor hop)
1 tsp. (5 ml) Irish moss

Boil for 15 minutes, remove pot from the stove, and cool for 15 minutes. Strain the cooled wort into the primary fermenter and add cold water to obtain 5 gallons (18.9 L). When the wort temperature is under 80°F (26.6°C), pitch your yeast.

**1st choice: Wyeast's 2007 Pilsen lager yeast
(Ferment at 40–52°F [4–11°C])**
**2nd choice: Wyeast's 2035 American lager yeast
(Ferment at 40–52°F [4–11°C])**

Ferment in the primary fermenter 5–7 days or until fermentation slows, then siphon into the secondary fermenter. Bottle when fermentation is complete with:

¾ cup (180 ml) corn sugar

 Serve this at 40°F (4°C) in a Pilsner glass.

 **Alternate Methods**

Mini-mash Method: Mash 2.75 lb. (1.25 kg) German 2-row Pilsner malt, 6 oz. (.17 kg) dextrin malt, and the specialty grain at 150°F (65.5°C) for 90 minutes. Then follow the extract recipe omitting 2 lb. (.9 kg) DME at the beginning of the boil.

All-grain Method: Mash 9.25 lb. (4.2 kg) German 2-row Pilsner malt, ½ lb. (.23 kg) dextrin malt, and the specialty grain at 150°F (65.5°C) for 90 minutes. Add 3.5 HBU (30% less than the extract recipe) of bittering hops for 90 minutes of the boil. Add the flavor hops and Irish moss for the last 15 minutes of the boil.

Grolsch Lager

Grolsche Bierbrouwerij, Groenlo, Holland

The Grolsch Brewery was started in 1898 and has been brewing their popular Pilsner ever since. Light-bodied, medium golden Grolsch has a stark white, frothy head with a fresh mown grass and light yeast nose. Smooth and light-bodied, the flavor is initially bitter with a strong hop and slight toasted grain flavor. The aftertaste is long and dry with a lingering bitterness. Grolsch is known for its bottles with ceramic swing-tops that are highly coveted by homebrewers today.

Yield: 5 gallons (18.9 L)	Final gravity: 1.012–1.014	SRM 3.5
Original gravity: 1.055–1.057	IBU 29	5.5% alcohol by volume

Crush and steep in ½ gallon (1.9 L) 150°F (65.5°C) water for 20 minutes:

> **4 oz. (113 g) 2.5°L German light crystal malt**
> **2 oz. (57 g) German Munich malt**

Strain the grain water into your brew pot. Sparge the grains with ½ gallon (1.9 L) water at 150°F (65.5°C). Add water to the brew pot for 1.5 gallons (5.7 L) total volume. Bring the water to a boil, remove the pot from the stove, and add:

> **6.5 lb. (3 kg) M&F extra-light DME**
> **1 oz. (28 g) Northern Brewer @ 8% AA (8 HBU)**
> **(bittering hop)**

Add water until total volume in the brew pot is 2.5 gallons (9 L). Boil for 45 minutes then add:

> **¼ oz. (7 g) German Hallertau Hersbrucker (flavor hop)**
> **1 tsp. (5 ml) Irish moss**

Boil for 5 minutes then add:

> **½ oz. (14 g) Czech Saaz (flavor hop)**

Boil for 10 minutes, remove pot from the stove, and cool for 15 minutes. Strain the cooled wort into the primary fermenter and add cold water to obtain 5 gallons (18.9 L). When the wort temperature is under 80°F (26.6°C), pitch your yeast.

> **1st choice: Wyeast's 2042 Danish lager yeast**
> **(Ferment at 42–52°F [6–11°C])**
> **2nd choice: Wyeast's 2247 Danish II lager yeast**
> **(Ferment at 42–52°F [6–11°C])**

Ferment in the primary fermenter 5–7 days or until fermentation slows, then siphon into the secondary fermenter. Bottle when fermentation is complete with:

> **¾ cup (180 ml) corn sugar**

 Serve at 40°F (4°C) in a Pilsner glass.

 **Alternate Methods**

Mini-mash Method: Mash 3.25 lb. (1.5 kg) German 2-row Pilsner malt and the specialty grains at 150°F (65.5°C) for 90 minutes. Then follow the extract recipe omitting 2.25 lb. (1 kg) DME at the beginning of the boil.

All-grain Method: Mash 10.25 lb. (4.6 kg) German 2-row Pilsner malt with the specialty grain at 150°F (65.5°C) for 90 minutes. Add 6 HBU (25% less than the extract recipe) of bittering hops for 90 minutes of the boil. Add flavor hops and Irish moss for the last 15 minutes of the boil and the second flavor hops for the last 10 minutes.

Heineken Lager

Heineken, Rotterdam, Holland

This popular Dutch lager has a bright straw-gold color and a nice white head. The smooth, medium-bodied beer has a refreshing light hop character. The taste balances a light malt flavor reminiscent of hay and herbs with a hint of toasted grain. Moderately carbonated, it finishes long with a hop aftertaste.

Yield: 5 gallons (18.9 L)	Final gravity: 1.011–1.013	SRM 3–4
Original gravity: 1.051–1.054	IBU 24	5% alcohol by volume

Crush and steep in ½ gallon (1.9 L) 150°F (65.5°C) water for 20 minutes:

4 oz. (113 g) 2.5°L German light crystal malt

Strain the grain water into your brew pot. Sparge the grains with ½ gallon (1.9 L) water at 150°F (65.5°C). Add water to the brew pot for 1.5 gallons (5.7 L) total volume. Bring the water to a boil, remove the pot from the stove, and add:

3.3 lb. (1.5 kg) Bierkeller light malt syrup
3.25 lb. (1.5 kg) M&F extra-light DME
½ oz. (14 g) Northern Brewer @ 8% AA (4 HBU) (bittering hop)
1 oz. (28 g) German Hallertau Hersbrucker @ 3% AA (3 HBU) (bittering hop)

Add water until total volume in the brew pot is 2.5 gallons (9 L). Boil for 50 minutes then add:

¼ oz. (7 g) German Hallertau Hersbrucker (flavor hop)
1 tsp. (5 ml) Irish moss

Boil for 10 minutes, remove pot from the stove, and cool for 15 minutes. Strain the cooled wort into the primary fermenter and add cold water to obtain 5 gallons (18.9 L). When the wort temperature is under 80°F (26.6°C), pitch your yeast.

1st choice: Wyeast's 2042 Danish lager yeast (Ferment at 42–52°F [6–11°C])
2nd choice: Wyeast's 2247 Danish II lager yeast (Ferment at 42–52°F [6–11°C])

Ferment in the primary fermenter 5–7 days or until fermentation slows, then siphon into the secondary fermenter. Bottle when fermentation is complete with:

¾ cup (180 ml) corn sugar

 Chill to 40°F (4°C) and serve in a Pilsner glass.

Alternate Methods

Mini-mash Method: Mash 3 lb. (1.36 kg) German 2-row Pilsner malt and the specialty grain at 150°F (65.5°C) for 90 minutes. Then follow the extract recipe omitting 2.25 lb. (1 kg) DME at the beginning of the boil.

All-grain Method: Mash 9.25 lb. (4.2 kg) German 2-row Pilsner malt with the specialty grain at 150°F (65.5°C) for 90 minutes. Add 5 HBU (28% less than the extract recipe) of bittering hops for 90 minutes of the boil. Add the flavor hops and Irish moss for the last 10 minutes of the boil.

La Trappe Quadrupel

Trappist Brewery De Schaapskooi, Tilburg, Holland

This quadrupel's full palate is mild and pleasantly bitter and spicy, laced with alcohol. The finish leaves you with an aftertaste that is slightly sweet and spicy.

Yield: 5 gallons (18.9 L)   Final gravity: 1.017–1.021   SRM 21
Original gravity: 1.096–1.100   IBU 24   10% alcohol by volume

Crush and steep in 1 gallon (3.8 L) 150°F (65.5°C) water for 20 minutes:

> **1 lb. (.45 kg) 65°L German dark crystal malt**
> **4 oz. (113 g) Belgian biscuit malt**
> **4 oz. (113 g) Belgian aromatic malt**

Strain the grain water into your brew pot. Sparge the grains with ½ gallon (1.9 L) water at 150°F (65.5°C). Add water to the brew pot for 1.5 gallons (5.7 L) total volume. Bring the water to a boil and add:

> **9.75 lb. (4.4 kg) M&F extra-light DME**
> **2 lb. (.9 kg) Belgian clear candi sugar**
> **1 oz. (28 g) Brewers Gold @ 7% AA (7 HBU)**
> **(bittering hop)**

Add water until total volume in the brew pot is 3.5 gallons (13 L). Boil for 45 minutes then add:

> **½ oz. (14 g) Styrian Goldings (flavor hop)**
> **1 tsp. (5 ml) Curacao bitter orange peel**
> **½ tsp. (2 ml) coriander seeds, crushed**
> **1 tsp. (5 ml) Irish moss**

Boil for 12 minutes then add:

> **½ oz. (14 g) Styrian Goldings (aroma hop)**
> **½ tsp. (2 ml) Curacao bitter orange peel**
> **½ tsp. (2 ml) coriander seeds, crushed**

Boil for 3 minutes. Cool for 15 minutes. Strain the cooled wort into the primary fermenter and add cold water to obtain 5 gallons (18.9 L). When the wort temperature is under 80°F (26.6°C), pitch yeast.

> **1st choice: Wyeast's 3787 Belgian Trappist ale yeast**
> **(Ferment at 68–72°F [20–22°C])**
> **2nd choice: Wyeast's 1388 Belgian strong ale yeast**
> **(Ferment at 68–72°F [20–22°C])**

Ferment in the primary fermenter 5–7 days or until fermentation slows, then siphon into the secondary fermenter. Bottle when fermentation is complete with:

> **1¼ cup (300 ml) M&F light dry malt extract**

 Serve in a wide-mouthed goblet at 60°F (16°C).

Alternate Methods

Mini-mash Method: Mash 2.5 lb. (1.1 kg) Belgian 2-row pale malt and the specialty grains at 150°F (65.5°C) for 90 minutes. Then follow the extract recipe omitting 2.5 lb. (1.1 kg) DME at the beginning of the boil.

All-grain Method: Mash 10 lb. (4.5 kg) Belgian 2-row Pilsner malt, 4.25 lb. (1.9 kg) Belgian 2-row pale malt, and the specialty grains at 150°F (65.5°C) for 90 minutes. Add 5 HBU (29% less than the extract recipe) of bittering hops and the candi sugar for 90 minutes of the boil. Add the flavor hops, spices and Irish moss for the last 15 minutes of the boil and the aroma hops and spices, for the last 3 minutes.

Guinness Extra Stout

Arthur Guinness & Sons, Dublin, Ireland

Guinness's light tan head and deep brown color with ruby highlights are recognized around the world. If you keg your beer, you might want to consider purchasing a G-mix tank (carbon dioxide and nitrogen mix), that will give you the creamy head that Guinness is famous for. This is a recipe for bottled Guinness as it sold in Great Britain, not the Extra Stout sold in the United States, which is 6 percent alcohol by volume.

Yield: 5 gallons (18.9 L)	Final gravity: 1.009–1.011	SRM 54
Original gravity: 1.042–1.045	IBU 40	4.2% alcohol by volume

Crush and steep in 1 gallon (3.8 L) 150°F (65.5°C) water for 20 minutes:

- **12 oz. (.34 kg) roasted barley**
- **4 oz. (113 g) 55°L British crystal malt**
- **4 oz. (113 g) flaked barley**
- **3 oz. (85 g) acid malt (optional: will give that slightly sour Guinness taste)**

Strain the grain water into your brew pot. Sparge the grains with ½ gallon (1.9 L) water at 150°F (65.5°C). Add water to the brew pot for 1.5 gallons (5.7 L) total volume. Bring the water to a boil, remove the pot from the stove, and add:

- **4 lb. (1.8 kg) Mountmellick light malt syrup**
- **1.75 lb. (.8 kg) M&F light DME**
- **1 oz. (28 g) Target @ 8.5% AA (8.5 HBU) (bittering hop)**
- **½ oz. (14 g) East Kent Goldings @ 5% AA (2.5 HBU) (bittering hop)**

Add water until total volume in the brew pot is 2.5 gallons (9 L). Boil for 45 minutes then add:

- **1 tsp. (5 ml) Irish moss**

Boil for 15 minutes, remove pot from the stove, and cool for 15 minutes. Strain the cooled wort into the primary fermenter and add cold water to obtain 5 gallons (18.9 L). When the wort temperature is under 80°F (26.6°C), pitch your yeast.

> **1st choice: Wyeast's 1084 Irish ale yeast (Ferment at 68–72°F [20–22°C])**
> **2nd choice: Wyeast's 1098 British ale yeast (Ferment at 68–72°F [20–22°C])**

Ferment in the primary fermenter 4–5 days or until fermentation slows, then siphon into the secondary fermenter. Bottle when fermentation is complete with:

- **1¼ cup (300 ml) M&F light DME**

 Serve at 55°F (13°C) in a pint glass.

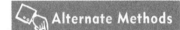

Alternate Methods

Mini-mash Method: Mash 1.5 lb. (.68 kg) British 2-row pale malt and the specialty grains at 150°F (65.5°C) for 90 minutes. Then follow the extract recipe omitting the 1.75 lb. (.8 kg) DME at the beginning of the boil.

All-grain Method: Mash 6 lb. (2.7 kg) British 2-row pale malt, ½ lb. (.23 kg) oat hulls, the specialty grains, and an additional 1 lb. (.45 kg) flaked barley at 150°F (65.5°C) for 90 minutes. Add 8 HBU (27% less than the extract recipe) of bittering hops for 90 minutes of the boil. Add the Irish moss for the last 15 minutes of the boil.

Harp Lager

Harp Brewery, Dundalk, Ireland

Harp is a deep gold, continental lager with a frothy white head. This lager has a light hop nose, is slightly bitter and has a long, bitter, hop aftertaste. This lager is topped with Guinness stout to create the classic Black n' Tan!

Yield: 5 gallons (18.9 L)　　　Final gravity: 1.012–1.013　　SRM 4–5
Original gravity: 1.051–1.054　　IBU 26　　　　　　　　　5% alcohol by volume

Crush and steep in ½ gallon (1.9 L) 150°F (65.5°C) water for 20 minutes:

10 oz. (.28 kg) 10°L crystal malt

Strain the grain water into your brew pot. Sparge the grains with ½ gallon (1.9 L) water at 150°F (65.5°C). Add water to the brew pot for 1.5 gallons (5.7 L) total volume. Bring the water to a boil, remove the pot from the stove, and add:

4 lb. (1.8 kg) Mountmellick light malt syrup
2.75 lb. (1.25 kg) M&F extra-light DME
2 oz. (57 g) German Hallertau Hersbrucker @ 3% AA
(6 HBU) (bittering hop)

Add water until total volume in the brew pot is 2.5 gallons (9 L). Boil for 45 minutes then add:

½ oz. (14 g) German Hallertau Hersbrucker (flavor hop)
½ oz. (14 g) Czech Saaz (flavor hop)
1 tsp. (5 ml) Irish moss

Add water until total volume in the brew pot is 2.5 gallons (9 L). After 55 minutes of the boil add:

¼ oz. (7 g) German Hallertau Hersbrucker (aroma hop)
¼ oz. (7 g) Czech Saaz (aroma hop)

Boil for 5 minutes, remove pot from the stove, and cool for 15 minutes. Strain the cooled wort into the primary fermenter and add cold water to obtain 5 gallons (18.9 L). When the wort temperature is under 80°F (26.6°C), pitch your yeast.

1st choice: Wyeast's 2206 Bavarian lager yeast
(Ferment at 47–52° [8–11°C])
2nd choice: Wyeast's 2565 Kolsch lager yeast
(Ferment at 52–62°F [11–17°C])

Ferment in the primary fermenter 5–7 days or until fermentation slows, then siphon into the secondary fermenter. Bottle when fermentation is complete with:

¾ cup (180 ml) corn sugar

 Serve at 40–42°F (4–6°C) in a pint glass.

Alternate Methods

Mini-mash Method: Mash 2.75 lb. (1.25 kg) British 2-row lager malt and the specialty grain at 150°F (65.5°C) for 90 minutes. Then follow the extract recipe omitting 2.25 lb. (1 kg) DME at the beginning of the boil.

All-grain Method: Mash 9 lb. (4.1 kg) British 2-row lager malt with the specialty grain at 150°F (65.5°C) for 90 minutes. Add 4.5 HBU (25% less than the extract recipe) of bittering hops for 90 minutes of the boil. Add the flavor hops and Irish moss for the last 15 minutes of the boil and the aroma hops for the last 5 minutes.

Murphy's Irish Stout

Murphy Brewery Ireland Ltd., Cork, Ireland

This easy drinking stout is now available in a bottle with a nitrogen cartridge that will pour out a dense, foamy, off-white head sitting on a blackish-brown beer. Imparting an aroma of toffee and coffee, the taste is smooth with mild bitterness and a flavor of roasted, toasted malt.

Yield: 5 gallons (18.9 L)	Final gravity: 1.008–1.010	SRM 81
Original gravity: 1.040–1.043	IBU 37	4.2% alcohol by volume

Crush and steep in 1 gallon (3.8 L) 150°F (65.5°C) water for 20 minutes:

> ½ lb. (.23 kg) British chocolate malt
> 7 oz. (.2 kg) roasted barley
> 4 oz. (113 g) 55°L British crystal malt

Strain the grain water into your brew pot. Sparge the grains with ½ gallon (1.9 L) water at 150°F (65.5°C). Add water to the brew pot for 1.5 gallons (5.7 L) total volume. Bring the water to a boil, remove the pot from the stove, and add:

> 4 lb. (1.8 kg) Mountmellick light malt syrup
> 1 lb. (.45 kg) M&F light DME
> ½ lb. (.23 kg) cane sugar
> 1 oz. (28 g) Target @ 9.5% AA (9.5 HBU) (bittering hop)

Add water until total volume in the brew pot is 2.5 gallons (9 L). Boil for 45 minutes then add:

> ¼ oz. (7 g) East Kent Goldings (flavor hop)
> 1 tsp. (5 ml) Irish moss

Boil for 15 minutes, remove pot from the stove, and cool for 15 minutes. Strain the cooled wort into the primary fermenter and add cold water to obtain 5 gallons (18.9 L). When the wort temperature is under 80°F (26.6°C), pitch your yeast.

> **1st choice: Wyeast's 1084 Irish ale yeast**
> **(Ferment at 68–72°F [20–22°C])**
> **2nd choice: Wyeast's 1098 British ale yeast**
> **(Ferment at 68–72°F [20–22°C])**

Ferment in the primary fermenter 4–6 days or until fermentation slows, then siphon into the secondary fermenter. Bottle when fermentation is complete with:

> 1¼ cup (300 ml) M&F light DME

 Serve in a pint glass at 55°F (13°C).

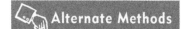 **Alternate Methods**

Mini-mash Method: Mash ¾ lb. (.34 kg) British 2-row pale malt and the specialty grains at 150°F (65.5°C) for 90 minutes. Then follow the extract recipe omitting the 1 lb. (.45 kg) DME at the beginning of the boil.

All-grain Method: Mash 5.75 lb. (2.6 kg) British 2-row pale malt with the specialty grains at 150°F (65.5°C) for 90 minutes. Add 7.5 HBU (21% less than the extract recipe) of bittering hops and the cane sugar for 90 minutes of the boil. Add the flavor hops and Irish moss for the last 15 minutes of the boil.

Moretti Doppio Malto

Moretti, Udine, Italy

This doppelbock's creamy, light-tan head sits on top of a dark-copper beer. The palate is brimming with a well-balanced flavor of hop bitterness and complex toasted malt combining with a sweet alcohol suggestion. It's long, dry finish reminds you of the hops and malt.

Yield: 5 gallons (18.9 L)	Final gravity: 1.021–1.023	SRM 25
Original gravity: 1.080–1.083	IBU 29	7.5% alcohol by volume

Crush and steep in 1 gallon (3.8 L) 150°F (65.5°C) water for 20 minutes:

> **½ lb. (.23 kg) 65°L German dark crystal malt**
> **2 oz. (57 g) chocolate malt**
> **6 oz. (.17 kg) German Munich malt**

Strain the grain water into your brew pot. Sparge the grains with ½ gallon (1.9 L) water at 150°F (65.5°C). Add water to the brew pot for 1.5 gallons (5.7 L) total volume. Bring the water to a boil, remove the pot from the stove, and add:

> **9 lb. (4.1 kg) M&F extra-light DME**
> **½ lb. (.23 kg) Malto-dextrin**
> **2 oz. (57 g) Styrian Goldings @ 5% AA (10 HBU)**
> **(bittering hop)**

Add water until total volume in the brew pot is 2.5 gallons (9 L). Boil for 45 minutes then add:

> **½ oz. (14 g) Styrian Goldings (flavor hop)**
> **1 tsp. (5 ml) Irish moss**

Add water until total volume in the brew pot is 2.5 gallons (9 L). After 55 minutes of the boil add:

> **½ oz. (14 g) Styrian Goldings (aroma hop)**

Boil for 5 minutes, remove pot from the stove, and cool for 15 minutes. Strain the cooled wort into the primary fermenter and add cold water to obtain 5 gallons (18.9 L). When the wort temperature is under 80°F (26.6°C), pitch your yeast.

> **Wyeast's 2308 Munich lager yeast**
> **(Ferment at 47–52° [8–11°C] for 14 days then at**
> **57–62°F [14–17°C] for the remainder of fermentation)**

Ferment in the primary fermenter 5–7 days or until fermentation slows, then siphon into the secondary fermenter. Bottle when fermentation is complete with:

> **1¼ cup (300 ml) M&F extra-light DME**

 Serve in a balloon glass at 55°F (13°C).

 **Alternate Methods**

Mini-mash Method: Mash 2 lb. (.9 kg) German 2-row Pilsner malt, ¾ lb. (.34 kg) dextrin malt, and the specialty grains at 150°F (65.5°C) for 90 minutes. Then follow the extract recipe omitting 2 lb. (.9 kg) DME and the Malto-dextrin at the beginning of the boil.

All-grain Method: Mash 13.33 lb. (6 kg) German 2-row Pilsner malt, ¾ lb. (.34 kg) dextrin malt, the specialty grains, and an additional 2 oz. of German dark crystal malt at 150°F (65.5°C) for 90 minutes. Add 6 HBU (40% less than the extract recipe) of bittering hops for 90 minutes of the boil. Add the flavor hops and Irish moss for the last 15 minutes of the boil and the aroma hops for the last 5 minutes.

Okocim Porter

Okocim Brewery, Okocim, Poland

Okocim Porter is dark black in color with a creamy, cappuccino-colored head. The nose is malty and sweet with traces of roasted malt. The full-bodied flavor is brimming with roasted malt and molasses with a nicely balanced hop presence. This porter finishes with an aftertaste dominated by dry roasted grains.

Yield: 5 gallons (18.9 L)	**Final gravity: 1.024–1.026**	**SRM 64**
Original gravity: 1.087–1.091	**IBU 29**	**8.1% alcohol by volume**

Crush and steep in 1 gallon (3.8 L) 150°F (65.5°C) water for 20 minutes:

> **12 oz. (.34 kg) 65°L German dark crystal malt**
> **4 oz. (113 g) black malt**
> **4 oz. (113 g) chocolate malt**
> **4 oz. (113 g) German Munich malt**

Strain the grain water into your brew pot. Sparge the grains with ½ gallon (1.9 L) water at 150°F (65.5°C). Add water to the brew pot for 1.5 gallons (5.7 L) total volume. Bring the water to a boil, remove the pot from the stove, and add:

> **9.75 lb. (4.4 kg) M&F extra-light DME**
> **12 oz. (.34 kg) Malto-dextrin**
> **2 oz. (57 g) Polishner Lublin @ 4.5% AA (9 HBU)**
> **(bittering hop)**

Add water until total volume in the brew pot is 3.5 gallons (13 L). Boil for 45 minutes then add:

> **½ oz. (14 g) Polishner Lublin (flavor hop)**
> **1 tsp. (5 ml) Irish moss**

Boil for 15 minutes, remove pot from the stove, and cool for 15 minutes. Strain the cooled wort into the primary fermenter and add cold water to obtain 5 gallons (18.9 L). When the wort temperature is under 80°F (26.6°C), pitch your yeast.

> **1st choice: Wyeast's 2308 Munich lager yeast**
> **(Ferment at 47–52° [8–11°C] for 14 days then at**
> **57–62°F [14–17°C] for the remainder of fermentation)**
> **2nd choice: Wyeast's 2206 Bavarian lager yeast**
> **(Ferment at 47–52° [8–11°C])**

Ferment in the primary fermenter 5–7 days or until fermentation slows, then siphon into the secondary fermenter. Bottle when fermentation is complete with:

> **1¼ cup (300 ml) M&F light DME**

 Serve at 55°F (13°C) in a wide-mouthed goblet.

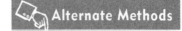

Alternate Methods

Mini-mash Method: Mash 2 lb. (.9 kg) German 2-row Pilsner malt and the specialty grains at 150°F (65.5°C) for 90 minutes. Then follow the extract recipe omitting 2.25 lb. (1 kg) DME at the beginning of the boil.

All-grain Method: Mash 15 lb. (6.8 kg) German 2-row Pilsner malt, ½ lb. (.23 kg) dextrin malt, and the specialty grains at 152°F (66.6°C) for 90 minutes. Add 7 HBU (22% less than the extract recipe) of bittering hops for 90 minutes of the boil. Add the flavor hops and Irish moss for the last 15 minutes of the boil.

Zywiec Beer

Zywiec Brewery, Zywiec, Poland

This deep-golden Pilsner has a finely-beaded white head and a slightly spicy, very aromatic hop aroma with traces of malt. Medium-bodied Zywiec has a pleasant balance of hop bitterness and toasted grain flavor with a hint of smoke. This highly carbonated beer finishes dry.

Yield: 5 gallons (18.9 L)	Final gravity: 1.012–1.013	SRM 4–5
Original gravity: 1.051–1.052	IBU 32	5% alcohol by volume

Crush and steep in ½ gallon (1.9 L) 150°F (65.5°C) water for 20 minutes:

>**6 oz. (.17 kg) 2.5°L German light crystal malt**
>**½ lb. (.23 kg) German Munich malt**

Strain the grain water into your brew pot. Sparge the grains with ½ gallon (1.9 L) water at 150°F (65.5°C). Add water to the brew pot for 1.5 gallons (5.7 L) total volume. Bring the water to a boil, remove the pot from the stove, and add:

>**6.6 lb. (3 kg) Ireks light malt syrup**
>**4 oz. (113 g) M&F extra-light DME**
>**2 oz. (57 g) Polishner Lublin @ 4.5% AA (9 HBU)**
>**(bittering hop)**

Add water until total volume in the brew pot is 2.5 gallons (9 L). Boil for 45 minutes then add:

>**¼ oz. (7 g) German Hallertau Hersbrucker (flavor hop)**
>**1 tsp. (5 ml) Irish moss**

Boil for 10 minutes then add:

>**¼ oz. (7 g) German Hallertau Hersbrucker (aroma hop)**

Boil for 5 minutes, remove pot from the stove, and cool for 15 minutes. Strain the cooled wort into the primary fermenter and add cold water to obtain 5 gallons (18.9 L). When the wort temperature is under 80°F (26.6°C), pitch your yeast.

>**1st choice: Wyeast's 2278 Czech Pilsner yeast**
>**(Ferment at 40–52°F [4–11°C])**
>**2nd choice: Wyeast's 2007 Pilsen lager yeast**
>**(Ferment at 40–52°F [4–11°C])**

Ferment in the primary fermenter 5–7 days or until fermentation slows, then siphon into the secondary fermenter. Bottle when fermentation is complete with:

>**1¼ cup (300 ml) M&F extra-light DME**

 Serve in a Pilsner glass at 45°F (7°C).

 **Alternate Methods**

Mini-mash Method: Mash 2.5 lb. (1.1 kg) German 2-row Pilsner malt and the specialty grains at 150°F (65.5°C) for 90 minutes. Then follow the extract recipe replacing the 6.6 lb. (3 kg) Ireks light malt syrup with 3.3 lb. (1.5 kg) Bierkeller light malt syrup. Also use an additional ¾ lb. (.34 kg) M&F extra-light DME at the beginning of the boil.

All-grain Method: Mash 9 lb. (4.1 kg) German 2-row Pilsner malt with the specialty grains at 150°F (65.5°C) for 90 minutes. Add 6.5 HBU (28% less than the extract recipe) of bittering hops for 90 minutes of the boil. Add the flavor hops and Irish moss for the last 15 minutes of the boil and the aroma hops for the last 5 minutes.

Unicer Super Bock

Unicer Uniao Cervejeria S.A., Leca do Balio, Portugal

Medium-bodied Unicer is deep-golden in color and has a white head. The aroma is a light combination of malt and hops. The smooth flavor is a nice blend of spicy hops and malt followed by a smooth malt finish. A very well-balanced Bock!

Yield: 5 gallons (18.9 L)   Final gravity: 1.012–1.015   SRM 3.5
Original gravity: 1.052–1.054   IBU 24   5% alcohol by volume

Crush and steep in ½ gallon (1.9 L) 150°F (65.5°C) water for 20 minutes:

4 oz. (113 g) 2.5°L German light crystal malt
4 oz. (113 g) German Munich malt

Strain the grain water into your brew pot. Sparge the grains with ½ gallon (1.9 L) water at 150°F (65.5°C). Add water to the brew pot for 1.5 gallons (5.7 L) total volume. Bring the water to a boil, remove the pot from the stove, and add:

6 lb. (2.7 kg) M&F extra-light DME
4 oz. (113 g) Malto-dextrin
1 oz. (28 g) German Hallertauer Northern Brewer @ 6.5% AA (6.5 HBU) (bittering hop)

Add water until total volume in the brew pot is 2.5 gallons (9 L). Boil for 45 minutes then add:

½ oz. (14 g) Spalt (flavor hop)
1 tsp. (5 ml) Irish moss

Boil for 10 minutes then add:

¼ oz. (7 g) Tettnanger (aroma hop)

Boil for 5 minutes, remove pot from the stove, and cool for 15 minutes. Strain the cooled wort into the primary fermenter and add cold water to obtain 5 gallons (18.9 L). When the wort temperature is under 80°F (26.6°C), pitch your yeast.

> **1st choice: Wyeast's 2206 Bavarian lager yeast (Ferment at 40–52°F [4–11°C])**
> **2nd choice: Wyeast's 2124 Bohemian lager yeast (Ferment at 40–52°F [4–11°C])**

Ferment in the primary fermenter 5–7 days or until fermentation slows, then siphon into the secondary fermenter. Bottle when fermentation is complete with:

¾ cup (180 ml) corn sugar

 Serve at 55°F (13°C) in a wide-mouthed goblet.

 **Alternate Methods**

Mini-mash Method: Mash 2.75 lb. (1.25 kg) German 2-row Pilsner malt, 6 oz. (.17 kg) dextrin malt, and the specialty grains at 150°F (65.5°C) for 90 minutes. Then follow the extract recipe omitting 2 lb. (.9 kg) DME at the beginning of the boil.

All-grain Method: Mash 9.25 lb. (4.2 kg) German 2-row Pilsner malt, 6 oz. dextrin malt, and the specialty grains at 150°F (65.5°C) for 90 minutes. Add 4.5 HBU (31% less than the extract recipe) of bittering hops for 90 minutes of the boil. Add the flavor hops and Irish moss for the last 15 minutes of the boil and the aroma hops for the last 5 minutes.

Estrella Galicia Especial

Estrella Galicia Brewery, Galicia, Spain

The brewery in La Coruna was founded by Don Jose Maria Rivera Corral in 1906. This pale gold beer with its bright, white head has a sweet smooth aroma with a light hop fruitiness. The flavor is slightly bitter with light malt overtones followed by a light hop aftertaste. This is a nicely carbonated and refreshing, light brew.

Yield: 5 gallons (18.9 L)	Final gravity: 1.009–1.012	SRM 3
Original gravity: 1.049–1.051	IBU 28	5% alcohol by volume

Crush and steep in ½ gallon (1.9 L) 150°F (65.5°C) water for 20 minutes:

> **4 oz. (113 g) 2.5°L German light crystal malt**
> **3 oz. (85 g) German Munich malt**

Strain the grain water into your brew pot. Sparge the grains with ½ gallon (1.9 L) water at 150°F (65.5°C). Add water to the brew pot for 1.5 gallons (5.7 L) total volume. Bring the water to a boil, remove the pot from the stove, and add:

> **4 lb. (1.8 kg) Alexander's pale malt syrup**
> **2 lb. (.9 kg) M&F extra-light DME**
> **¾ lb. (.34 kg) corn sugar**
> **1.5 oz (42 g) Tettnanger @ 4.7% AA (7 HBU)**
> **(bittering hop)**

Add water until total volume in the brew pot is 2.5 gallons (9 L). Boil for 45 minutes then add:

> **½ oz. (14 g) Styrian Goldings (flavor hop)**
> **1 tsp. (5 ml) Irish moss**

Boil for 5 minutes then add:

> **½ oz. (14 g) Czech Saaz (aroma hop)**

Boil for 10 minutes, remove pot from the stove, and cool for 15 minutes. Strain the cooled wort into the primary fermenter and add cold water to obtain 5 gallons (18.9 L). When the wort temperature is under 80°F (26.6°C), pitch your yeast.

> **1st choice: Wyeast's 2124 Bohemian lager yeast**
> **(Ferment at 42–52°F [6–11°C])**
> **2nd choice: Wyeast's 2206 Bavarian lager yeast**
> **(Ferment at 42–52°F [6–11°C])**

Ferment in the primary fermenter 5–7 days or until fermentation slows, then siphon into the secondary fermenter. Bottle when fermentation is complete with:

> **¾ cup (180 ml) corn sugar**

 Serve at 40°F (4°C) in a Pilsner glass.

Alternate Methods

Mini-mash Method: Mash 2.75 lb. (1.25 kg) German 2-row Pilsner malt and the specialty grains at 150°F (65.5°C) for 90 minutes. Then follow the extract recipe omitting the DME at the beginning of the boil.

All-grain Method: Mash 7.25 lb. (3.3 kg) German 2-row Pilsner malt, 1.25 lb. (.57 kg) flaked maize, ½ lb. (.23 kg) rice hulls, and the specialty grains at 150°F (65.5°C) for 90 minutes. Add 5 HBU (28% less than the extract recipe) of bittering hops for 90 minutes of the boil. Add the flavor hops and Irish moss for the last 15 minutes of the boil and the aroma hops for the last 5 minutes.

D. Carnegie and Co. Porter

AB Pripps Brygerreri, Sundsvall, Sweden

This porter is fermented for six months in the fermentation tank and then bottle-matured for six more months. The flavor is richly complex with hints of roasted malt, toffee, chocolate, coffee, and Madeira. It finishes long and dry.

Yield: 5 gallons (18.9 L)	Final gravity: 1.014–1.016	SRM 105
Original gravity: 1.062–1.063	IBU 45	6.1% alcohol by volume

Crush and steep in 1 gallon (3.8 L) 150°F (65.5°C) water for 20 minutes:

12 oz. (.34 kg) 65°L German dark crystal malt
10 oz. (.28 kg) chocolate malt
4 oz. (113 g) black malt
3 oz. (85 g) kiln coffee malt

Strain the grain water into your brew pot. Sparge the grains with ½ gallon (1.9 L) water at 150°F (65.5°C). Add water to the brew pot for 1.5 gallons (5.7 L) total volume. Bring the water to a boil, remove the pot from the stove, and add:

6.6 lb. (3 kg) Ireks light malt syrup
1.5 lb. (.68 kg) M&F light DME
1.7 oz. (48 g) German Northern Brewer @ 8 AA (13.5 HBU)
(bittering hop)

Add water until total volume in the brew pot is 2.5 gallons (9 L). Boil for 45 minutes then add:

½ oz. (14 g) Styrian Goldings (flavor hop)
1 tsp. (5 ml) Irish moss

Boil for 15 minutes, remove pot from the stove, and cool for 15 minutes. Strain the cooled wort into the primary fermenter and add cold water to obtain 5 gallons (18.9 L). When the wort temperature is under 80°F (26.6°C), pitch your yeast.

1st choice: Wyeast's 1742 Swedish ale yeast
(Ferment at 68–72°F [20–22°C])
2nd choice: Wyeast's 1007 German ale yeast
(Ferment at 68–72°F [20–22°C])

Ferment in the primary fermenter 5–7 days or until fermentation slows, then siphon into the secondary fermenter. Bottle when fermentation is complete with:

1¼ cup (300 ml) M&F extra-light DME

 Serve in a wide-mouthed goblet at 55°F (13°C).

 **Alternate Methods**

Mini-mash Method: Mash 2 lb. (.9 kg) British 2-row pale malt and the specialty grains at 150°F (65.5°C) for 90 minutes. Then follow the extract recipe replacing the Ireks light malt syrup with 3.3 lb. (1.5 kg) Bierkeller light malt syrup. Also add an additional ½ lb. (.23 kg) M&F light DME at the beginning of the boil.

All-grain Method: Mash 10 lb. (4.5 kg) British 2-row pale malt with the specialty grains at 150°F (65.5°C) for 90 minutes. Add 9.5 HBU (27% less than the extract recipe) of bittering hops for 90 minutes of the boil. Add the flavor hops and Irish moss for the last 15 minutes of the boil.

Caesarus Imperator Heller Bock

Brauerei Hurlimann AG, Zurich, Switzerland

Caesarus has a dense, off-white head with a deep gold color. The intense aroma is one of fruit, malt, and alcohol. This single bock's taste is full of sweet malt balanced by alcohol tapering off with a sweet malt finish.

Yield: 5 gallons (18.9 L)   Final gravity: 1.019–1.021   SRM 9
Original gravity: 1.072–1.075   IBU 26   6.8% alcohol by volume

Crush and steep in ½ gallon (1.9 L) 150°F (65.5°C) water for 20 minutes:

> ½ lb. (.23 kg) German Vienna malt
> 4 oz. (113 g) Belgian aromatic malt
> 3 oz. (85 g) 65°L German dark crystal malt

Strain the grain water into your brew pot. Sparge the grains with ½ gallon (1.9 L) water at 150°F (65.5°C). Add water to the brew pot for 1.5 gallons (5.7 L) total volume. Bring the water to a boil, remove the pot from the stove, and add:

> 6.6 lb. (3 kg) Ireks light malt syrup
> 2.5 lb. (1.1 kg) M&F extra-light DME
> ½ lb. (.23 kg) Malto-dextrin
> 2 oz. (57 g) Spalt @ 4.25% AA (8.5 HBU) (bittering hop)

Add water until total volume in the brew pot is 2.5 gallons (9 L). Boil for 45 minutes then add:

> ½ oz. (14 g) German Hallertau Hersbrucker (flavor hop)
> 1 tsp. (5 ml) Irish moss

Boil for 13 minutes then add:

> ¼ oz. (7 g) Hallertauer Mittelfrüh (aroma hop)

Boil for 2 minutes, remove pot from the stove, and cool for 15 minutes. Strain the cooled wort into the primary fermenter and add cold water to obtain 5 gallons (18.9 L). When the wort temperature is under 80°F (26.6°C), pitch your yeast.

> Wyeast's 2308 Munich lager yeast
> (Ferment at 47–52° [8–11°C] for the first two weeks,
> then ferment at 57–62°F (14–17°C) for the rest of
> fermentation)

Ferment in the primary fermenter 5–7 days or until fermentation slows, then siphon into the secondary fermenter. Bottle when fermentation is complete with:

> 1¼ cup (300 ml) M&F extra-light DME

 Serve in a pint glass at 55°F (13°C).

Alternate Methods

Mini-mash Method: Mash 3 lb. (1.36 kg) German 2-row Pilsner malt and the specialty grains at 150°F (65.5°C) for 90 minutes. Then follow the extract recipe the omitting the 2.5 lb. (1.13 kg) DME at the beginning of the boil.

All-grain Method: Mash 11 lb. (5 kg) German 2-row Pilsner malt, 1 lb. (.45 kg) German Munich malt, ¾ lb. (.34 kg) dextrin malt, and the specialty grains at 150°F (65.5°C) for 90 minutes. Add 5.5 HBU (35% less than the extract recipe) of bittering hops for 90 minutes of the boil. Add the flavor hops and Irish moss for the last 15 minutes of the boil and the aroma hops for the last 2 minutes.

Samiclaus Bier

Brauerei Hurlimann AG, Zurich, Switzerland

Samiclaus (Santa Claus) is the world's strongest lager at 14 percent alcohol by volume. It is brewed once a year on December 6 in honor of St. Nicholas and released one year later. Samiclaus is a wonderful alternative to brandy.

Yield: 5 gallons (18.9 L)   Final gravity: 1.028–1.034   SRM 21
Original gravity: 1.138–1.144   IBU 29   14% alcohol by volume

Crush and steep in 1 gallon (3.8 L) 150°F (65.5°C) water for 20 minutes:

1 lb. (.45 kg) 65°L German dark crystal malt
½ lb. (.23 kg) German Vienna malt

Strain the grain water into your brew pot. Sparge the grains with ½ gallon (1.9 L) water at 150°F (65.5°C). Add water to the brew pot for 2.5 gallons (9 L) total volume. Bring the water to a boil, remove the pot from the stove, and add:

15.5 lb. (7 kg) M&F extra-light DME
1 lb. (.45 kg) clear candi sugar
1.5 oz. (42 g) Northern Brewer @ 7.3% AA (11 HBU) (bittering hop)

Add water until total volume in the brew pot is 4 gallons (15 L). Boil for 45 minutes then add:

½ oz. (14 g) Tettnanger (flavor hop)
1 tsp. (5 ml) Irish moss

Boil for 13 minutes then add:

½ oz. (14 g) Hallertauer Mittelfrüh (aroma hop)

Boil for 2 minutes, remove pot from the stove, and cool for 15 minutes. Strain the cooled wort into the primary fermenter and add cold water to obtain 5 gallons (18.9 L). When the wort temperature is under 80°F (26.6°C), pitch your yeast.

Wyeast's 2308 Munich lager yeast
(Ferment at 57–62° [14–17°C] for the first 2 weeks,
then ferment at 42–52°F (6–11°C) for 6 weeks)

Ferment in the primary fermenter 5–7 days or until fermentation slows, then siphon into the secondary fermenter. After 8 weeks add:

champagne yeast

Ferment at 65°F (18°C). Bottle when fermentation is complete with:

1¼ cup (300 ml) M&F light DME

Lager the bottles at 47–52°F [8.3–11°C] for 9 to 10 months.

 Serve in a brandy snifter at 60°F (16°C).

Alternate Methods

Mini-mash Method: Mash 3 lb. (1.36 kg) German 2-row Pilsner malt and the specialty grains at 150°F (65.5°C) for 90 minutes. Then follow the extract recipe omitting 2.75 lb. (1.25 kg) DME at the beginning of the boil.

All-grain Method: Mash 23.75 lb. (10.8 kg) German 2-row Pilsner malt with the specialty grain at 150°F (65.5°C) for 90 minutes. Add 8 HBU (27% less than the extract recipe) of bittering hops and the candi sugar for 90 minutes of the boil. Add the flavor hops and Irish moss for the last 15 minutes of the boil and the aroma hops for the last 2 minutes.

Keo Beer

Keo Ltd., Limassol, Cyprus

Pale golden Keo has a tightly beaded head of white bubbles. It arrives with a light floral hop nose and traces of malt. Highly carbonated with a light body, Keo has a malty flavor with bitterness in the back. Light and very refreshing!

Yield: 5 gallons (18.9 L)	Final gravity: 1.010–1.012	SRM 3
Original gravity: 1.046–1.048	IBU 21	4.6% alcohol by volume

Crush and steep in ½ gallon (1.9 L) 150°F (65.5°C) water for 20 minutes:

> ½ lb. (.23 kg) 2.5°F German light crystal malt

Strain the grain water into your brew pot. Sparge the grains with ½ gallon of water at 150°F (65.5°C). Add water to the brew pot for 1.5 gallons (5.7 L) total volume. Bring the water to a boil, remove the pot from the stove, and add:

> 5.5 lb. (2.5 kg) M&F extra-light DME
> 2 oz. (57 g) Czech Saaz at 2.75% AA
> (5.5 HBU) (bittering hop)

Add water until total volume in the brew pot is 2.5 gallons (9 L). Boil for 45 minutes then add:

> ¼ oz. (7 g) Czech Saaz (flavor hop)
> 1 tsp. (5 ml) Irish moss

Boil for 10 minutes then add:

> ¼ oz. (7 g) Czech Saaz (aroma hop)

Boil for 5 minutes, remove pot from the stove, and cool for 15 minutes. Strain the cooled wort into the primary fermenter and add cold water to obtain 5 gallons (18.9 L). When the wort temperature is under 80°F (26.6°C), pitch your yeast.

> 1st choice: Wyeast's 2278 Czech Pilsner lager yeast
> (Ferment at 40–52°F [4–11°C])
> 2nd choice: Wyeast's 2007 Pilsen lager yeast
> (Ferment at 40–52°F [4–11°C])

Ferment in the primary fermenter 5–7 days or until fermentation slows, then siphon into the secondary fermenter. Bottle when fermentation is complete with:

> 1 cup (240 ml) corn sugar

 Serve in a Pilsner glass at 40°F (4°C).

 **Alternate Methods**

Mini-mash Method: Mash 3 lb. (1.36 kg) German 2-row Pilsner malt and the specialty grain at 150°F (65.5°C) for 90 minutes. Then follow the extract recipe omitting 2.25 lb. (1 kg) DME at the beginning of the boil.

All-grain Method: Mash 8.33 lb. (3.8 kg) German 2-row Pilsner malt with the specialty grain at 150°F (65.5°C) for 90 minutes. Add 4 HBU (27% less than the extract recipe) of bittering hops for 90 minutes of the boil. Add the flavor hops and Irish moss for the last 15 minutes of the boil and the aroma hops for the last 5 minutes.

Maccabee Premium Beer

Temp Beer Industries, Netanya, Israel

This highly carbonated kosher beer has a long-lasting creamy white head and a lovely golden color. Maccabee starts with a whiff of soft, sweet malt aroma. It is a medium-bodied lager, with an initial hop bitterness followed by a light harmonious blend of malt and hops, ending with a dry aftertaste.

Yield: 5 gallons (18.9 L)	Final gravity: 1.016–1.019	SRM 4
Orginal gravity: 1.067–1.070	IBU 26	6.5% alcohol by volume

Crush and steep in ½ gallon (1.9 L) 150°F (65.5°C) water for 20 minutes:

> **½ lb. (.23 kg) 2.5°L German light crystal malt**
> **2 oz. (57 g) Belgian aromatic malt**

Strain the grain water into your brew pot. Sparge the grains with ½ gallon (1.9 L) water at 150°F (65.5°C). Add water to the brew pot for 1.5 gallons (5.7 L) total volume. Bring the water to a boil, remove the pot from the stove, and add:

> **7.75 lb. (3.5 kg) M&F extra-light DME**
> **4 oz. (113 g) Malto-dextrin**
> **2 oz. (57 g) Tettnanger @ 4% AA (8 HBU)**
> **(bittering hop)**

Add water until total volume is 2.5 gallons (9 L) Boil for 45 minutes then add:

> **½ oz. (14 g) Tettnanger (flavor hop)**
> **1 tsp. (5 ml) Irish moss**

Boil for 15 minutes, remove pot from the stove, and cool for 15 minutes. Strain the cooled wort into the primary fermenter and add cold water to obtain 5 gallons. When the wort temperature is under 80°F (26.6°C), pitch your yeast.

> **1st choice: Wyeast's 2278 Czech Pilsner yeast**
> **(Ferment at 42–52°F [6–11°C])**
> **2nd choice: Wyeast's 2124 Bohemian lager yeast**
> **(Ferment at 42–52°F [6–11°C])**

Ferment in the primary fermenter 5–7 days or until fermentation slows, then siphon into the secondary fermenter. Bottle when fermentation is complete with:

> **⅞ cup (200 ml) corn sugar**

 Serve in a Pilsner glass at 50°F (10°C).

Alternate Methods

Mini-mash Method: Mash 2.5 lb. (1.1 kg) 2-row British lager malt and the specialty grains at 150°F (65.5°C) for 90 minutes. Then follow the extract recipe omitting 2 lb. (.9 kg) DME at the beginning of the boil.

All-grain Method: Mash 11.75 lb. (5.3 kg) 2-row British lager malt and ½ lb. (.23 kg) dextrin malt with the specialty grains at 150°F (65.5°C) for 90 minutes. Use 5.5 HBU (31% less than the extract recipe) of bittering hops for 90 minutes of the boil. Add the flavor hops and Irish moss for the last 15 minutes of the boil.

Almaza Pilsener Beer

Brasserie et malterie Almaza SAL, Beirut, Lebanon

Pale gold Almaza has a white, frothy head and a mild hop aroma. Crisply flavored with hops up front and malt in the background, it leaves a semi-dry aftertaste. A real thirst quencher.

Yield: 5 gallons (18.9 L)   Final gravity: 1.008–1.009   SRM 2–3
Original gravity: 1.040   IBU 20   4% alcohol by volume

Crush and steep in ½ gallon (1.9 L) 150°F (65.5°C) water for 20 minutes:

> ⅓ lb. (.15 kg) 2.5°L German light crystal malt
> 3 oz. (85 g) German Munich malt

Strain the grain water into your brew pot. Sparge the grains with ½ gallon (1.9 L) water at 150°F (65.5°C). Add water to the brew pot for 1.5 gallons (5.7 L) total volume. Bring the water to a boil, remove the pot from the stove, and add:

> 4 lb. (1.8 kg) M&F extra-light DME
> ⅔ lb. (.3 kg) corn sugar
> 1 oz. (28 g) Tettnanger @ 4.5% AA (4.5 HBU)
>   (bittering hop)

Add water until total volume is 2.5 gallons (9 L) Boil for 45 minutes then add:

> ¼ oz. (7 g) Czech Saaz (flavor hop)
> ¼ oz. (7 g) Tettnanger (flavor hop)
> 1 tsp. (5 ml) Irish moss

Boil for 10 minutes then add:

> ¼ oz. (7 g) Czech Saaz (aroma hop)

Boil for 5 minutes, remove pot from the stove, and cool for 15 minutes. Strain the cooled wort into the primary fermenter and add cold water to obtain 5 gallons (18.9 L). When the wort temperature is under 80°F (26.6°C), pitch your yeast.

> **1st choice: Wyeast's 2206 Bavarian lager yeast**
> **(Ferment at 42–52°F [6–11°C])**
> **2nd choice: Wyeast's 2007 Pilsen lager yeast**
> **(Ferment at 42–52°F [6–11°C])**

Ferment in the primary fermenter 5–7 days or until fermentation slows, then siphon into the secondary fermenter. Bottle when fermentation is complete with:

> ¾ cup (180 ml) corn sugar

 Pour into a Pilsner glass and serve at 45°F (7°C).

Alternate Methods

Mini-mash Method: Mash 2.75 lb. (1.25 kg) British 2-row lager malt and the specialty grains at 150°F (65.5°C) for 90 minutes. Then follow the extract recipe omitting 2 lb. (.9 kg) DME at the beginning of the boil.

All-grain Method: Mash 5.75 lb. (2.6 kg) British 2-row lager malt, 1.25 lb. (.57 kg) flaked maize, and ½ lb. (.23 kg) rice hulls with the specialty grains at 122°F (50°C) for 30 minutes and 150°F (65.5°C) for 90 minutes. Use 3.5 HBU (23% less than the extract recipe) of bittering hops for 90 minutes of the boil. Add the flavor hops and Irish moss for the last 15 minutes of the boil and the aroma hops for the last 5 minutes.

Efes Pilsener

Efes Breweries, Istanbul, Izmir and Adana, Turkey

Pale gold Efes Pilsener sports a brilliant white head and is nicely carbonated with a light body. There is a hint of sweet malt in the nose. It balances an initial bitterness with a buttered toast–malt taste and a dry aftertaste. This is a pleasant, well-balanced beer that complements Middle Eastern food perfectly.

Yield: 5 gallons (18.9 L)   Final gravity: 1.010–1.011   SRM 3–4
Original gravity: 1.051–1.052   IBU 21   5.1% alcohol by volume

Crush and steep in ½ gallon (1.9 L) 150°F (65.5°C) water for 20 minutes:

6 oz. (.17 kg) 2.5°L German light crystal malt
5 oz. (142 g) German Munich malt

Strain the grain water into your brew pot. Sparge the grains with ½ gallon (1.9 L) water at 150°F (65.5°C). Add water to the brew pot for 1.5 gallons (5.7 L) total volume. Bring the water to a boil, remove the pot from the stove, and add:

4.5 lb. (2 kg) M&F extra-light DME
1.5 lb. (.68 kg) rice solids
1 oz. (28 g) Tettnanger @ 5.5% AA (5.5 HBU) (bittering hop)

Add water until total volume is 2.5 gallons (9 L). Boil for 45 minutes then add:

¼ oz. (7 g) Tettnanger (flavor hop)
1 tsp. (5 ml) Irish moss

Boil for 12 minutes then add:

¼ oz. (7 g) Tettnanger (aroma hop)

Boil for 3 minutes, remove pot from the stove, and cool for 15 minutes. Strain the cooled wort into the primary fermenter and add cold water to obtain 5 gallons (18.9 L). When the wort temperature is under 80°F (26.6°C), pitch your yeast.

1st choice: Wyeast's 2278 Czech Pilsner yeast (Ferment at 40–52°F [4–11°C])
2nd choice: Wyeast's 2124 Bohemian lager yeast (Ferment at 42–52°F [6–11°C])

Ferment in the primary fermenter 5–7 days or until fermentation slows, then siphon into the secondary fermenter. Bottle when fermentation is complete with:

⅞ cup (200 ml) corn sugar

 Serve in a Pilsner glass at 45°F (7°C).

 **Alternate Methods**

Mini-mash Method: Mash 2.5 lb. (1.1 kg) British 2-row lager malt and the specialty grains at 150°F (65.5°C) for 90 minutes. Then follow the extract recipe omitting 2 lb. (.9 kg) DME at the beginning of the boil.

All-grain Method: Grind 2.5 lb. (1.1 kg) rice, then cook it for 20 minutes until soft. Mash 7 lb. (4.2 kg) 6-row pale malt, the rice, and 1 lb. (.45 kg) rice hulls with the specialty grains at 122°F (50°C) for 30 minutes and 150°F (65.5°C) for 60 minutes. Use 4.5 HBU (19% less than the extract recipe) of bittering hops for 60 minutes of the boil. Add the flavor hops and Irish moss for the last 15 minutes of the boil and aroma hops for the last 3 minutes.

Blanche de Chambly

Unibroue, Chambly, Quebec, Canada

This bottle-conditioned white beer has a stark-white Belgian-lace head, a hazy straw color with a light, lemony refreshing nose. The beer has bittersweet hints with a mellow, light taste. Brewed in Canada in Belgian style.

Yield: 5 gallons (18.9 L)   Final gravity: 1.010–1.011   SRM 3.5
Original gravity: 1.051   IBU 10.5   5.2% alcohol by volume

Bring 1.5 gallons of water to a boil, remove the pot from the stove, and add:

- **3.3 lb. (1.5 kg) M&F wheat syrup (55% wheat, 45% barley malt)**
- **2.25 lb. (1 kg) M&F wheat DME (55% wheat malt, 45% barley malt)**
- **4 oz. (113 g) Belgian clear candi sugar**
- **1 oz. (28 g) German Hallertau Hersbrucker @ 3% AA (3 HBU) (bittering hop)**

Add water until total volume in the brew pot is 2.5 gallons (9 L). Boil for 50 minutes then add:

- **1 tsp. (5 ml) Curacao bitter orange peel**
- **½ tsp. (2 ml) coriander, crushed**
- **1 tsp. (5 ml) Irish moss**

Boil for 10 minutes, remove pot from the stove, and cool for 15 minutes. Strain the cooled wort into the primary fermenter and add cold water to obtain 5 gallons (18.9 L). When the wort temperature is under 80°F (26.6°C), pitch your yeast.

- **Wyeast's 3944 Belgian White Beer yeast (Ferment at 68–72°F [20–22°C])**

Ferment in the primary fermenter 5–7 days or until fermentation slows, then siphon into the secondary fermenter. Bottle when fermentation is complete with:

- **1¼ cup (300 ml) M&F wheat DME**

 Serve in a footed tall goblet at 50°F (10°C).

 **Alternate Methods**

Mini-mash Method: Mash 2 lb. (.9 kg) British 2-row lager malt and 1.75 lb. (.8 kg) wheat malt at 150°F (65.5°C) for 90 minutes. Then follow the extract recipe omitting the wheat DME at the beginning of the boil.

All-grain Method: Mash 4.75 lb. (2.2 kg) British 2-row lager malt and 4.5 lb. (2 kg) wheat malt at 150°F (65.5°C) for 90 minutes. Add 3 HBU (14% less than the extract recipe) of bittering hops and the candi sugar for 90 minutes of the boil. Add the spices and Irish moss for the last 10 minutes of the boil.

Brasal Bock

Brasserie Brasal, La Salle, Quebec, Canada

This brilliant amber bock with shades of garnet has a creamy, light tan head and a huge malt aroma. The flavor is initially very malty with a fruity hop background, followed by some alcohol and roasted malt. The aftertaste is dry and is filled with roasted malt and hops. A glorious bock from Canada!

Yield: 5 gallons (18.9 L)	Final gravity: 1.020–1.022	SRM 24
Original gravity: 1.082–1.083	IBU 20	7.8% alcohol by volume

Crush and steep in 1 gallon (3.8 L) 150°F (65.5°C) water for 20 minutes:

6 oz. (.17 kg) 80°L crystal malt
6 oz. (.17 kg) Vienna malt
3 oz. (85 g) chocolate malt

Strain the grain water into your brew pot. Sparge the grains with ½ gallon (1.9 L) water at 150°F (65.5°C). Add water to the brew pot for 1.5 gallons (5.7 L) total volume. Bring the water to a boil, remove the pot from the stove, and add:

9.25 lb. (4.2 kg) M&F extra-light DME
4 oz. (113 g) Malto-dextrin
2 oz. (57 g) Tettnanger @ 4.5% AA (9 HBU)
(bittering hop)

Add water until total volume in the brew pot is 2.5 gallons (9 L). Boil for 45 minutes then add:

½ oz. (14 g) German Hallertau Hersbrucker (flavor hop)
1 tsp. (5 ml) Irish moss

Boil for 15 minutes, remove pot from the stove, and cool for 15 minutes. Strain the cooled wort into the primary fermenter and add cold water to obtain 5 gallons (18.9 L). When the wort temperature is under 80°F (26.6°C), pitch your yeast.

1st choice: Wyeast's 2206 Bavarian lager yeast
(Ferment at 47–52° [8–11°C])
2nd choice: Wyeast's 2124 Bohemian lager yeast
(Ferment at 47–52° [8–11°C])

Ferment in the primary fermenter 5–7 days or until fermentation slows, then siphon into the secondary fermenter. Bottle when fermentation is complete with:

1¼ cups (300 ml) M&F extra-light DME

 Serve in a stemmed tumbler at 50°F (10°C).

 **Alternate Methods**

Mini-mash Method: Mash 2.5 lb. (1.1 kg) Canadian 2-row pale malt and the specialty grains at 122°F (50°C) for 30 minutes and 150°F (65.5°C) for 60 minutes. Then follow the extract recipe omitting 2 lb. (.9 kg) DME at the beginning of the boil.

All-grain Method: Mash 14.5 lb. (6.6 kg) Canadian 2-row pale malt, ½ lb. (.23 kg) dextrin malt, and the specialty grains at 122°F (50°C) for 30 minutes and 150°F (65.5°C) for 60 minutes. Add 5.5 HBU (39% less than the extract recipe) of bittering hops for 90 minutes of the boil. Add the flavor hops and Irish moss for the last 15 minutes.

Maple Wheat Ale

Niagara Falls Brewing Co., Niagara Falls, Ontario, Canada

Deep gold Maple Wheat has a white head of large bubbles. It has a sweet, wheat malt and fruity hop aroma. The flavor is big and rich with initial sweetness, followed by wheat, maple, and some gentle spices. The aftertaste is dry and spicy. This is a potent, well balanced beer.

Yield: 5 gallons (18.9 L)   Final gravity: 1.016–1.018   SRM 8–9
Original gravity: 1.084   IBU 21   8.5% alcohol by volume

Bring 1.5 gallons of water to a boil, remove the pot from the stove and add:

> **9.25 lb. (4.2 kg) M&F wheat DME (55% wheat, 45% barley malt)**
> **½ lb. (.23 kg) maple syrup**
> **1.5 oz. (42 g) Willamette @ 5% AA (7.5 HBU) (bittering hop)**

Add water until total volume is 2.5 gallons (9 L). After 45 minutes of the boil:

> **½ oz. (14 g) Willamette (flavor hop)**
> **1 tsp. (5 ml) Irish moss**

Boil for 15 minutes, remove pot from the stove, and cool for 15 minutes. Strain the cooled wort into the primary fermenter and add cold water to obtain 5 gallons (18.9 L). When the wort temperature is under 80°F (26.6°C), pitch your yeast.

> **1st choice: Wyeast's 3056 Bavarian wheat yeast (Ferment at 68–72°F [20–22°C])**
> **2nd choice: Wyeast's 3944 White Beer yeast (Ferment at 68–72°F [20–22°C])**

Ferment in the primary fermenter 4–5 days or until fermentation slows, then siphon into the secondary fermenter. Bottle when fermentation is complete with:

> **½ cup (120 ml) corn sugar**
> **⅓ cup (180 ml) maple syrup**

 Chill to 45°F (7°C) and serve in a champagne flute.

 **Alternate Methods**

Mini-mash Method: Mash 1.75 lb. (.8 kg) wheat malt and 1.5 lb. (.68 kg) Canadian 2-row pale malt at 150°F (65.5°C) for 90 minutes. Then follow the extract recipe omitting 2 lb. (.9 kg) wheat DME at the beginning of the boil.

All-grain Method: Mash 7.5 lb. (3.4 kg) Canadian 2-row pale malt and 8 lb. (3.6 kg) wheat malt at 150°F (65.5°C) for 90 minutes. Add 4.5 HBU (40% less than the extract recipe) of bittering hops and the maple syrup for 90 minutes of the boil. Add the flavor hops and Irish moss for the last 15 minutes of the boil.

Molson Ice

Molson Breweries of Canada Ltd., Vancouver, Toronto, and Montreal, Canada

Molson Ice beer, first brewed in 1993, is fermented very cold so that ice crystals are formed. These are then removed, resulting in a smoother, less bitter beer with high alcohol. Medium-bodied Molson Ice has a white, creamy head, is golden in color, and enters with an aroma of fruit and perfume with hints of grain. The flavor is smooth with traces of hops and malt. Molson Ice finishes with a smooth, dry hop aftertaste.

Yield: 5 gallons (18.9 L)	Final gravity: 1.011–1.014	SRM 4
Original gravity: 1.055–1.059	IBU 14	5.6% alcohol by volume

Crush and steep in ½ gallon (1.9 L) 150°F (65.5°C) water for 20 minutes:

6 oz. (.17 kg) 10°L crystal malt

Strain the grain water into your brew pot. Sparge the grains with ½ gallon (1.9 L) water at 150°F (65.5°C). Add water to the brew pot for 1.5 gallons (5.7 L) total volume. Bring the water to a boil, remove the pot from the stove, and add:

6.25 lb. (2.8 kg) M&F extra-light DME
½ lb. (.23 kg) corn sugar
¾ oz. (21 g) Tettnanger @ 4.5% AA (3.5 HBU) (bittering hop)

Add water until total volume in the brew pot is 2.5 gallons (9 L). Boil for 45 minutes then add:

½ oz. (14 g) German Hallertau Hersbrucker (flavor hop)
1 tsp. (5 ml) Irish moss

Boil for 5 minutes then add:

½ oz. (28 g) Tettnanger (aroma hop)

Boil for 10 minutes, remove pot from the stove, and cool for 15 minutes. Strain the cooled wort into the primary fermenter and add cold water to obtain 5 gallons (18.9 L). When the wort temperature is under 80°F (26.6°C), pitch your yeast.

1st choice: Wyeast's 2007 Pilsen lager yeast (Ferment at 47–52° [8–11°C])
2nd choice: Wyeast's 2035 American lager yeast (Ferment at 47–52° [8–11°C])

Ferment in the primary fermenter 5–7 days or until fermentation slows, then siphon into the secondary fermenter. When fermentation is complete, store secondary fermenter at 35°F (1.6°C) for 2 weeks. Then bottle with:

¾ cup (180 ml) corn sugar

 Serve in a frosty mug at 40°F (4°C).

 **Alternate Methods**

Mini-mash Method: Mash 3 lb. (1.36 kg) Canadian 2-row pale malt and the specialty grain at 122°F (50°C) for 30 minutes and 150°F (65.5°C) for 60 minutes. Then follow the extract recipe omitting 2.25 lb. (1 kg) DME at the beginning of the boil.

All-grain Method: Mash 9.5 lb. (4.3 kg) Canadian 2-row pale malt, ¾ lb. (.34 kg) flaked maize, ½ lb. (.23 kg) rice hulls, and the specialty grain at 122°F (50°C) for 30 minutes and 150°F (65.5°C) for 60 minutes. Add 2.5 HBU (29% less than the extract recipe) of bittering hops for 90 minutes of the boil. Add the flavor hops and Irish moss for the last 15 minutes of the boil and the aroma hops for the last 5 minutes.

Bohemia Beer

Cerveceria Cuauhtemoc S. A., Monterrey, N. L., Mexico

Bohemia was introduced to the market in 1905. Its name refers to the great brewing region in the Czech Republic. Pale gold in color, it has a dense snow-white head and a crisp off-dry malt aroma. This medium-bodied Pilsner brings forth a complex taste with a slight bitterness, balancing it with a fresh, sweet malt flavor. The finish is long and dry.

Yield: 5 gallons (18.9 L)   Final gravity: 1.012–1.014   SRM 3–4
Original gravity: 1.054–1.057   IBU 26   5.4% alcohol by volume

Crush and steep in ½ gallon (1.9 L) 150°F (65.5°C) water for 20 minutes:

12 oz. (.34 kg) 2.5°L German light crystal malt

Strain the grain water into your brew pot. Sparge the grains with ½ gallon (1.9 L) water at 150°F (65.5°C). Add water to the brew pot for 1.5 gallons (5.7 L) total volume. Bring the water to a boil, remove the pot from the stove, and add:

4 lb. (1.8 kg) Alexander's pale malt syrup
3.25 lb. (1.5 kg) M&F extra-light DME
2 oz. (57 g) Czech Spalt @ 3.5% AA (7 HBU)
(bittering hop)

Add water until the total volume in the brew pot is 2.5 gallons (9 L). Boil for 45 minutes then add:

½ oz. (14 g) Tettnanger (flavor hop)
1 tsp. (5 ml) Irish moss

Boil for 15 minutes, remove pot from the stove, and cool for 15 minutes. Strain the cooled wort into the primary fermenter and add cold water to obtain 5 gallons (18.9 L). When the wort temperature is under 80°F (26.6°C), pitch your yeast.

1st choice: Wyeast's 2124 Bohemian lager yeast
(Ferment at 42–52°F [6–11°C])
2nd choice: Wyeast's 2007 Pilsen lager yeast
(Ferment at 42–52°F [6–11°C])

Ferment in the primary fermenter 5–7 days or until fermentation slows, then siphon into the secondary fermenter. Bottle when fermentation is complete with:

1¼ cups (300 ml) M&F extra-light DME

 Serve at 40–45°F (4–7°C) in a frosty mug.

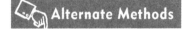 **Alternate Methods**

Mini-mash Method: Mash 2 lb. (.9 kg) German 2-row Pilsner malt with the specialty grain at 122°F (50°C) for 30 minutes and 150°F (65.5°C) for 60 minutes. Then follow the extract recipe but omit 1.75 lb. DME at the beginning of the boil.

All-grain Method: Mash 9.75 lb. (4.4 kg) German 2-row Pilsner malt with the specialty grain at 122°F (50°C) for 30 minutes and 150°F (65.5°C) for 60 minutes. Use 5 HBU (29% less than the extract recipe) bittering hops for 90 minutes of the boil. Add the flavor hops and Irish moss for the last 15 minutes of the boil.

Dos Equis

Cerveceria Moctezuma, S.A. de C.V. Orizaba, Veracruz, Mexico

Dos Equis has been brewed since 1900. It is one of the more famous reddish-amber Vienna-style lagers from Mexico. With a light tan head, it starts with a soft, clean, malt nose and leads into a palate that bursts with malt, caramel, and toasted malt. This well-balanced medium-bodied lager leaves you with a wonderful hop finish and long dry malt aftertaste. The original name for Dos Equis was Singlox which means a beer for the next century. It was then changed to Dos Equis which signifies the year 2000.

Yield: 5 gallons (18.9 L)	Final gravity: 1.013–1.014	SRM 10
Original gravity: 1.049–1.050	IBU 22	4.6% alcohol by volume

Crush and steep in 1 gallon (3.8 L) 150°F (65.5°C) water for 20 minutes:

> **6 oz. (.17 kg) 2.5°L German light crystal malt**
> **1 lb. (.45 kg) German Vienna malt**
> **1 oz. (28 g) black malt**

Strain the grain water into your brew pot. Sparge the grains with ½ gallon (1.9 L) water at 150°F (65.5°C). Add water to the brew pot for 1.5 gallons (5.7 L) total volume. Bring the water to a boil, remove the pot from the stove, and add:

> **5.5 lb. (2.5 kg) M&F light DME**
> **¼ lb. (113 g) Malto-dextrin**
> **1.2 oz. (34 g) Tettnanger @ 5% AA (6 HBU) (bittering hop)**

Add water until the total volume is 2.5 gallons (9 L). Boil for 50 minutes then add:

> **¼ oz. (7 g) Tettnanger (flavor hop)**
> **¼ oz. (7 g) Czech Saaz (flavor hop)**
> **1 tsp. (5 ml) Irish moss**

Boil for 10 minutes, remove pot from the stove, and cool for 15 minutes. Strain the cooled wort into the primary fermenter and add cold water to obtain 5 gallons (18.9 L). When the wort temperature is under 80°F (26.6°C), pitch your yeast.

> **1st choice: Wyeast's 2124 Bohemian lager yeast**
> **(Ferment at 42–52°F [6–11°C])**
> **2nd choice: Wyeast's 2206 Bavarian lager yeast**
> **(Ferment at 42–52°F [6–11°C])**

Ferment in the primary fermenter 5–7 days or until fermentation slows, then siphon into the secondary fermenter. Bottle when fermentation is complete with:

> **1¼ cups (300 ml) M&F extra-light DME**

 Serve at 45°F (7°C) in a mug or a stein.

 **Alternate Methods**

Mini-mash Method: Mash 1.75 lb. (.8 kg) German 2-row Pilsner malt with the specialty grains at 122°F (50°C) for 30 minutes and 150°F (65.5°C) for 60 minutes. Then follow the extract recipe but omit 2 lb. (.9 kg) DME at the beginning of the boil.

All-grain Method: Mash 6.75 lb. (3.1 kg) German 2-row Pilsner malt and 1 lb. (.45 kg) additional Vienna malt with the specialty grains at 122°F (50°C) for 30 minutes and 150°F (65.5°C) for 60 minutes. Use 4.5 HBU (25% less than the extract recipe) bittering hops for 90 minutes of the boil. Add the flavor hops and Irish moss for the last 10 minutes of the boil.

Negra Modelo Dark Beer

Cerveceria Modelo, S.A., Mexico City, Mexico

This impressive dark amber lager displays an off-white head. Negra Modelo has a smooth, dry, chocolate, malty taste and finish. It is a very well-balanced beer, brewed in the Vienna style, although a touch lighter in body, darker in color, and less malty than its German counterparts. This is the perfect Mexican beer to drink if you desire something with more body and flavor than the traditional light lagers from this region.

Yield: 5 gallons (18.9 L)   Final gravity: 1.011–1.013   SRM 21
Original gravity: 1.050–1.051   IBU 27   4.9% alcohol by volume

Crush and steep in 1 gallon (3.8 L) 150°F (65.5°C) water for 20 minutes:

6 oz. (.17 kg) 60°L crystal malt
½ lb. (.23 kg) German Vienna malt
2 oz. (57 g). chocolate malt

Strain the grain water into your brew pot. Sparge the grains with ½ gallon (1.9 L) water at 150°F (65.5°C). Add water to the brew pot for 1.5 gallons (5.7 L) total volume. Bring the water to a boil, remove the pot from the stove, and add:

3 lb. (1.4 kg) M&F light DME
3.3 lb. (1.5 kg) Bierkeller light malt syrup
1 oz. (28 g) German Hallertau Hersbrucker @ 3% AA (3 HBU) (bittering hop)
1 oz. (28 g) Tettnanger @ 4% AA (4 HBU) (bittering hop)

Add water until the total volume is 2.5 gallons (9 L). Boil for 50 minutes then add:

½ oz. (14 g) Tettnanger (flavor hop)
1 tsp. (5 ml) Irish moss

Boil for 10 minutes, remove pot from the stove, and cool for 15 minutes. Strain the cooled wort into the primary fermenter and add cold water to obtain 5 gallons (18.9 L). When the wort temperature is under 80°F (26.6°C), pitch your yeast.

1st choice: Wyeast's 2124 Bohemian lager yeast
(Ferment at 42–52°F [6–11°C])
2nd choice: Wyeast's 2206 Bavarian lager yeast
(Ferment at 42–52°F [6–11°C])

Ferment in the primary fermenter 5–7 days or until fermentation slows, then siphon into the secondary fermenter. Bottle when fermentation is complete with:

1¼ cups (300 mg) M&F extra-light DME

 Serve in a pint glass at 50°F (10°C).

Alternate Methods

Mini-mash Method: Mash 2.25 lb. (1 kg) German 2-row Pilsner malt with the specialty grains at 122°F (50°C) for 30 minutes and 150°F (65.5°C) for 60 minutes. Then follow the extract recipe but omit 2 lb. (.9 kg) DME at the beginning of the boil.

All-grain Method: Mash 7.75 lb. (3.5 kg) German 2-row Pilsner malt and 1 lb. (.45 kg) additional Vienna malt with the specialty grains at 122°F (50°C) for 30 minutes and 150°F (65.5°C) for 60 minutes. Use 5 HBU (28% less than the extract recipe) bittering hops for 90 minutes of the boil. Add the flavor hops and Irish moss for the last 10 minutes of the boil.

Anchor Steam Beer

Anchor Brewing Co., San Francisco, California, U.S.A.

Steam beer is one of the few beer styles to have originated in the United States. The use of lager yeast gives Anchor Steam the smoothness of a lager with the fruitiness of an ale. The full-bodied beer has high carbonation with a creamy off-white head, a deep amber color, and a fruity, citrus hop aroma with some malt. It has a clean, smooth, slightly bitter flavor with a refreshing finish.

Yield: 5 gallons (18.9 L)   Final gravity: 1.012–1.013   SRM 18
Original gravity: 1.051–1.052   IBU 40   5% alcohol by volume

Crush and steep in ½ gallon (1.9 L) 150°F (65.5°C) water for 20 minutes:

14 oz. (.4 kg) 80°L US crystal malt

Strain the grain water into your brew pot. Sparge the grains with ½ gallon (1.9 L) water at 150°F (65.5°C). Add water to the brew pot for 1.5 gallons (5.7 L) total volume. Bring the water to a boil, remove the pot from the stove, and add:

4 lb. (1.8 kg) Alexander's pale malt syrup
2.75 lb. (1.25 kg) M&F light DME
1.25 oz. (35 g) Northern Brewer @ 8% AA (10 HBU)
(bittering hop)

Add water until total volume in the brew pot is 2.5 gallons (9 L). Boil for 45 minutes then add:

½ oz. (14 g) Northern Brewer (flavor hop)
1 tsp. (5 ml) Irish moss

After 59 minutes of the boil add:

½ oz. (14 g) Northern Brewer (aroma hop)

Boil for 1 minute, remove pot from the stove and cool for 15 minutes. Strain the cooled wort into the primary fermenter and add cold water to obtain 5 gallons (18.9 L). When the wort temperature is under 80°F (26.6°C), pitch your yeast.

1st choice: Wyeast's 2112 California lager yeast
(Ferment at 60–66°F [16–19°C])
2nd choice: Wyeast's 2565 Kölsch yeast
(Ferment at 60–66°F [16–19°C])

Ferment in the primary fermenter 5–7 days or until fermentation slows, then siphon into the secondary fermenter. Bottle when fermentation is complete with:

1¼ cup (300 ml) M&F extra-light DME

 Serve in a pub mug at 50°F (10°C).

Alternate Methods

Mini-mash Method: Mash 2.5 lb. (1.1 kg) US 2-row pale malt and the specialty grain at 122°F (50°C) for 30 minutes and at 150°F (65.5°C) for 60 minutes. Then follow the extract recipe omitting 2 lb. (.9 kg) DME at the beginning of the boil.

All-grain Method: Mash 9 lb. (4.1 kg) US 2-row pale malt with the specialty grain at 122°F (50°C) for 30 minutes and at 150°F (65.5°C) for 90 minutes. Add 7 HBU (30% less than the extract recipe) of bittering hops for 60 minutes of the boil. Add the flavor hops and Irish moss for the last 15 minutes of the boil and the aroma hops for the last 1 minute.

Atlantic Amber

New England Brewing Company, Norwalk, Connecticut, U.S.A.

Atlantic Amber is the flagship beer of the New England Brewery, which has been in business since 1989. Medium-bodied, it displays a creamy beige head and is brilliant amber in color. Atlantic Amber has a nice hop nose with hints of sweet malt and a complex hop palate with malt and fruit in the back. There is a dry hop finish with a long, dry hop aftertaste. This is a well-crafted beer with lots of character.

Yield: 5 gallons (18.9 L)
Original gravity: 1.048–1.051

Final gravity: 1.010–1.013
IBU 35

SRM 22
4.8% alcohol by volume

Crush and steep in ½ gallon (1.9 L) 150°F (65.5°C) water for 20 minutes:

12 oz. (.34 kg) 120°L crystal malt

Strain the grain water into your brew pot. Sparge the grains with ½ gallon (1.9 L) water at 150°F (65.5°C). Add water to the brew pot for 1.5 gallons (5.7 L) total volume. Bring the water to a boil, remove the pot from the stove, and add:

5.75 lb. (2.6 kg) M&F light DME
1 oz. (28 g) Northern Brewer @ 9% AA (9 HBU) (bittering hop)

Add water until total volume in the brew pot is 2.5 gallons (9 L). Boil for 45 minutes then add:

½ oz. (14 g) Cascade (flavor hop)
1 tsp. (5 ml) Irish moss

Boil for 12 minutes then add:

¼ oz. (7 g) Czech Saaz (aroma hop)

Boil for 3 minutes, remove pot from the stove, and cool for 15 minutes. Strain the cooled wort into the primary fermenter and add cold water to obtain 5 gallons (18.9 L). When the wort temperature is under 80°F (26.6°C), pitch your yeast.

1st choice: Wyeast's 2112 California lager yeast (Ferment at 60–65°F [16–18°C])
2nd choice: Wyeast's 2565 Kölsch yeast (Ferment at 60–65°F [16–18°C])

Ferment in the primary fermenter 5–7 days or until fermentation slows, then siphon into the secondary fermenter. Bottle when fermentation is complete with:

1¼ cup (300 ml) M&F extra-light DME

 Serve at 50°F (10°C) in a pint glass.

Alternate Methods

Mini-mash Method: Mash 2.75 lb. (1.25 kg) British 2-row pale malt and the specialty grain at 150°F (65.5°C) for 90 minutes. Then follow the extract recipe omitting 2.25 lb. (1 kg) DME at the beginning of the boil.

All-grain Method: Mash 8.33 lb. (3.8 kg) British 2-row pale malt with the specialty grain at 150°F (65.5°C) for 90 minutes. Add 7 HBU (22% less than the extract recipe) of bittering hops for 90 minutes of the boil. Add the flavor hops and Irish moss for the last 15 minutes of the boil and the aroma hops for the last 3 minutes.

Bert Grant's Imperial Stout

Bert Grant's Real Ales, Yakima, Washington, U.S.A.

Bert Grant's medium-bodied Imperial Stout pours with a light brown head and is espresso-black in color. The aroma is full of hops and roasted grains. The clean, crisp flavor is a complex mixture of fruit, coffee, malt, and hops. The dry aftertaste has hints of honey.

Yield: 5 gallons (18.9 L)	**Final gravity:** 1.015–1.018	**SRM 104**
Original gravity: 1.071–1.074	**IBU 75**	**7.1% alcohol by volume**

Crush and steep in 1 gallon (3.8 L) 150°F (65.5°C) water for 20 minutes:

1 lb. (.45 kg) 120°L US crystal malt
12 oz. (.34 kg) US black malt

Strain the grain water into your brew pot. Sparge the grains with ½ gallon (1.9 L) water at 150°F (65.5°C). Add water to the brew pot for 1.5 gallons (5.7 L) total volume. Bring the water to a boil, remove the pot from the stove, and add:

5 lb. (2.3 kg) M&F light DME
4 lb. (1.8 kg) Alexander's pale malt syrup
4 oz. (113 g) clover honey
2 oz. (57 g) Galena @ 12% AA (24 HBU) (bittering hop)

Add water until total volume in the brew pot is 2.5 gallons (9 L). Boil for 45 minutes then add:

½ oz. (14 g) Cascade (flavor hop)
1 tsp. (5 ml) Irish moss

Boil for 14 minutes then add:

½ oz. (14 g) Cascade (aroma hop)

Boil for 1 minute, remove pot from the stove, and cool for 15 minutes. Strain the cooled wort into the primary fermenter and add cold water to obtain 5 gallons (18.9 L). When the wort temperature is under 80°F (26.6°C), pitch your yeast.

**Wyeast's 1056 American ale yeast
(Ferment at 68–72°F [20–22°C])**

Ferment in the primary fermenter 5–7 days or until fermentation slows, then siphon into the secondary fermenter and add:

½ oz. (14 g) East Kent Goldings (dry hop)
½ oz. (14 g) Cascade (dry hop)

Bottle when fermentation is complete with:

1¼ cup (300 ml) M&F light DME

 Serve in a goblet at 55°F (13°C).

 **Alternate Methods**

Mini-mash Method: Mash 2.25 lb. (1 kg) US 2-row pale malt and the specialty grains at 122°F (50°C) for 30 minutes and 150°F (65.5°C) for 60 minutes. Then follow the extract recipe omitting 2.25 lb. (1 kg) DME at the beginning of the boil.

All-grain Method: Mash 12 lb. (5.4 kg) US 2-row pale malt with the specialty grains at 122°F (50°C) for 30 minutes and 150°F (65.5°C) for 60 minutes. Add 16 HBU (33% less than the extract recipe) of bittering hops and the honey for 90 minutes of the boil. Add the flavor hops and Irish moss for the last 15 minutes of the boil and the aroma hops for the last 1 minute.

Copper Ale

Otter Creek Brewing Company, Middlebury, Vermont, U.S.A.

This delicious alt beer has a malt flavor that balances nicely with sharp, spicy hops.

Yield: 5 gallons (18.9 L)   Final gravity: 1.014–1.016   SRM 21

Original gravity: 1.055–1.058   IBU 21   5.2% alcohol by volume

Crush and steep in 1 gallon (3.8 L) 150°F (65.5°C) water for 20 minutes:

- ½ lb. (.23 kg) US 80°L crystal malt
- ½ lb. (.23 kg) US Munich malt
- 1 oz. (28 g) US chocolate malt
- 1 oz. (28 g) US roasted barley

Strain the grain water into your brew pot. Sparge the grains with ½ gallon (1.9 L) water at 150°F (65.5°C). Add water to the brew pot for 1.5 gallons (5.7 L) total volume. Bring the water to a boil and add:

- 4 lb. (1.8 kg) Superbrau light malt syrup
- 3 lb. (1.36 kg) M&F light DME
- 4 oz. (113 g) Malto-dextrin
- ½ oz (14 g) Chinook @ 11% AA (5.5 HBU) (bittering hop)

Add water until total volume in the brew pot is 2.5 gallons (9 L). Boil for 45 minutes then add:

- ½ oz. (14 g) German Hallertau Hersbrucker (flavor hop)
- 1 tsp. (5 ml) Irish moss

Boil for 12 minutes then add:

- ½ oz. (14 g) Tettnanger (aroma hop)

Boil for 3 minutes. Cool for 15 minutes. Strain the cooled wort into the primary fermenter and add cold water to obtain 5 gallons (18.9 L). When the wort temperature is under 80°F (26.6°C), pitch yeast.

Wyeast's 1007 German ale yeast
(Ferment at 68–72°F [20–22°C])

Ferment in the primary fermenter 5–7 days or until fermentation slows, then siphon into the secondary fermenter and add:

- ½ oz. Tettnanger (dry hop)

Bottle when fermentation is complete with:

- 1¼ cup (300 ml) M&F extra-light DME

After bottling, store at 60–72°F (16–22°C) for 3 weeks to carbonate, then cold-condition bottles at 47–52°F (8–11°C) for 4 weeks.

 Serve in an alt beer or pint glass at 50°F (10°C).

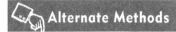 **Alternate Methods**

Mini-mash Method: Mash 2 lb. (.9 kg) US 2-row pale malt and the specialty grains at 122°F (50°C) for 30 minutes and 150°F (65.5°C) for 60 minutes. Then follow the extract recipe omitting 2 lb. (.9 kg) DME at the beginning of the boil.

All-grain Method: Mash 9.25 lb. (4.2 kg) US 2-row pale malt, ½ lb. (.23 kg) dextrin malt, and the specialty grains at 122°F (50°C) for 30 minutes and 150°F (65.5°C) for 60 minutes. Add 4 HBU (27% less than the extract recipe) of bittering hops for 90 minutes of the boil. Add the flavor hops and Irish moss for the last 15 minutes of the boil and the aroma hops for the last 3 minutes.

Dixie Blackened Voodoo Lager

Dixie Brewing Co. Inc., New Orleans, Louisiana, U.S.A.

This lager has an aroma that is malty with light fruit overtones leading into a good body with toasted malt and a hint of hops.

Yield: 5 gallons (18.9 L)	Final gravity: 1.011–1.014	SRM 27
Original gravity: 1.053–1.056	IBU 25	5.4% alcohol by volume

Crush and steep in ½ gallon (1.9 L) 150°F (65.5°C) water for 20 minutes:

> ½ lb. (.23 kg) US 80°L crystal malt
> 1 oz. (28 g) US black malt
> 2 oz. (57 g) US chocolate malt

Strain the grain water into your brew pot. Sparge the grains with ½ gallon (1.9 L) water at 150°F (65.5°C). Add water to the brew pot for 1.5 gallons (5.7 L) total volume. Bring the water to a boil, remove the pot from the stove, and add:

> 4 lb. (1.8 kg) Superbrau light malt syrup
> 2.75 lb. (1.25 kg) M&F light DME
> ⅓ lb. (.15 kg) rice solids
> 1.5 oz. (42 g) Mt. Hood @ 4.3% AA (6.5 HBU)
> (bittering hop)

Add water until total volume in the brew pot is 2.5 gallons (9 L). Boil for 45 minutes then add:

> ¼ oz. (7 g) Cascade (flavor hop)
> ¼ oz. (7 g) Mt. Hood (flavor hop)
> 1 tsp. (5 ml) Irish moss

Boil for 10 minutes then add:

> ¼ oz. (7 g) Cascade (aroma hop)
> ¼ oz. (7 g) Mt. Hood (aroma hop)

Boil for 5 minutes, remove pot from the stove, and cool for 15 minutes. Strain the cooled wort into the primary fermenter and add cold water to obtain 5 gallons (18.9 L). When the wort temperature is under 80°F (26.6°C), pitch your yeast.

> 1st choice: Wyeast's 2035 American lager yeast
> (Ferment at 42–52°F [6–11°C])
> 2nd choice: Wyeast's 2007 Pilsen lager yeast
> (Ferment at 42–52°F [6–11°C])

Ferment in the primary fermenter 5–7 days or until fermentation slows, then siphon into the secondary fermenter. Bottle when fermentation is complete with:

> ¾ cup (180 ml) corn sugar

 Serve in a tumbler at 50°F (10°C).

 **Alternate Methods**

Mini-mash Method: Mash 2.5 lb. (1.1 kg) US 2-row pale malt and the specialty grains at 122°F (50°C) for 30 minutes and 150°F (65.5°C) for 60 minutes. Then follow the extract recipe omitting 2 lb. (.9 kg) DME at the beginning of the boil.

All-grain Method: Grind ½ lb. (.23 kg) rice, then boil for 20 minutes until soft. Mash 7.25 lb. (3.3 kg) British 2-row lager malt and 2 lb. (.9 kg) US 6-row pale malt with the specialty grains at 122°F (50°C) for 30 minutes and 150°F (65.5°C) for 60 minutes. Add 4.5 HBU (31% less than the extract recipe) of bittering hops for 90 minutes of the boil. Add the flavor hops and Irish moss for the last 15 minutes of the boil and the aroma hops for the last 5 minutes.

Elliot Ness Lager

Great Lakes Brewing Co., Cleveland, Ohio, U.S.A.

Great Lakes Brewing was established in 1988 in a former feed store that was once a bar the untouchable G-man Elliot Ness visited. Their Elliot Ness is a Vienna-style lager that has great malt aroma with fruity hops in the background. The flavor is initially smooth, malty, and reminiscent of nuts.

Yield: 5 gallons (18.9 L)   Final gravity: 1.013–1.016   SRM 10–11
Original gravity: 1.063–1.065   IBU 35   6.2% alcohol by volume

Crush and steep in 1 gallon (3.8 L) 150°F (65.5°C) water for 20 minutes:

> ½ lb. (.23 kg) US 40°L crystal malt
> ½ lb. (.23 kg) US Munich malt

Strain the grain water into your brew pot. Sparge the grains with ½ gallon (1.9 L) water at 150°F (65.5°C). Add water to the brew pot for 1.5 gallons (5.7 L) total volume. Bring the water to a boil, remove the pot from the stove, and add:

> 4 lb. (1.8 kg) Superbrau light malt syrup
> 4 lb. (1.8 kg) M&F light DME
> 1 oz. (28 g) Tettnanger @ 4.5% AA (4.5 HBU)
>   (bittering hop)
> 2 oz. (57 g) German Hallertau Hersbrucker @ 3% AA
>   (6 HBU) (bittering hop)

Add water until total volume in the brew pot is 2.5 gallons (9 L). Boil for 45 minutes then add:

> ½ oz. (14 g) German Hallertau Hersbrucker (flavor hop)
> 1 tsp. (5 ml) Irish moss

Boil for 5 minutes then add:

> ¼ oz. (7 g) Tettnanger (flavor hop)

Boil for 10 minutes, remove pot from the stove, and cool for 15 minutes. Strain the cooled wort into the primary fermenter and add cold water to obtain 5 gallons (18.9 L). When the wort temperature is under 80°F (26.6°C), pitch your yeast.

> 1st choice: Wyeast's 2206 Bavarian lager yeast
>   (Ferment at 47–52° [8–11°C])
> 2nd choice: Wyeast's 2124 Bohemian lager yeast
>   (Ferment at 47–52° [8–11°C])

Ferment in the primary fermenter 5–7 days or until fermentation slows, then siphon into the secondary fermenter. Bottle when fermentation is complete with:

> 1¼ cup (300 ml) M&F light DME

 Serve this lager in a mug at 50°F (10°C).

 **Alternate Methods**

Mini-mash Method: Mash 2.25 lb. (1 kg) British 2-row lager malt and the specialty grains at 122°F (50°C) for 30 minutes and 150°F (65.5°C) for 60 minutes. Then follow the extract recipe omitting 2 lb. (.9 kg) DME at the beginning of the boil.

All-grain Method: Mash 10.25 lb. (4.6 kg) British 2-row lager malt, the specialty grains, and an additional 1 lb. (.45 kg) US Munich malt at 122°F (50°C) for 30 minutes and 150°F (65.5°C) for 60 minutes. Add 7 HBU (33% less than the extract recipe) of bittering hops for 90 minutes of the boil. Add the flavor hops and Irish moss for the last 15 minutes of the boil and the additional flavor hops for the last 10 minutes.

Elm City Connecticut Ale

New Haven Brewing Company, New Haven, Connecticut, U.S.A.

This pale amber ale has an off-white head with big bubbles and an enticing aroma of hops and malt. The flavor is malty with traces of caramel and it finishes with malt on the palate. The aftertaste is long and malty with hops in the back. Very clean and well balanced.

Yield: 5 gallons (18.9 L)   Final gravity: 1.010–1.013   SRM 12
Original gravity: 1.048–1.051   IBU 33   4.8% alcohol by volume

Crush and steep in ½ gallon (1.9 L) 150°F (65.5°C) water for 20 minutes:

6 oz. (.17 kg) US 80°L crystal malt
2 oz. (57 g) US Munich malt
½ oz. (14 g) roasted barley

Strain the grain water into your brew pot. Sparge the grains with ½ gallon (1.9 L) water at 150°F (65.5°C). Add water to the brew pot for 1.5 gallons (5.7 L) total volume. Bring the water to a boil, remove the pot from the stove, and add:

5.75 lb. (2.6 kg) M&F light DME
1 oz. (28 g) Northern Brewer @ 7% AA (7 HBU)
(bittering hop)

Add water until total volume in the brew pot is 2.5 gallons (9 L). Boil for 45 minutes then add:

1 oz. (14 g) Willamette (flavor hop)
1 tsp. (5 ml) Irish moss

Boil for 14 minutes then add:

1 oz. (14 g) East Kent Goldings (aroma hop)

Boil for 1 minute, remove pot from the stove and cool for 15 minutes. Strain the cooled wort into the primary fermenter and add cold water to obtain 5 gallons (18.9 L). When the wort temperature is under 80°F (26.6°C), pitch your yeast.

1st choice: Wyeast's 1098 British ale yeast
(Ferment at 68–72°F [20–22°C])
2nd choice: Wyeast's 1028 London ale yeast
(Ferment at 68–72°F [20–22°C])

Ferment in the primary fermenter 5–7 days or until fermentation slows, then siphon into the secondary fermenter. Bottle when fermentation is complete with:

1¼ cup (300 ml) M&F extra-light DME

 Serve in a frosty mug at 45°F (7°C).

 **Alternate Methods**

Mini-mash Method: Mash 3 lb. (1.36 kg) British 2-row pale malt and the specialty grains at 150°F (65.5°C) for 90 minutes. Then follow the extract recipe omitting 2.25 lb. (1 kg) DME at the beginning of the boil.

All-grain Method: Mash 8.5 lb. (3.9 kg) British 2-row pale malt with the specialty grains at 150°F (65.5°C) for 90 minutes. Add 5 HBU (29% less than the extract recipe) of bittering hops for 90 minutes of the boil. Add the flavor hops and Irish moss for the last 15 minutes of the boil and the aroma hops for the last 1 minute.

Geary's Pale Ale

D. L. Geary Brewing Co., Portland, Maine, U.S.A.

This English-style ale starts off with a nice hoppy, fruity nose as you admire this brilliant golden-copper beer and its off-white head. It has a crisp, refreshing hop taste on the bitter side with a dry hop finish and hop bitterness in the aftertaste.

Yield: 5 gallons (18.9 L)   **Final gravity: 1.010–1.012**   **SRM 24**
Original gravity: 1.046–1.048   **IBU 35**   **4.5% alcohol by volume**

Crush and steep in ½ gallon (1.9 L) 150°F (65.5°C) water for 20 minutes:
> **10 oz. (.28 kg) 55°L British crystal malt**
> **3 oz. (85 g) British chocolate malt**

Strain the grain water into your brew pot. Sparge the grains with ½ gallon (1.9 L) water at 150°F (65.5°C). Add water to the brew pot for 1.5 gallons (5.7 L) total volume. Bring the water to a boil and add:
> **5.5 lb. (2.5 kg) M&F light DME**
> **1 oz. (28 g) Cascade @ 5% AA (5 HBU) (bittering hop)**
> **1 oz. (28 g) Mt Hood @ 3% AA (3 HBU) (bittering hop)**

Add water until total volume in the brew pot is 2.5 gallons (9 L). Boil for 45 minutes then add:
> **½ oz. (14 g) Tettnanger (flavor hop)**
> **1 tsp. (5 ml) Irish moss**

Boil for 5 minutes then add:
> **½ oz. (14 g) Fuggles (flavor hop)**

Boil for 9 minutes then add:
> **½ oz. (14 g) Fuggles (aroma hop)**

Boil for 1 minute. Cool for 15 minutes. Strain the cooled wort into the primary fermenter and add cold water to obtain 5 gallons (18.9 L). When the wort temperature is under 80°F (26.6°C), pitch yeast.
> **1st choice: Wyeast's 1056 American ale yeast**
> **(Ferment at 68–72°F [20–22°C])**
> **2nd choice: Wyeast's 1272 American ale II yeast**
> **(Ferment at 68–72°F [20–22°C])**

Ferment in the primary fermenter 4–5 days or until fermentation slows, then siphon into the secondary fermenter and add:
> **½ oz. (14 g) Cascade (dry hop)**

Bottle when fermentation is complete with:
> **1¼ cup (300 ml) M&F extra-light DME**

Serve in a pint glass at 45°F (7°C).

Alternate Methods

Mini-mash Method: Mash 2.25 lb. (1 kg) British 2-row pale malt and the specialty grains at 150°F (65.5°C) for 90 minutes. Then follow the extract recipe omitting 2 lb. (.9 kg) DME at the beginning of the boil.

All-grain Method: Mash 8 lb. (3.6 kg) British 2-row pale malt with the specialty grains at 150°F (65.5°C) for 90 minutes. Add 6 HBU (25% less than the extract recipe) of bittering hops for 90 minutes of the boil. Add the flavor hops and Irish moss for the last 15 minutes of the boil, the additional flavor hops for the last 10 minutes, and the aroma hops for the last 1 minute.

Harpoon IPA

The Massachusetts Bay Brewing Company, Boston, Massachusetts, U.S.A.

This deep copper-gold IPA enters with a big, white head followed by an exciting fruity hop aroma. The big flavor is initially hop-dominated followed by a balanced hop and malt combination. The aftertaste is long, crisp, and very satisfying, dominated by dry hop flavor.

Yield: 5 gallons (18.9 L)   Final gravity: 1.014–1.016   SRM 13
Original gravity: 1.061–1.063   IBU 49   6% alcohol by volume

Crush and steep in 1 gallon (3.8 L) 150°F (65.5°C) water for 20 minutes:

> **8 oz. (.23 kg) 60°L US crystal malt**
> **4 oz. (113 g) toasted 2-row pale malt**
> **1 oz. (28 g) roasted barley**

Strain the grain water into your brew pot. Sparge the grains with ½ gallon (1.9 L) water at 150°F (65.5°C). Add water to the brew pot for 1.5 gallons (5.7 L) total volume. Bring the water to a boil, remove the pot from the stove, and add:

> **4 lb. (1.8 kg) Alexander's pale malt syrup**
> **4 lb. (1.8 kg) M&F Light DME**
> **2 oz. (57 g) Clusters @ 6.5% AA (13 HBU) (bittering hop)**

Add water until total volume in the brew pot is 2.5 gallons (9 L). Boil for 45 minutes then add:

> **½ oz. (14 g) Fuggles (flavor hop)**
> **½ oz. (14 g) Cascade (flavor hop)**
> **1 tsp. (5 ml) Irish moss**

Boil for 14 minutes then add:

> **½ oz. (14 g) Fuggles (aroma hop)**
> **½ oz. (14 g) Cascade (aroma hop)**

Boil for 1 minute, remove pot from the stove, and cool for 15 minutes. Strain the cooled wort into the primary fermenter and add cold water to obtain 5 gallons (18.9 L). When the wort temperature is under 80°F (26.6°C), pitch your yeast.

> **1st choice: Wyeast's 1098 British ale yeast**
> **(Ferment at 68–72°F [20–22°C])**
> **2nd choice: Wyeast's 1084 Irish ale yeast**
> **(Ferment at 68–72°F [20–22°C])**

Ferment in the primary fermenter 4–5 days or until fermentation slows, then siphon into the secondary fermenter. Bottle when fermentation is complete with:

> **1¼ cup (300 ml) M&F extra-light DME**

 Serve in a pint glass at 50°F (10°C).

Mini-mash Method: Mash 3.25 lb. (1.5 kg) British 2-row pale malt and the specialty grains at 150°F (65.5°C) for 90 minutes. Then follow the extract recipe omitting 2.5 lb. (1.1 kg) DME at the beginning of the boil.

All-grain Method: Mash 11 lb. (5 kg) British 2-row pale malt with the specialty grain at 150°F (65.5°C) for 90 minutes. Add 9 HBU (31% less than the extract recipe) of bittering hops for 90 minutes of the boil. Add the flavor hops and Irish moss for the last 15 minutes of the boil and the aroma hops for the last 1 minute.

Hatuey

The Hatuey Brewery, Winston-Salem, North Carolina, U.S.A.

This light lager, pronounced "Ah-Twee," is referred to as the beer of free Cuba. It is brewed by the Bacardi family from their original 1926 recipe first brewed at their Santiago Brewery in Cuba. Hatuey is named after a legendary Taino Indian chief, who became a symbol of Cuban independence after leading several rebellions against the Spanish in the early 16th century. The beer that bears his name has a bright white head, a dark straw color, and a clean, mild hop aroma with a whiff of sweet malt. This refreshing lager has a mild, light malt taste with faint hops in the background.

Yield: 5 gallons (18.9 L)	Final gravity: 1.010–1.011	SRM 3–4
Original gravity: 1.053–1.054	IBU 16	5.4% alcohol by volume

Crush and steep in ½ gallon (1.9 L) 150°F (65.5°C) water for 20 minutes:

> ½ lb. (.23 kg) 20°L crystal malt

Strain the grain water into your brew pot. Sparge the grains with ½ gallon (1.9 L) water at 150°F (65.5°C). Add water to the brew pot for 1.5 gallons (5.7 L) total volume. Bring the water to a boil, remove the pot from the stove, and add:

> 5 lb. (2.3 kg) M&F extra-light DME
> 1.33 lb. (.6 kg) corn sugar
> 2 oz. (57 g) Czech Saaz @ 2% AA (4 HBU)
> (bittering hop)

Add water until the total water in the brew pot is 2.5 gallons (9 L). Boil for 45 minutes then add:

> ½ oz. (14 g) Tettnanger (flavor hop)
> 1 tsp. (5 ml) Irish moss

Boil for 15 minutes, remove pot from the stove, and cool for 15 minutes. Strain the cooled wort into the primary fermenter and add cold water to obtain 5 gallons (18.9 L). When the wort temperature is under 80°F (26.6°C), pitch your yeast.

> 1st choice: Wyeast's 2035 American lager yeast
> (Ferment at 42–52°F [6–11°C])
> 2nd choice: Wyeast's 2007 Pilsen lager yeast
> (Ferment at 42–52°F [6–11°C])

Ferment in the primary fermenter 5–7 days or until fermentation slows, then siphon into the secondary fermenter. Bottle when fermentation is complete with:

> ¾ cup (180 ml) corn sugar

 Chill to 45°F (7°C) and pour into a Pilsner glass.

Alternate Methods

Mini-mash Method: Mash 2.75 lb. (1.25 kg) British 2-row lager malt with the specialty grain at 150°F (65.5°C) for 90 minutes. Then follow the extract recipe but omit 2 lb. (.9 kg) DME at the beginning of the boil.

All-grain Method: Mash 8.25 lb. (3.75 kg) US 2-row lager malt, 2 lb. (.9 kg) flaked maize, and the specialty grains at 122°F (50°C) for 30 minutes and 150°F (65.5°C) for 60 minutes. Use 3 HBU (25% less than the extract recipe) bittering hops for 90 minutes of the boil. Add the flavor hops and Irish moss for the last 15 minutes of the boil.

Magic Hat #9

Magic Hat Brewing Co., South Burlington, Vermont, U.S.A.

Magic Hat #9 is a unique and mysterious brew with a hint of apricot. It is orange-amber in color with a creamy, white head. It has a roasted malt aroma followed by a complex malt, apricot fruit, and hop flavor. This self-described "not quite pale ale" finishes dry with a slight fruit aftertaste. It is dry, crisp, fruity, and very refreshing.

Yield: 5 gallons (18.9 L)	Final gravity: 1.011–1.013	SRM 13
Original gravity: 1.051–1.053	IBU 25	5.1% alcohol by volume

Crush and steep in ½ gallon (1.9 L) 150°F (65.5°C) water for 20 minutes:

½ lb. (.23 kg) US 60°L crystal malt

Strain the grain water into your brew pot. Sparge the grains with ½ gallon (1.9 L) water at 150°F (65.5°C). Add water to the brew pot for 1.5 gallons (5.7 L) total volume. Bring the water to a boil, remove the pot from the stove, and add:

5.5 lb. (2.5 kg) M&F light DME
½ lb. (.23 kg) M&F wheat DME (55% wheat, 45% barley)
1.5 oz (42 g) Tettnanger @ 4.3% AA (6.5 HBU)
　　(bittering hop)

Add water until total volume in the brew pot is 2.5 gallons (9 L). Boil for 45 minutes then add:

¼ oz. (7 g) Willamette (flavor hop)
¼ oz. (7 g) Cascade (flavor hop)
1 tsp. (5 ml) Irish moss

Boil for 15 minutes, remove pot from the stove, and cool for 15 minutes. Strain the cooled wort into the primary fermenter and add cold water to obtain 5 gallons (18.9 L). When the wort temperature is under 80°F (26.6°C), pitch your yeast.

　　1st choice: Wyeast's 1056 American ale yeast
　　(Ferment at 68–72°F [20–22°C])
　　2nd choice: Wyeast's 1272 American ale II yeast
　　(Ferment at 68–72°F [20–22°C])

Ferment in the primary fermenter 4–5 days or until fermentation slows, then siphon into the secondary fermenter and add:

3 oz. (85 g) apricot beer flavoring

Bottle when fermentation is complete with:

1¼ cup (300 ml) M&F extra-light DME

 Serve in a pint glass at 50°F (10°C).

 **Alternate Methods**

Mini-mash Method: Mash 2.75 lb. (1.25 kg) British 2-row pale malt and the specialty grain at 150°F (65.5°C) for 90 minutes. Then follow the extract recipe omitting 2 lb. (.9 kg) DME at the beginning of the boil.

All-grain Method: Mash 8.75 lb. (4 kg) British 2-row pale malt, 6 oz. (.17 kg) US wheat malt, and the specialty grain at 150°F (65.5°C) for 90 minutes. Add 5 HBU (23% less than the extract recipe) of bittering hops for 90 minutes of the boil. Add the flavor hops and Irish moss for the last 15 minutes of the boil.

Pete's Wicked Ale

Pete's Brewing Company, Palo Alto, California, U.S.A.

Pete Slosberg, a homebrewer, started Pete's Brewing Company in 1986 with Wicked Ale, now his flagship brew. This American brown ale has a tan head and deep amber color with tints of red. The fruity hop aroma leads into a malty flavor that is nutty and bittersweet. It finishes with malt and hops and has a long, dry aftertaste.

Yield: 5 gallons (18.9 L) Final gravity: 1.011–1.013 SRM 27
Original gravity: 1.052–1.054 IBU 30 5.2% alcohol by volume

Crush and steep in ½ gallon (1.9 L) 150°F (65.5°C) water for 20 minutes:

½ lb. (.23 kg) 60°L US crystal malt
4 oz. (113 g) US chocolate malt

Strain the grain water into your brew pot. Sparge the grains with ½ gallon (1.9 L) water at 150°F (65.5°C). Add water to the brew pot for 1.5 gallons (5.7 L) total volume. Bring the water to a boil, remove the pot from the stove, and add:

4 lb. (1.8 kg) Superbrau light malt syrup
2.75 lb. (1.25 kg) M&F light DME
1 oz. (28 g) Brewer's Gold @ 8% AA (8 HBU)
**   (bittering hop)**

Add water until total volume in the brew pot is 2.5 gallons (9 L). Boil for 45 minutes then add:

½ oz. (14 g) East Kent Goldings (flavor hop)
1 tsp. (5 ml) Irish moss

Boil for 15 minutes, remove pot from the stove, and cool for 15 minutes. Strain the cooled wort into the primary fermenter and add cold water to obtain 5 gallons (18.9 L). When the wort temperature is under 80°F (26.6°C), pitch your yeast.

1st choice: Wyeast's 1028 London ale yeast
**   (Ferment at 68–72°F [20–22°C])**
2nd choice: Wyeast's 1056 American ale yeast
**   (Ferment at 68–72°F [20–22°C])**

Ferment in the primary fermenter 5–7 days or until fermentation slows, then siphon into the secondary fermenter and add:

1 oz. (28 g) Cascade (dry hop)

Bottle when fermentation is complete with:

1¼ cup (300 ml) M&F light DME

 Serve in a pint glass at 50°F (10°C).

Alternate Methods

Mini-mash Method: Mash 2.25 lb. (1 kg) US 2-row pale malt and the specialty grains at 122°F (50°C) for 30 minutes and 150°F (65.5°C) for 60 minutes. Then follow the extract recipe omitting 1.75 lb. (.8 kg) DME at the beginning of the boil.

All-grain Method: Mash 9.33 lb. (4.2 kg) US 2-row pale malt with the specialty grains at 122°F (50°C) for 30 minutes and 150°F (65.5°C) for 60 minutes. Add 6 HBU (25% less than the extract recipe) of bittering hops for 90 minutes of the boil. Add the flavor hops and Irish moss for the last 15 minutes of the boil.

Red Hook ESB

Redhook Ale Brewery, Seattle, Washington, and Portsmouth, New Hampshire, U.S.A.

This popular Extra Special Bitter is a deep copper-orange color with an off-white, creamy head. It is medium-bodied, with a fruity, hop and malt aroma. The well-balanced hop and malt flavor ends with a sweet, hop finish. The aftertaste is complex, dry, and hoppy. A well-integrated ESB.

Yield: 5 gallons (18.9 L)   Final gravity: 1.012–1.014   SRM 13
Original gravity: 1.054–1.057   IBU 37   5.4% alcohol by volume

Crush and steep in ½ gallon (1.9 L) 150°F (65.5°C) water for 20 minutes:

13 oz. (.37 kg) 60°L US crystal malt

Strain the grain water into your brew pot. Sparge the grains with ½ gallon (1.9 L) water at 150°F (65.5°C). Add water to the brew pot for 1.5 gallons (5.7 L) total volume. Bring the water to a boil, remove the pot from the stove, and add:

4 lb. (1.8 kg) Alexander's pale malt syrup
3.25 lb. (1.5 kg) M&F light DME
2 oz. (57 g) Tettnanger @ 4.75% AA (9.5 HBU)
(bittering hop)

Add water until total volume in the brew pot is 2.5 gallons (9 L). Boil for 45 minutes then add:

½ oz. (14 g) Willamette (flavor hop)
1 tsp. (5 ml) Irish moss

Boil for 10 minutes then add:

1 oz. (28 g) Tettnanger (aroma hop)

Boil for 5 minutes, remove pot from the stove, and cool for 15 minutes. Strain the cooled wort into the primary fermenter and add cold water to obtain 5 gallons (18.9 L). When the wort temperature is under 80°F (26.6°C), pitch your yeast.

1st choice: Wyeast's 1056 American ale yeast
(Ferment at 68–72°F [20–22°C])
2nd choice: Wyeast's 1272 American ale II yeast
(Ferment at 68–72°F [20–22°C])

Ferment in the primary fermenter 4–5 days or until fermentation slows, then siphon into the secondary fermenter. Bottle when fermentation is complete with:

1¼ cup (300 ml) M&F extra-light DME

 Serve in a pint glass at 45°F (7°C).

 **Alternate Methods**

Mini-mash Method: Mash 2.5 lb. (1.1 kg) US 2-row pale malt and the specialty grain at 122°F (50°C) for 30 minutes and 150°F (65.5°C) for 60 minutes. Then follow the extract recipe omitting 2 lb. (.9 kg) DME at the beginning of the boil.

All-grain Method: Mash 9.67 lb. (4.4 kg) US 2-row pale malt with the specialty grain at 122°F (50°C) for 30 minutes and 150°F (65.5°C) for 60 minutes. Add 7 HBU (26% less than the extract recipe) of bittering hops for 90 minutes of the boil. Add the flavor hops and Irish moss for the last 15 minutes of the boil and the aroma hops for the last 5 minutes.

Rogue Old Crustacean Barley Wine

Rouge Ales, Newport, Oregon, U.S.A.

Rogue Old Crustacean's strong aroma is full of malt, fruit, and alcohol followed by the rich, strong flavor full of hops and malt. This barley wine finishes powerfully with fruit, followed by a long, dry, hoppy, bitter aftertaste.

Yield: 5 gallons (18.9 L)	**Final gravity: 1.019–1.024**	**SRM 36**
Original gravity: 1.090–1.094	**IBU 100**	**9% alcohol by volume**

Crush and steep in 1 gallon (3.8 L) 150°F (65.5°C) water for 20 minutes:

> **10 oz. (.28 kg) 120°L US crystal malt**
> **10 oz. (.28 kg) US Munich malt**
> **3 oz. (85 g) US chocolate malt**

Strain the grain water into your brew pot. Sparge the grains with ½ gallon (1.9 L) water at 150°F (65.5°C). Add water to the brew pot for 1.5 gallons (5.7 L) total volume. Bring the water to a boil, remove the pot from the stove, and add:

> **4 lb. (1.8 kg) Alexander's pale malt syrup**
> **7.5 lb. (3.4 kg) M&F light DME**
> **2 oz. (85 g) Chinook @ 14% AA (28 HBU)**
> **(bittering hop)**

Add water until total volume in the brew pot is 3.5 gallons (13 L). Boil for 45 minutes then add:

> **1 oz. (28 g) Centennial (flavor hop)**
> **1 tsp. (5 ml) Irish moss**

Boil for 10 minutes then add:

> **1 oz. (28 g) Centennial (aroma hop)**

Boil for 5 minutes, remove pot from the stove, and cool for 15 minutes. Strain the cooled wort into the primary fermenter and add cold water to obtain 5 gallons (18.9 L). When the wort temperature is under 80°F (26.6°C), pitch your yeast.

> **1st choice: Wyeast's 1272 American ale II yeast**
> **(Ferment at 68–72°F [20–22°C])**
> **2nd choice: Wyeast's 1056 American ale yeast**
> **(Ferment at 68–72°F [20–22°C])**

Ferment in the primary fermenter 5–7 days or until fermentation slows, then siphon into the secondary fermenter. Bottle when fermentation is complete with:

> **1¼ cup (300 ml) M&F light DME**

Age in the bottle at least 1 year before drinking.

 Serve in a brandy snifter at 60°F (16°C).

 **Alternate Methods**

Mini-mash Method: Mash 2 lb. (.9 kg) US 2-row pale malt and the specialty grains at 122°F (50°C) for 30 minutes and 150°F (65.5°C) for 60 minutes. Then follow the extract recipe omitting 2 lb. (.9 kg) DME at the beginning of the boil.

All-grain Method: Mash 15.25 lb. (6.9 kg) US 2-row pale malt, the specialty grains, and an additional 1 lb. (.45 kg) US Munich malt at 122°F (50°C) for 30 minutes and 150°F (65.5°C) for 60 minutes. Add 21 HBU (25% less than the extract recipe) of bittering hops for 90 minutes of the boil. Add the flavor hops and Irish moss for the last 15 minutes of the boil and the aroma hops for the last 5 minutes.

Samuel Adams Boston Lager

Boston Beer Company, Boston, Massachusetts, U.S.A.

This popular golden Pilsner-type lager uses 100 percent Noble hops. It has a hoppy, floral aroma with some malt leading into a soft, malty mouthfeel that hints at sweetness. This well-balanced flagship beer of the Boston Beer Company lingers with a complex, dry finish.

Yield: 5 gallons (18.9 L)   Final gravity: 1.011–1.013   SRM 9.5
Original gravity: 1.049–1.052   IBU 35   4.9% alcohol by volume

Crush and steep in ½ gallon (1.9 L) 150°F (65.5°C) water for 20 minutes:

½ lb. (.23 kg) 60°L US crystal malt

Strain the grain water into your brew pot. Sparge the grains with ½ gallon (1.9 L) water at 150°F (65.5°C). Add water to the brew pot for 1.5 gallons (5.7 L) total volume. Bring the water to a boil, remove the pot from the stove, and add:

4 lb. (1.8 kg) Superbrau light malt syrup
2.5 lb. (1.1 kg) M&F light DME
2 oz. (57 g) Tettnanger @ 4.5% AA (9 HBU)
(bittering hop)

Add water until total volume in the brew pot is 2.5 gallons (9 L). Boil for 45 minutes then add:

½ oz. (14 g) Hallertauer Mittelfrüh (flavor hop)
1 tsp. (5 ml) Irish moss

Boil for 13 minutes then add:

½ oz. (14 g) Tettnanger (aroma hop)

Boil for 2 minutes, remove pot from the stove, and cool for 15 minutes. Strain the cooled wort into the primary fermenter and add cold water to obtain 5 gallons (18.9 L). When the wort temperature is under 80°F (26.6°C), pitch your yeast.

1st choice: Wyeast's 2206 Bavarian lager yeast
(Ferment at 47–52° [8–11°C])
2nd choice: Wyeast's 2124 Bohemian lager yeast
(Ferment at 47–52° [8–11°C])

Ferment in the primary fermenter 5–7 days or until fermentation slows, then siphon into the secondary fermenter and add:

¼ oz. (7 g) Hallertauer Mittelfrüh (dry hop)

Bottle when fermentation is complete with:

1¼ cup (300 ml) M&F extra-light DME

 Serve at 40°F (4°C) in a mug or pint glass.

 **Alternate Methods**

Mini-mash Method: Mash 2.75 lb. (1.25 kg) US 2-row pale malt and the specialty grain at 122°F (50°C) for 30 minutes and 150°F (65.5°C) for 60 minutes. Then follow the extract recipe omitting 2 lb. (.9 kg) DME at the beginning of the boil.

All-grain Method: Boston Beer uses a decoction mash but a two stage infusion mash will be fine. Mash 9 lb. (4.1 kg) US 2-row pale malt with the specialty grain at 122°F (50°C) for 30 minutes and 150°F (65.5°C) for 60 minutes. Add 7 HBU (22% less than the extract recipe) of bittering hops for 90 minutes of the boil. Add the flavor hops and Irish moss for the last 15 minutes of the boil and the aroma hops for the last 2 minutes.

Sierra Nevada Pale Ale

Sierra Nevada Brewing Company, Chico, California, U.S.A.

Deep amber Sierra Nevada pours with a white, frothy head. The aroma has a huge, complex bouquet of spicy flower and citrus from whole Cascade hops. The bold hop flavor balances out with smooth, rich malt. There is an endless hop finish and aftertaste from this classic, full-bodied beer.

Yield: 5 gallons (18.9 L)   Final gravity: 1.014–1.016   SRM 7
Original gravity: 1.057–1.059   IBU 32   5.5% alcohol by volume

Crush and steep in ½ gallon (1.9 L) 150°F (65.5°C) water for 20 minutes:

4 oz. (113 g) US 60°L crystal malt

Strain the grain water into your brew pot. Sparge the grains with ½ gallon (1.9 L) water at 150°F (65.5°C). Add water to the brew pot for 1.5 gallons (5.7 L) total volume. Bring the water to a boil, remove the pot from the stove, and add:

6.5 lb. (3 kg) M&F light DME
¼ lb. (113 g) Malto-dextrin
1 oz. (28 g) Nugget @ 8.5% AA (8.5 HBU)
(bittering hop)

Add water until total volume in the brew pot is 2.5 gallons (9 L). Boil for 45 minutes then add:

½ oz. (14 g) Perle (flavor hop)
1 tsp. (5 ml) Irish moss

Boil for 14 minutes then add:

1 oz. (28 g) Cascade (aroma hop)

Boil for 1 minute, remove pot from the stove and cool for 15 minutes. Strain the cooled wort into the primary fermenter and add cold water to obtain 5 gallons (18.9 L). When the wort temperature is under 80°F (26.6°C), pitch your yeast.

1st choice: Wyeast's 1056 American ale yeast
(Ferment at 68–72°F [20–22°C])
2nd choice: Wyeast's 1098 British ale yeast
(Ferment at 68–72°F [20–22°C])

Ferment in the primary fermenter 5–7 days or until fermentation slows, then siphon into the secondary fermenter and add:

½ oz. (14 g) Cascade (dry hop)

Bottle when fermentation is complete with:

1¼ cup (300 ml) M&F extra-light DME

 Serve in a pint glass at 45°F (7°C).

 **Alternate Methods**

Mini-mash Method: Mash 3 lb. (1.36 kg) US 2-row pale malt and the specialty grains at 122°F (50°C) for 30 minutes and 150°F (65.5°C) for 60 minutes. Then follow the extract recipe omitting 2 lb. (.9 kg) DME at the beginning of the boil.

All-grain Method: Mash 10.33 lb. (4.7 kg) US 2-row pale malt, ½ lb. (.23 kg) dextrin malt, and the specialty grains at 122°F (50°C) for 30 minutes and 150°F (65.5°C) for 60 minutes. Add 6 HBU (32% less than the extract recipe) of bittering hops for 90 minutes of the boil. Add the flavor hops and Irish moss for the last 15 minutes of the boil and the aroma hops for the last 1 minute.

Wit Black

Spring Street Brewing Co., Inc., St. Paul, Minnesota, U.S.A.

Wit Black is the only black wheat beer brewed in the United States. It is 25 percent wheat and 75 percent barley. Moderately full-bodied, it pours with a frothy, tan head and is mahogany in color. The aroma is malty with hints of roasted coffee. This mildly bitter, smooth wheat beer has a well-balanced flavor of roasted grain and coffee with a hint of subtle spice. It finishes smooth with a slight spiciness. Deceptively soft and light.

Yield: 5 gallons (18.9 L)	Final gravity: 1.011–1.012	SRM 54
Original gravity: 1.053–1.054	IBU 11	5.3% alcohol by volume

Crush and steep in ½ gallon (1.9 L) 150°F (65.5°C) water for 20 minutes:

> **½ lb. (.23 kg) roasted wheat malt (Or roast wheat malt in an oven until brown, about 60 minutes at 325°F [163°C] turning every 15 minutes.)**
> **2 oz. (57 g) roasted barley**

Strain the grain water into your brew pot. Sparge the grains with ½ gallon (1.9 L) water at 150°F (65.5°C). Add water to the brew pot for 1.5 gallons (5.7 L) total volume. Bring the water to a boil, remove the pot from the stove, and add:

> **2.5 lb. (1.1 kg) M&F wheat DME (55% wheat, 45% barley)**
> **3.67 lb. (1.66 kg) M&F light DME**
> **1 oz. (28 g) Tettnang @ 3.5% AA (3.5 HBU) (bittering hop)**

Add water until total volume in the brew pot is 2.5 gallons (9 L). Boil for 45 minutes then add:

> **⅛ tsp. (.5 ml) crushed anise**
> **1 tsp. (5 ml) Irish moss**

Boil for 15 minutes, remove pot from the stove, and cool for 15 minutes. Strain the cooled wort into the primary fermenter and add cold water to obtain 5 gallons (18.9 L). When the wort temperature is under 80°F (26.6°C), pitch your yeast.

> **1st choice: Wyeast's 1056 American ale yeast (Ferment at 68–72°F [20–22°C])**
> **2nd choice: Wyeast's 1272 American ale II ale yeast (Ferment at 68–72°F [20–22°C])**

Ferment in the primary fermenter 5–7 days or until fermentation slows, then siphon into the secondary fermenter. Bottle when fermentation is complete with:

> **1¼ cup (300 ml) M&F light DME**

 Serve at 45°F (7°C) in a wheat beer glass.

Alternate Methods

Mini-mash Method: Mash 1.33 lb. (.6 kg) US 2-row pale malt, 15 oz. (.43 kg) US wheat malt, and the specialty grains at 122°F (50°C) for 30 minutes and 150°F (65.5°C) for 60 minutes. Then follow the extract recipe omitting 1.75 lb. (.8 kg) wheat DME at the beginning of the boil.

All-grain Method: Mash 7.33 lb. (3.3 kg) US 2-row pale malt, 2.25 lb. (1 kg) US wheat malt, and the specialty grains at 122°F (50°C) for 30 minutes and at 150°F (65.5°C) for 90 minutes. Add 2.5 HBU (29% less than the extract recipe) of bittering hops for 60 minutes of the boil. Add the flavor hops and Irish moss for the last 15 minutes of the boil.

Yuengling Porter

D. G. Yuengling & Son Inc., Pottsville, Pennsylvania, U.S.A.

Yuengling, the oldest brewery in the United States, was established in 1829 and is still family owned. Their porter has been brewed since the brewery's inception. The aroma is one of smooth, roasted grains with a bit of licorice in the background. The flavor is smooth and dry with roasted grains dominating, followed by a dry aftertaste.

Yield: 5 gallons (18.9 L)	Final gravity: 1.010–1.011	SRM 48
Original gravity: 1.048–1.049	IBU 22	4.7% alcohol by volume

Crush and steep in ½ gallon (1.9 L) 150°F (65.5°C) water for 20 minutes:

> ½ lb. (.23 kg) 80°L US crystal malt
> 6 oz. (.17 kg) US black malt

Strain the grain water into your brew pot. Sparge the grains with ½ gallon (1.9 L) water at 150°F (65.5°C). Add water to the brew pot for 1.5 gallons (5.7 L) total volume. Bring the water to a boil, remove the pot from the stove, and add:

> 4 lb. (1.8 kg) Superbrau light malt syrup
> 1.75 lb. (.8 kg) M&F light DME
> ½ lb. (.23 kg) corn sugar
> ½ oz. (14 g) Cluster @ 6% AA (3 HBU) (bittering hop)
> ½ oz. (14 g) Cascade @ 5% AA (2.5 HBU) (bittering hop)

Add water until total volume in the brew pot is 2.5 gallons (9 L). Boil for 45 minutes then add:

> ½ oz. (14 g) Cascade (flavor hop)
> 1 tsp. (5 ml) Irish moss

Boil for 15 minutes, remove pot from the stove, and cool for 15 minutes. Strain the cooled wort into the primary fermenter and add cold water to obtain 5 gallons (18.9 L). When the wort temperature is under 80°F (26.6°C), pitch your yeast.

> 1st choice: Wyeast's 2308 Munich lager yeast
> (Ferment primary at 50–55°F [10–13°C], secondary at 57–65°F [14–18°C])
> 2nd choice: Wyeast's 2042 Danish lager yeast
> (Ferment primary at 50–55°F [10–13°C], secondary at 57–65°F [14–18°C])

Ferment in the primary fermenter 5–7 days or until fermentation slows, then siphon into the secondary fermenter. Bottle when fermentation is complete with:

> 1½ cup (300 ml) M&F light DME

 Serve in a pint glass at 50°F (10°C).

 **Alternate Methods**

Mini-mash Method: Mash 2 lb. (.9 kg) US 2-row pale malt and the specialty grains at 122°F (50°C) for 30 minutes and 150°F (65.5°C) for 60 minutes. Then follow the extract recipe omitting the 1.75 lb. (.8 kg) DME at the beginning of the boil.

All-grain Method: Mash 7.75 lb. (3.5 kg) US 2-row pale malt, ¾ lb. (.34 kg) corn grits or flaked maize, ½ lb. (.23 kg) oat hulls, and the specialty grains at 122°F (50°C) for 30 minutes and 150°F (65.5°C) for 60 minutes. Add 4 HBU (27% less than the extract recipe) of bittering hops for 90 minutes of the boil. Add the flavor hops and Irish moss for the last 15 minutes of the boil.

Xingu Black Beer

Cervejaria Sul Brasileira Ltd., Toledo, Brazil

This Brazilian black lager pronounced "Shin-goo," is named after a tributary of the Amazon River. Xingu introduces itself with a creamy, deep tan head, is opaque dark brown to black in color, and has a whiff of malt in the nose. Medium in body, this lager comes forth with a flavor of toasted grain and roasted malt. Mild in the hop department with sweet, malt overtones, this refreshing lager is perfectly balanced.

Yield: 5 gallons (18.9 L)	Final gravity: 1.017–1.018	SRM 110
Original gravity: 1.062–1.063	IBU 23	5.8% alcohol by volume

Crush and steep in 1 gallon (3.8 L) 150°F (65.5°C) water for 20 minutes:

> ½ lb. (.23 kg) German Vienna malt
> 12 oz. (.34 kg) 80°L crystal malt
> 12 oz. (.34 kg) US chocolate malt
> 2 oz. (57 g) US black malt

Strain the grain water into your brew pot. Sparge the grains with ½ gallon (1.9 L) water at 150°F (65.5°C). Add water to the brew pot for 1.5 gallons (5.7 L) total volume. Bring the water to a boil, remove the pot from the stove, and add:

> 6.5 lb. (3 kg) M&F light DME
> 4 oz. (113 g) dark brown sugar
> ½ oz. (14 g) Yakima Magnum @ 14% AA (7 HBU)
> (bittering hop)

Add water until the total volume is 2.5 gallons (9 L). Boil for 50 minutes then add:

> ½ oz. (14 g) German Hallertau Hersbrucker (flavor hop)
> 1 tsp. (5 ml) Irish moss

Boil for 10 minutes, remove pot from the stove, and cool for 15 minutes. Strain the cooled wort into the primary fermenter and add cold water to obtain 5 gallons (18.9 L). When the wort temperature is under 80°F (26.6°C), pitch your yeast.

> Wyeast's 2308 Munich lager yeast
> (Ferment at 42–52°F [6–11°C] for 14 days, then
> 57–62°F [14–17°C] for the remainder of fermentation)

Ferment in the primary fermenter 5–7 days or until fermentation slows, then siphon into the secondary fermenter. Bottle when fermentation is complete with:

> 1.25 cups (300 ml) M&F wheat DME
> (55% wheat, 45% barley).

 Serve at 55°F (13°C) in a goblet or pint glass.

 **Alternate Methods**

Mini-mash Method: Mash 1.5 lb. (.68 kg) British 2-row lager malt and ¾ lb. (.34 kg) dextrin malt with the specialty grains at 150°F (65.5°C) for 90 minutes. Then follow the extract recipe but omit 2.5 lb. (1.1 kg) DME at the beginning of the boil.

All-grain Method: Mash 8 lb. (3.6 kg) British 2-row lager malt and ¾ lb. (.34 kg) dextrin malt with the specialty grains at 122°F (50°C) for 30 minutes and 150°F (65.5°C) for 60 minutes. Use 5.5 HBU (21% less than the extract recipe) bittering hops for 60 minutes of the boil. Add the flavor hops and Irish moss for the last 10 minutes of the boil.

Cuzco Dark Premium

Compania Cerveceria del Sur del Peru, Cuzco, Peru
This dark, reddish-brown ale has a creamy, luscious, dark tan head followed by a wonderfully complex aroma of rich malt and chocolate. The aroma is repeated in the flavor of this unique brew. This is a true dessert beer.

Yield: 5 gallons (18.9 L) Final gravity: 1.021 SRM 69
Original gravity: 1.065–1.066 IBU 15 5.7% alcohol by volume

Crush and steep in 1 gallon (3.8 L) 150°F (65.5°C) water for 20 minutes:
> ½ lb. (.23 kg) chocolate malt
> 1.5 lb. (.68 kg) 60°L crystal malt

Strain the grain water into your brew pot. Sparge the grains with ½ gallon of 150°F water. Add water to the brew pot for 1.5 gallons (5.7 L) total volume. Bring the water to a boil, remove the pot from the stove, and add:
> 6.75 lb. (3.1 kg) M&F light DME
> ½ lb. (.23 kg) Malto-dextrin
> 6 oz. (.17 kg) lactose
> 1 oz. (28 g) Willamette @ 5% AA (5 HBU) (bittering hop)

Add water until total volume is 2.5 gallons (9 L). Boil for 45 minutes then add:
> 3 Tb. (45 ml) Ghirardelli's chocolate powder
> 1 tsp. (5 ml) Irish moss

Boil for 14 minutes then add:
> 2 Tb. (30 ml) Ghirardelli's chocolate powder

Boil for 1 minute, remove pot from the stove and cool for 15 minutes. Strain the cooled wort into the primary fermenter and add cold water to obtain 5 gallons (18.9 L). When the wort temperature is under 80°F (26.6°C), pitch your yeast.
> 1st choice: Wyeast's 1028 London ale yeast
> (Ferment at 68–73°F [20–23°C])
> 2nd choice: Wyeast's 1968 Special London ale yeast
> (Ferment at 68–73°F [20–23°C])

Ferment in the primary fermenter 3–5 days or until fermentation slows, then siphon into the secondary fermenter. Bottle when fermentation is complete with:
> 1¼ cups (300 ml) wheat DME (55% wheat, 45% barley)

 Serve in a goblet at 55°F (13°C).

Alternate Methods

Mini-mash Method: Mash 1 lb. (.45 kg) British 2-row pale malt with the specialty grains at 150°F (65.5°C) for 90 minutes. Then follow the extract recipe but omit 1.75 lb. (.9 kg) DME at the beginning of the boil.

All-grain Method: Mash 9.25 lb. (4.2 kg) British 2-row pale malt and ¾ lb. (.34 kg) dextrin malt with the specialty grains at 150°F (65.5°C) for 90 minutes. Use 3.5 HBU (30% less than the extract recipe) bittering hops for 60 minutes of the boil. Add chocolate powder and Irish moss for the last 15 minutes of the boil and the aroma chocolate powder for the last minute.

APPENDIX 1
Beer Style Guidelines

ALES

Ales use a top-fermenting *Saccharomyces cerevisiae* yeast strain. They ferment at warmer temperatures and faster than lagers. Ales have a pronounced palate where esters and fruity qualities are part of their makeup.

Style	Original Gravity	Final Gravity	Alcohol by Volume	Bitterness (IBU)*	Color (SRM)**	Body
BARLEY WINES						
English-Style Barley Wine	1.085–1.120	1.024–1.032	8.5–12.2%	50–100	14–22	Very Full
American-Style Barley Wine	1.085–1.120	1.024–1.032	8.5–12.2%	50–100	14–22	Very Full
BELGIAN/FRENCH ALES						
Flanders Brown/ Oud Bruin	1.044–1.056	1.008–1.016	4.8–5.2%	15–25	12–18	Light to Medium
Dubbel	1.050–1.070	1.012–1.016	6–7.5%	18–25	10–14	Medium to Full
Tripel	1.060–1.096	1.016–1.024	7–10.1%	20–25	4–6	Medium to Full
Belgian Pale Ale	1.044–1.054	1.008–1.014	4.1–6.2%	20–30	4–12	Light to Medium
Belgian Strong Ale	1.064–1.096	1.012–1.024	7–11%	20–50	4–20	Medium
White (Wit)	1.044–1.050	1.006–1.010	4.8–5.2%	15–25	2–4	Light to Medium
Bière de Garde	1.060–1.080	1.012–1.016	4.5–8%	25–30	8–12	Light to Medium
BELGIAN-STYLE LAMBICS						
Lambic	1.044–1.056	1.000–1.010	5.1–6.4%	11–23	6–13	Light
Gueuze	1.044–1.056	1.000–1.010	5.1–6.4%	11–23	6–13	Light
Fruit Lambic	1.040–1.072	1.008–1.016	5.1–7.0%	15–21	N/A	Light to Medium
MILD AND BROWN ALES						
English Light Mild	1.030–1.038	1.004–1.008	3.4–4.1%	10–24	8–17	Light
English Dark Mild	1.030–1.038	1.004–1.008	3.4–4.1%	10–24	17–34	Light
English Brown	1.040–1.050	1.008–1.014	4.2–6%	15–25	15–22	Medium
American Brown	1.040–1.055	1.010–1.018	4.2–6.0%	25–60	15–22	Medium
Classic English Pale Ale	1.044–1.056	1.008–1.016	4.5–5.4%	20–40	4–11	Medium
India Pale Ale	1.050–1.070	1.012–1.018	5.1–7.6%	40–60	8–14	Medium
AMERICAN-STYLE ALES						
American Pale Ale	1.044–1.056	1.008–1.016	4.5–5.5%	20–40	4–11	Medium
American Amber Ale	1.044–1.056	1.006–1.016	4.5–5.5%	20–40	11–18	Medium
ENGLISH BITTERS						
English Ordinary	1.033–1.038	1.006–1.012	3.1–3.8%	20–35	8–12	Light to Medium
English Special Bitter	1.038–1.045	1.006–1.012	4.2–4.8%	28–46	12–14	Medium

* For an explanation of bitterness, measured in International Bittering Units (abbreviated IBU), see page 3.
** Color is measured by the Standard Research Method (SRM), described on page 6.

ALES (continued)

Style	Original Gravity	Final Gravity	Alcohol by Volume	Bitterness (IBU)*	Color (SRM)	Body
ENGLISH BITTERS (continued)						
English Extra Special Strong Bitter	1.046–1.060	1.010–1.016	4.8–5.9%	30–55	12–14	Medium
SCOTTISH ALES						
Scottish Light Ale	1.030–1.035	1.006–1.012	2.8–3.6%	9–20	8–17	Light
Scottish Heavy Ale	1.035–1.040	1.010–1.014	3.6–4.1%	12–20	10–19	Medium
Scottish Export Ale	1.040–1.050	1.010–1.018	4.1–4.6%	15–25	10–19	Medium
PORTERS						
Brown Porter	1.045–1.060	1.008–1.016	4.5–6.0%	20–30	20–30	Light to Medium
Robust Porter	1.045–1.060	1.008–1.016	5.1–6.6%	25–40	30+	Medium to Full
ENGLISH AND SCOTTISH STRONG ALES						
Old Ale/Strong Ale	1.055–1.075	1.012–1.020	6.1–8.2%	30–40	10–16	Medium to Full
Strong Scotch Ale	1.072–1.085	1.016–1.028	6.8–8.5%	25–35	10–25	Full
STOUTS						
Classic Irish Dry Stout	1.038–1.048	1.008–1.014	4.1–5.4%	30–40	40+	Light to Medium
Foreign-Style Stout	1.052–1.072	1.008–1.020	6.1–7.6%	30–60	40+	Medium to Full
Sweet/Cream Stout	1.045–1.056	1.012–1.020	3.2–6.4%	15–25	40+	Medium to Full
Oatmeal Stout	1.038–1.056	1.008–1.020	3.6–6.1%	20–40	20+	Medium to Full
Imperial Stout	1.075–1.090	1.020–1.030	7.8–9%	50–80	20+	Full

LAGERS

Lagers are produced with bottom-fermenting *Saccharomyces uvarum* strains of yeast at colder fermentation temperatures than ales. This cooler environment inhibits the natural production of esters and other fermentation byproducts, creating a "cleaner-tasting" beer.

Style	Original Gravity	Final Gravity	Alcohol by Volume	Bitterness (IBU)	Color (SRM)	Body
BOCKS						
Traditional Bock	1.066–1.074	1.018–1.024	6.4–7.6%	20–30	15–30	Medium to Full
German-Style Helles/Maibock	1.066–1.068	1.012–1.020	6.4–7.6%	20–30	4–10	Medium to Full
Doppelbock	1.074–1.080	1.020–1.028	6.6–7.9%	17–27	12–30	Full
Eisbock	1.090–1.116	N/A	8.7–14.4%	26–33	18–50	Full
GERMAN DARK LAGERS						
Munich Dunkel	1.052–1.056	1.014–1.018	4.8–5.4%	16–25	17–20	Medium
Schwarzbier	1.044–1.052	1.012–1.016	3.8–5%	22–30	25–30	Medium
GERMAN LIGHT LAGERS						
Munich Helles	1.044–1.050	1.008–1.012	4.8–5.6%	18–25	3–5	Medium
Dortmunder/ European Export	1.048–1.056	1.010–1.014	5.1–6.1%	23–29	3–5	Medium to Full

LAGERS (continued)

Style	Original Gravity	Final Gravity	Alcohol by Volume	Bitterness (IBU)	Color (SRM)	Body
CLASSIC PILSNERS						
German Pilsner	1.044–1.050	1.006–1.012	4.6–5.4%	30–40	3–4	Medium
Bohemian Pilsner	1.044–1.056	1.014–1.020	4.1–5.1%	35–45	3–5	Medium
American Pilsner	1.045–1.060	1.012–1.018	5.0–6.0%	20–40	3–6	Medium
AMERICAN LAGERS						
American Lager	1.040–1.046	1.006–1.010	4.1–4.8%	5–17	2–4	Light
American Light Lager	1.024–1.040	1.002–1.008	3.6–4.5%	8–15	2–4	Light
American Premium Lager	1.046–1.050	1.010–1.014	4.6–5.1%	13–23	2–8	Medium
American Dark Lager	1.040–1.050	1.008–1.012	4.1–5.6%	14–20	10–20	Light
VIENNAS/MÄRZENS/OKTOBERFESTS						
Vienna	1.048–1.056	1.012–1.018	4.8–5.5%	22–28	8–12	Light to Medium
Märzen/Oktoberfest	1.050–1.056	1.012–1.010	5.1–6.0%	18–25	5–15	Medium

HYBRID STYLES (LAGER AND ALE)

Style	Original Gravity	Final Gravity	Alcohol by Volume	Bitterness (IBU)	Color (SRM)	Body
AMERICAN-STYLE HYBRIDS						
American Wheat Ale/Lager	1.030–1.050	1.004–1.018	3.6–4.6%	12–17	2–8	Light to Medium
American Lager/ Ale/Cream Ale	1.044–1.056	1.004–1.010	4.3–5.7%	10–22	2–5	Light
GERMAN-STYLE ALES						
Kölsch	1.042–1.046	1.006–1.010	4.8–5.2%	20–30	4–5	Light
Düsseldorf Altbier	1.044–1.048	1.008–1.014	4.6–5.1%	25–48	11–19	Medium
GERMAN WHEAT BEERS						
Berliner Weisse	1.028–1.032	1.004–1.006	2.8–3.4%	3–6	2–4	Very Light
Weizen/Weissbier	1.046–1.056	1.008–1.016	5.0–5.6%	10–15	3–9	Medium to Full
Dunkel Weizen	1.048–1.056	1.008–1.016	4.8–5.5%	10–15	16–23	Medium to Full
Weizenbock	1.066–1.080	1.016–1.028	7.0–9.6%	10–15	5–30	Medium to Full
SMOKED BEERS						
Bamberg Rauchbier Lager	1.048–1.052	1.012–1.016	4.3–4.8%	20–30	10–20	Full
MISCELLANEOUS BEERS						
Fruit and Vegetable Beer	1.030–1.110	1.006–1.030	2.5–12.1%	5–70	5–50	Light to Full
Herb and Spice Beer	1.030–1.110	1.006–1.030	2.5–12.1%	5–70	5–50	Light to Full
California Common (Steam)	1.040–1.055	1.012–1.018	3.6–5%	35–45	8–17	Medium

Hop Chart

Hop	Origin	Use	Alpha Acid % Range	Hop Substitute
B.C. Goldings	Canada, U.S.	flavor, aroma	4–7%	English Kent Goldings
Brambling Cross	U.K., Canada	primarily aroma, occasional bittering	5–7%	English Kent Goldings
Brewers Gold	U.S., U.K., Germany	bittering	6–10 %	Bullion, Northern Brewer
Bullion	U.S., U.K .	bittering	6–11%	Brewers Gold, Northern Brewer, Galena
Cascade	U.S.	bittering, flavor, aroma, dry hop	4–8%	Centennial
Centennial	U.S.	bittering , aroma, dry hop	9–11%	Cascade
Challenger	U.K.	bittering , flavor , aroma	6–9%	Northern Brewer (bittering)
Chinook	U.S.	bittering	11–14%	Brewers Gold, Nugget
Cluster	U.S.	bittering	5–9%	Chinook, Galena
Columbus	U.S.	bittering	12–16%	Eroica
Crystal	U.S.	aroma	2.5–4.5%	German Hallertau Hersbrucker, Hallertauer Mittelfrüh
Czech Saaz	Czechoslovakia	flavor, aroma, dry hop	2.5–5.5%	U.S. Saaz, Lublin
Eroica	U.S.	bittering	9–13%	Brewers Gold
First Gold	U.K.	flavor, aroma	6.5–8.5%	East Kent Goldings
Fuggles	U.K., U.S.	flavor , aroma	3.5–5.5%	Willamette or Kent Goldings
Galena	U.S.	bittering	10–14%	Brewers Gold, Bullion
Hallertau Hersbrucker	Germany	bittering, flavor, aroma	2.3–5%	Hallertauer Mittelfrüh
Hallertau	U.S.	flavor, aroma	3-5–4.5%	German Hallertau Hersbrucker
Hallertauer Mittelfrüh	Germany	bittering, flavor , aroma	3.5–5.5%	Hallertau Hersbrucker
Kent Goldings	U.K.	flavor, finishing, dry hop	4–7%	B.C. Goldings, Fuggles
Liberty	U.S.	aroma	2.5–6 %	Hallertauer Mittelfrüh, Crystal
Lublin	Poland	flavor, aroma	3–6%	Czech Saaz
Mt. Hood	U.S.	flavor , aroma	3–6%	Hallertauer Hersbruck, Mittelfrüh
Northdown	U.K.	bittering, flavor, aroma, dry hop	8–11%	Northern Brewer
Northern Brewer	Germany, U.S., U.K.	bittering, flavor, aroma	7–10%	Northdown
Nugget	U.S.	bittering	10–14%	Chinook

(Hop Chart continued on page 166)

Hop	Origin	Use	Alpha Acid % Range	Hop Substitute
Orion	Germany	bittering	6–7.5%	Northern Brewer
Omega	U.K.	bittering	9–13%	Northdown
Perle	Germany , U.S.	flavor, aroma	6–8%	Hallertauer Mittelfrüh (do not use in Pilsners)
Pride of Ringwood	New Zealand	bittering	8–12%	Galena
Progress	U.K.	flavor, aroma	5–7.5%	Fuggles
Spalt	Germany, U.S.	bittering, flavor, aroma	3–6%	Czech Saaz
Strisselspalt	France	aroma	2.5–4%	Hallertau Hersbrucker
Styrian Goldings	Slovenia	bittering, flavor, aroma	4.5–7.5%	Fuggles
Target	U.K.	bittering	8–10%	Northdown, Yeoman
Tettnanger	Germany, U.S.	bittering,flavor, aroma	3–6.5%	Spalt, Czech Saaz
Ultra	U.S.	aroma	2–4%	Czech Saaz
U.S. Saaz	U.S.	aroma	2–4%	Czech Saaz
Whitbread Golding	U.K.	flavor, aroma	4.5–7.5%	Fuggles
Willamette	U.S.	flavor, aroma	3.5–6%	Fuggles
Yakima Magnum	U.S.	bittering	14–15%	Columbus
Yeoman	U.K.	bittering	6.5–8%	Northdown, Target

APPENDIX 3
Grains and Adjuncts Chart

Grain/ Adjunct	Color (Lovibond)	Gravity (1 lb. in 1 gal.)	Characteristics	Beer Styles
Acid (Sauer) malt	1.3–2.3	1.033	sour taste	Lambics
Amber malt	35	1.032	copper color, biscuit taste	brown ales, mild ales, old ales
Aromatic malt	20	1.036	malt aroma	brown ales
Biscuit malt	25	1.035	baked biscuit flavor and aroma	Belgian
Black barley	500	1.023–1.027	dry, sharp barley flavor	stouts
Black malt / Black patent malt	500	1.026	dry, burnt, chalky character and dark head color	porters, stouts, brown ales, dark lagers
Brown malt	65	1.032	dry biscuit flavor	porters, Belgian ales
Cara-Munich malt	56	1.033	caramel sweetness and aroma, copper color	Belgian ales, German smoked beers, bocks
Cara-Vienne malt	21	1.034	light crystal malt	Belgian Tripels
Cara-wheat	32	1.035	nutty, toasted wheat flavor, improves head retention	dunkel weizen
Chocolate malt	British 475, U.S. 350	1.034	nutty, toasted flavor, brown color	brown ales, porters, stouts, bocks
Crystal or caramel malt	Light:10–20, Med.: 40–60, Dark: 70–120	1.033–1.035	sweet caramel flavor, mouthfeel, amber color, helps head retention	Light: light lagers and ales, Medium: pale ales, Dark: brown ales, porters, stouts
Dextrin malt	British and American: 1.5, Belgian: 7.8	1.033	adds a fuller body, helps head retention	porters, stouts, and heavier-bodied beers
Dry malt extract (DME)	Extra Light: 2.5, Light: 3.5, Amber: 10, Dark: 30	1.044	Varies with style/brand	All styles
Flaked barley	1.5	1.032	helps head retention, creamy smoothness	porters, stouts
Flaked maize	1	1.037	lightens body and color	light pilsners and ales
Flaked oats	1	1.033	Adds body, smoothness and creamy head	stouts, Belgian ales
Flaked rye	2	1.036	dry, crisp character	rye beers
Flaked wheat	2	1.036	wheat flavor, hazy color, adds body and head retention	wheat and Belgian white beers
Grits	1–1.5	1.037	corn/grain taste	American lagers
Honey malt	25	1.034	nutty, honey, toasted flavor and aroma	brown ales, Belgian wheats, bocks, many other styles

(Grains and Adjuncts Chart continued on page 168)

Grain/ Adjunct	Color (Lovibond)	Gravity (1 lb. in 1 gal.)	Characteristics	Beer Styles
Irish moss	N/A	N/A	prevents chill haze	all lighter colored beers
Kiln-Amber malt	22	1.034	malty, grainy flavor	bocks, Oktoberfests, brown ales, mild ales, Scottish ales
Kiln-Coffee malt	170	1.034	coffee flavor	stouts, porters, brown ales, Scottish ales
Lager malt	1.4	1.038	light color and flavor	lagers
Malto-dextrin	N/A	1.043	adds body and mouthfeel	all extract beers
Maris Otter pale malt	2.2–3	1.038	pale color	pale ales
Melanoiden malt	33	1.033	reddish color	red ales
Mild ale malt	3.2	1.037	dry, nutty, malty flavor	English mild ales
Munich malt	8	1.034	amber color, sweet toasted, flavor and aroma	dark lagers, Oktoberfests, Scottish ales, porters
Oak chips	N/A	N/A	recreates cask-conditioned aroma	IPAs, Belgian ales, Scottish ales
Pale ale malt/Pale 2-row British malt	2.2	1.038	malt flavor	most English and Scottish ales
Pale 2-row American malt	1.8	1.037	moderate malt flavor	most beer styles
Pale 6-row American malt	1.8	1.035	moderate malt flavor	most beer styles
Peat-smoked malt	2.8	1.034	robust smoky flavor	Scottish ales
Pilsner malt	Belgian and German: 1.5, British: 1.75	1.037	light color and flavor	Pilsners and other light-colored beers
Rauch malt	25	1.037	smoky flavor	rauch beers, smoked porters, Scottish ales, barley wines
Roasted barley	500	1.025	dry, roasted flavor, amber color	stouts, porters, Scottish ales
Rye malt	3	1.029	dry, crisp character	rye beers
Special B malt	130–220	1.030	extreme caramel taste and aroma	dark Belgian ales, other dark beers
Syrup malt extract	Light: 3.5, Amber: 10, Dark: 30	1.037	varies with style/brand	all beer styles
Toasted malt	25	1.038	nutty flavor and aroma	IPAs, Scottish ales
Torrified wheat	1	1.036	helps head retention and mouthfeel	pale ales
Scottish ale malt	3	1.038	malt flavor and aroma	Scottish ales

(Grains and Adjuncts Chart continued on page 169)

Grain/ Adjunct	Color (Lovibond)	Gravity (1 lb. in 1 gal.)	Characteristics	Beer Styles
Victory malt	25	1.034	slightly toasted, biscuit flavor and aroma	IPAs, Scottish ales and nut brown ales
Vienna malt	German: 2.5, U.S.:4	German: 1.037, U.S.: 1.035	gold to amber color, toasted, malty, caramel flavor	Vienna, Märzen and Oktoberfest beers
Wheat malt	1.8	German: 1.039, US: 1.038	light flavor, creamy head	all wheat beers, stouts, doppelbocks, and alt

Sugars Chart

Sugar	Color (Lovibond)	Gravity (1 lb. in 1 gal.)	Characteristics	Beer Styles
Brown sugar	Brown: 40, Dark brown: 60	1.046	rich, sweet flavor	Scottish ales, old ales, holiday beers
Candi sugar or rock candi	Clear: 0.5, Amber: 75, Dark: 275	1.036	smooth taste, good head retention, sweet aroma and high gravity without being apparent	Belgian and holiday ales
Corn sugar	1	1.037	priming ingredient	all beer styles
Demerara Sugar	1	1.041–1.042	mellow, sweet flavor	English ales
Dextrose or glucose	1	1.037	mild sweet taste	English beers
Honey	varies with style (clover is .09)	1.032	sweet and dry taste	many beer styles
Invert sugar	N/A	1.046	increases alcohol	Belgian ales

Use as an adjunct or for priming before bottling. It is made from sucrose and is 5–10% less fermentable than sucrose. It does not contain dextrins. Use ³/₄ to 1 cup for priming.

Lactose	N/A	1.043	adds sweetness and body	sweet or milk stouts
Lyle's golden syrup	zero	1.036	increases alcohol without flavor	Belgian (Chimay) and English beers
Maple syrup	35	1.030	dry, woodsy flavor	pales ales, porters
Maple sap	3	1.009	crisp, dry, earthy flavor	pale ales, porters
Molasses	80	1.036	strong sweet flavor	stout, porter
Rice solids	.01	1.040	lightens flavor without taste	American and Asian lagers
Sucrose	N/A	1.046	white table sugar increases alcohol	Australian lagers, English bitters
Treacle	100	1.036	intense, sweet flavor	many English ales

Beer Style Index

STOUT
ABC Extra Stout, 27
Bert Grant's Imperial Stout, 144
Cooper's Best Extra Stout, 31
Dragon Stout, 38
Guinness Extra Stout, 120
John Courage Imperial Stout, 96
Mackeson XXX Stout, 99
Marston's Oyster Stout, 100
Murphy's Irish Stout, 122
Samuel Smith's Oatmeal Stout, 106
Sapporo Black Stout Draft, 26
Watney's Cream Stout, 115

WHEAT AND WHITE BEER
Aventinus Wheat-Doppelbock, 76
Blanche de Bruges, 49
Blanche de Chambly, 135
Edelweiss Dunkel Weissbier, 45
Maple Wheat Ale, 137
Paulaner Hefe-Weizen, 82
Rodenbach Grand Cru, 60
Wit Black, 158

LAGERS

BOCK AND DOUBLE BOCK
Ayinger Maibock, 77
Brasal Bock, 136
Caesarus Imperator Heller Bock, 129
Celebrator Doppelbock, 80
Moretti Doppio Malto, 123
Unicer Super Bock, 126

DARK LAGERS
Dixie Blackened Voodoo Lager, 146
St. Pauli Girl Dark, 84
Xingu Black Beer, 160

LIGHT LAGERS
33 Export, 30
Asahi Dry Draft Beer, 24
Bin Tang Pilsner Lager, 22
Castle Lager, 16
Cerveza Imperial, 41
Cerveza Panama Lager Alemania style, 44
Elephant Malt Liquor, 71
Estrella Galicia Especial, 127
Famosa Lager, 43
Foster's Lager, 33
Golden Eagle Lager Beer, 23
Grolsch Lager, 117

Gulder Export Premium, 15
Harp Lager, 121
Hatuey, 151
Heineken Lager, 118
Keo Beer, 131
Kirin Lager, 25
Lion Lager, 17
Maccabee Premium Beer, 132
Mamba Malt Liquor, 12
Marathon, 116
Medalla Light Cerveza, 39
Molson Ice, 138
O. B. Lager Beer, 28
Razor Edge Lager, 34
Samuel Adams Boston Lager, 156
Singha Malt Liquor, 29
Steinlager, 36
Tsing-Tao, 21
West End Export Lager, 35
Windhoek Special, 14
Zambezi Premium Export Lager, 20

PILSNER
Almaza Pilsener Beer, 133
Bitburger Premium Pils, 79
Bohemia Beer, 139
Efes Pilsener, 134
Kumburak Bohemian Pilsner, 70
Ngoma Togo Pils, 19
Pilsener of El Salvador Lager Bier, 42
Pilsner Urquell, 69
Tafel Pilsner Lager, 13
Warsteiner Premium Verum, 85
Zywiec Beer, 125

VIENNA, MARZEN/OCTOBERFEST, HELLES
Ayinger Oktober Fest-Märzen, 78
Dos Equis, 140
Elliot Ness Lager, 147
Negra Modelo Dark Beer, 141
Ngoma Malt Liquor Awooyo Special, 18

ESOTERIC BEERS
Anchor Steam Beer, 142
Carib Shandy Lager Flavored with Ginger, 40
Cuzo Dark Premium, 161
Cooper's Sparkling Ale, 32
Fraoch Heather Ale, 93
Kaiserdom Rauchbier, 81
La Trappe Quadrupel, 119
Samiclaus Bier, 130

Other Storey Titles You Will Enjoy

Brew Ware: How to Find, Adapt & Build Homebrewing Equipment, by Karl F. Lutzen and Mark Stevens. Contains step-by-step plans for building your own homebrewing equipment as well as reviews of commercially available equipment. 272 pages. Paperback. ISBN 0-88266-926-5.

Dave Miller's Homebrewing Guide: Everything you need to know to make great-tasting beer, by Dave Miller. Comprehensive guide covers extract to all grain brewing including equipment, recipe formulation, and troubleshooting. 368 pages. Paperback. ISBN 0-88266-905-2.

Homebrew Favorites, by Karl F. Lutzen & Mark Stevens. This guide to creating more than 240 unusual brews at home includes award-winning recipes culled from homebrew clubs, brewing suppliers, and homebrewers across North America. 256 pages. Paperback. ISBN 0-88266-613-4.

The Homebrewer's Garden: How to easily grow, prepare and use your own hops, brewing herbs and malts, by Joe Fisher and Dennis Fisher. 176 pages. Paperback. ISBN 1-58017-010-2.

More Homebrew Favorites: More than 260 New Brews!, by Karl F. Lutzen and Mark Stevens. All-new compilation of recipes from homebrewers across North America. 256 pages. Paperback. ISBN 0-88266-968-0.

North American CloneBrews, by Scott R. Russell. Clone the best 150 beers in North America without leaving your kitchen! Each recipe comes complete with partial mash, all extract, and all-grain ingredients. 176 pages. Paperback. ISBN 1-58017-246-6.

Homemade Root Beer, Soda & Pop, by Stephen Cresswell. Easy-to-follow instructions for making more than 60 traditional and modern soft drinks at home including root beer, sarsaparilla, and birch beer. 128 pages. Paperback. ISBN 1-58017-052-8.

These and other books from Storey Publishing are available wherever quality books are sold or by calling 1-800-441-5700. Visit us at www.storey.com.